The Unreliable Life of Harry the Valet: The Great Victorian Jewel Thief

The
Unreliable Life of
Harry the Valet:
The Great Victorian
Jewel Thief

Duncan Hamilton

Century · London

Published by Century 2011

2 4 6 8 10 9 7 5 3 1

First published in Great Britain in 2011 by
Century
Random House, 20 Vauxhall Bridge Road,
London SW1V 2SA

www.randomhouse.co.uk

Addresses for companies within The Random House Group Limited
can be found at: www.randomhouse.co.uk

The Random House Group Limited Reg. No. 954009

A CIP catalogue record for this book
is available from the British Library

Hardback ISBN: 9781846058134
Trade Paperback ISBN: 9781846058141

The Random House Group Limited supports The Forest Stewardship
Council (FSC), the leading international forest certification organisation.
All our titles that are printed on Greenpeace approved FSC certified paper carry
the FSC logo. Our paper procurement policy can be found at:
www.randomhouse.co.uk/environment

Mixed Sources
Product group from well-managed
forests and other controlled sources
www.fsc.org Cert no. TT-COC-2139
© 1996 Forest Stewardship Council
FSC

Typeset by SX Composing DTP, Rayleigh, Essex
Printed and bound in Great Britain by
Clays Ltd, St Ives plc

To Mandy with my love.
Without you nothing would have come of nothing.

Contents

Foreword

The 'greatest of the Pre-Raffleites'

He was an immaculately dapper and suave man; stylish without being showy. Everything about him was neat and precise, as though he'd only just left the fitting room of his Savile Row tailor.

All his suits were sharply bespoke – sombre black, sober charcoal-grey or formal navy, always three-piece and cut from English wool. His shoes were handmade too, and polished to mirrored perfection. His shirts were soft white cotton with stiff collars. His ties were dark silk, tightly knotted and decorated with a gold pin or clasp. The hat he wore – a bowler or a coachman depending on his mood – was scrupulously brushed, and its shiny silk band matched the shade of whichever suit he'd chosen from his wardrobe that day.

He was handsome too, the type of figure who expected admiring glances and naturally received them. The face was round and comely with high, well-defined cheekbones. The black moustache was waxed and twisted slightly upward at the corners. The pale skin was so smooth that even the crow's feet around the hazel eyes were as light as paper-creases. The only tangible sign of

I

ageing were peppery flecks of grey in his short dark hair, which further accentuated the impression of experience and distinction.

He walked with a long stride, and at a brisk, efficient pace, as if always trying to beat the clock in the race to an appointment. But there was a natural grace and snap authority about each step and his bearing was almost regal. He possessed a hard-muscled frame, the shoulders pinned back to emphasise his height of almost 6 feet, and he jauntily raised his chin whenever he turned his gaze. With a gleaming Gladstone bag in his left hand, he resembled a prosperous banker or a city broker about to close yet another deal before retiring to the leather armchairs of his club and indulging in a long, late and very expensive lunch there.

Here was someone who looked and acted as though he belonged in whichever stratum of high society he blessed with his presence. It was as if – either through birthright, the accumulation of 'new money' or from the brilliance of his own wit and acumen – he had an indisputable right to swank and be taken seriously in London's black-tie world. There was a haughty, grand edge to the circles in which he mixed. But he was equipped to flourish within its rigidly hierarchical structure because he demonstrated a broad education, a genteel charm and a gentle manner. He was punctilious about social conventions. At the sight of a jewelled lady, he would touch the curled brim of his hat and dip his head in deference, as if Queen Victoria herself were passing by. Sometimes his courtesy tipped on purpose into over-politeness in a willingness to please and flatter. Words slipped like oil off his tongue.

He could talk about finances. Its labyrinthine complexities seemed a familiar and easy language to him. He could talk expertly about the allure of horses and the turf and the glories of the shooting season, as if he owned both a thoroughbred being trained for the Epsom Derby and a heathery slice of the Scottish grouse moors. He could talk about lords and earls and debutantes and dowager duchesses as though he, too, was the owner of a title (which he didn't wish to flaunt) and had shared a silver-plated dinner with his aristocratic friends just the previous evening. Moreover, in one room he could have persuaded the Temperance Society that he abhorred both the grape and the grain, and in the next convinced the most knowledgeable licensed victualler in London of his credentials as a wine connoisseur.

Which is why, at first sight and on first meeting, no one ever guessed the truth about him.

He wasn't a banker or a businessman. His wealth didn't stem from any orthodox entrepreneurial know-how. There wasn't a spot of blue blood in his family lineage. Nor did he have the privilege of an inheritance and a country estate. While he gave the impression of knowing his way around stocks and shares and the price of gold, he dealt instead in denial and deception. For he lived in the half-light, and the gift he possessed was successfully pretending to be someone – and something – he wasn't. The talent he had to go with it was the ability to steal some of the most beautiful jewellery in Europe. He was a chancer, a scammer, a con man – and remarkably brilliant at all three. When he wrote about his extraordinary 'career' the newspaper that bought and published his memoir promoted it as:

THE LIFE STORY OF A SUPER-CROOK

'No living man has such a record of crime to his discredit,' it said proudly of its scoop. Every day for him was a well-rehearsed performance of stupendous skill and actorly poise. His wardrobe of fine suits were work clothes, designed to conceal his trade in the places where he practised it: hotels and restaurants, garden parties and gallery openings, charity functions and lavish dinners, which catered for the rich and the super-rich and the aristocracy. He needed to blend, chameleon-like, into any occasion to the extent that the person to whom he was speaking believed, without hesitation or doubt, that he was entitled to be there.

All this came as easily to him as flight does to a bird. He was in complete charge of his profession, an expert in the art of subtle distraction – the ability to persuade whoever he'd decided to liberate of money or jewels to follow his eyes and facial movements or the set of his body rather than the path of his velvet hands. It was a form of mesmerism, like dangling a pocket watch in front of audience volunteers and lulling them into a shallow trance. He would steal what he wanted and then offer a gracious excuse to explain his sudden departure. He left with a smile, a slight bow and a light handshake. The recipient of the handshake didn't know that he or she was touching the lean fingers of thievery. These were the fingers that had picked a thousand pockets, filched wallets and purses and caressed away diamonds, rubies and emeralds from women too implicitly trusting – or too flattered by his warm voice – to notice what was happening to them until he and the jewels were long gone, and only the faint scent of his cologne hung in the air. He had the dextrous touch of the stage magician; around him things just disappeared. And he disappeared too – without a backward glance. An hour later, the host or hostess would be counting the spoons and nervously asking guests: 'Who was that nice gentleman? Surely you know him?' Heads would shake and there would be amazed replies: 'But I thought you knew him?' Finally, and usually after an embarrassed pause, there'd be a half-choked whisper: 'So who was he?'

His street name was Harry the Valet – though almost everyone who came only briefly into his circle never knew it. He relied on multiple identities. To some he was Mr James. To others he was Mr Jackson. A few knew him as Mr Williams, Mr William or Mr Matthews. Occasionally he was plain Mr Jones. In a career spanning almost half a century – from 1876 to 1923 – he routinely robbed dukes and duchesses, earls and baronets, a maharaja, one of Britain's most revered actresses and countless diamond merchants, businessmen and businessmen's wives. He always focused on what he called the 'upper ten' – the top 10 per cent, for whom almost unlimited amounts of wealth made life in Britain and abroad a non-stop, whirling cabaret. He could claim, with justification, 'I must have worked my way half way through the pages of *Debrett's.*' On the continent, especially at the roulette and card tables of Monte Carlo, he became Mr Villiers or occasionally Mr de Villiers. He chose his names carefully, as though each one brought with it slightly different characteristics, which he then assimilated into his complex personality. He once called himself William Wilson. No one noticed that 'William Wilson' was the eponymous character in an Edgar Allan Poe short story originally published in 1839. The plot, which Poe set in London, turns on Wilson meeting someone who shares the same name and birthday and is capable of copying his dress, gait and voice almost exactly. With a growing, bewildered helplessness, Wilson finds the discovery of a doppelgänger robs him of his uniqueness. He cannot separate himself emotionally from someone who is on the one hand a total stranger and on the other a living and breathing copy of himself. Using the name suited the Valet's dry sense of humour. William Wilson was a private joke.

Under whichever name he used, the Valet acted like a real-life and charmingly rakish A. J. Raffles – finessing his way through the corridors and smoke rooms of society long before E. W. Hornung introduced his gentleman thief in *The Amateur Cracksman* in 1899. The Valet fitted the description that the fictional Raffles gave to the rogue Charles Peace, who was the most famous burglar in Victorian Britain before being caught and hanged for murder in 1879. Every waking hour for Peace was spent on the lookout for something which didn't belong to him. He knew no other way to live. Tongue pressed firmly into cheek, Hornung has Raffles calling Peace the 'greatest of the pre-Raffleites'. But he was wrong. The title belonged to the Valet. He was closer in spirit to Raffles too. The Valet stole with elegance, as if the very 'art' contained within it was important to him. Like Raffles, he knew how to behave in exalted company. Like Raffles, he was slavishly devoted to, and always in pursuit of, the finer things – in his case suites at West End hotels and the membership of drinking clubs in Oxford Street and Regent Street. And, also like Raffles, there was a curious, if dubious, code of honour attached to his crimes.

The Valet didn't exactly adhere to the Robin Hood-like philosophy of the redistribution of wealth; but he never took from anyone he believed was unable to bear the loss. He thought those from whom he stole could well afford the damage inflicted on them. To take jewels from the wealthy was no greater a sin to him than scrumping an apple from their orchard. He spoke about it as if altruistically highlighting the hideous imbalance between the haves and have-nots of Victorian London. The argument suited the Valet's purpose. Not only did it provide him with a form of justification, it also elicited sympathy. The poverty-stricken saw the thefts as good deeds – small acts of retribution on their behalf. He was one of them, and he robbed from the rich to give to 'the poor'; though, in every instance, 'the poor' in question was exclusively himself.

In these subtle ways, he worked hard to emphasise the virtue in his vice and to portray himself as a cheeky rascal – a Very English Rogue embroiled in some playful skulduggery – rather than the sort of dark-caped villain who appeared weekly in the *Illustrated Police News* or the shock-horror editions of the penny-dreadfuls which were sold on street corners. To burnish the image, he insisted that he was an adjunct to the society crowd from which he stole and classed his 'recreation' as that of 'sportsman', as though an Olympic medal existed for such audacity. But he was neither the embodiment of the Corinthian spirit nor an amateur pilferer devoted to the fun of the chase. He was a hardened and dedicated professional fixed on the main chance.

He would airily describe himself nonetheless as 'an artist' or an 'expert in precious stones'. The thefts themselves were 'little adventures', as if he were taking part in a Ripping Yarn. The sobriquet 'The Valet' gave a theatrical swish and swagger and also a degree of romance to what he did. It was as though he were an invented character, made up specifically for the purpose of a racy story, rather than a flesh and blood thief. The name was bestowed early on by the criminal underworld as a sign of his acceptance within it. It was preserved to reflect his status as the finest jewel thief of his – and most other – generations. His contemporaries thought him adroit and intelligent enough to succeed where Captain Blood had failed in 1671. The Valet, it was said, could have palmed the Black Prince's Ruby from the Imperial State Crown and dropped it into his pocket before the Beefeaters in the Tower of London realised he was among them, let alone that a theft had taken place. He had the daring – and the dash – to do it.

'The big jobs are the easiest,' he claimed. His mind once quickly calculated 'four different ways of stealing the Scottish Crown Jewels' from Edinburgh Castle – even though 'an armed sentry was walking backwards and forwards under the window' as he studied them. Reluctantly he concluded that the difficulty was not in actually 'lifting them', but 'in not knowing how to dispose of them'. Which fence would be stupid enough to handle the jewels? Who could possibly re-cut the stones to make them unrecognisable and saleable on the open market? And who would ever buy – and then never display – what every policeman on God's earth would immediately be tasked to find? The Queen's jewels and the Koh-i-noor diamond in the Tower fell into the same category: 'Capable of being stolen – but too hot for anyone to handle afterwards,' he said. He shaped a strategy to steal them nonetheless.

'I would have done too,' he added, 'if they had been worth the effort.'

There were elaborate and conflicting accounts of why the label of the Valet was originally given to him, and also why it stuck so solidly. Even the police referred to him almost exclusively as Harry, as though he'd become a matey drinking acquaintance, or half admiringly as the Valet. Some said the name was given to him because he'd once worked as a valet to a duke, which is where he'd perfected his lordly language and white-gloved manner. The story was untrue. He dismissed it as 'So much rubbish', insisting, 'I have never been a gentleman's gentleman.' With a transparent sliver of pride, he added: 'Nor have I done an honest job of work outside the walls of French or English prisons.' Others said that in his early criminal days he'd often posed as a valet to gain access to hotels where liveried doormen and over-eager managers, suspicious of strangers, barred his way. That story was only partly true. There was the theory that he acted as an underworld valet, capable of bringing whatever was ordered by a fence or buyer. That story was true – but it had nothing to do with his nickname. But he confessed that over time even his friends – and especially the police – came to believe: 'That my success in getting away with the jewel cases of the peerage lay in the fact that I was thoroughly acquainted with the habits of titled people and because I looked the part of a real life valet'.

The truth is more prosaic. He became Harry the Valet because he was given criminal schooling by a prolific fence in London's Middlesex Street. He became inseparable from him. The Valet euphemistically described his tutor as one of his 'closet acquaintances'. The fence was called Abraham Mitchell, who gave his occupation as 'general dealer'. He drove around London in a smart, yellow-wheeled gig drawn by a black cob called Irish Prince. Rather in the way that the Artful Dodger did Fagin's bidding, so the apprentice crook fetched and carried for his master; as reliably and as punctually as a valet appearing in the panelled study with the drinks tray after the servant's bell has been rung. 'A nickname in criminal circles is lightly bestowed, and once acquired is not easily shaken off,' he said. 'Mine was simply as the result of a joking remark.' He and Mitchell had been visiting a horse dealer's in the Strand. Another fence, strolling by, saw teacher and nascent pupil together for the umpteenth time. As he passed them, he half turned, 'jerked his thumb over his shoulder' and said with a snarl, 'You're his valet – you are always with him.' And then he repeated it to other fences and crooks, as though delivering a pearl of polished thought.

The Valet took the name as a compliment and wore it like a laurel crown. It appealed to his self-worth and self-esteem. There was something unmistakably catchy about it, like a popular tune of the period. Newspapers came to appreciate the fact that Harry the Valet could be turned into an appealing headline. The public came to like the assonance of the phrase on the ear. The police liked it because by the early 1890s every uniformed and plain-clothes officer in London knew of the Valet – if not by sight then definitely through deed. For them the Valet was a form of short-hand requiring no further elaboration. Even the phenomenally successful writer Edgar Wallace – for whom the phrase 'best-seller' is pitifully inadequate – would later use Harry the Valet as a character. In the 1920s, it was said, only the Bible outsold Wallace's books around the globe. He produced work at machine-like speed, writing 175 novels and twenty-four plays and creating King Kong. In the 1930s he turned Harry the Valet from society crook to bent copper in *The Man at the Carlton* purely on the basis that he liked the lyrical quality of the name.

Frequently the Valet heard himself talked about in a tone of fear and awe – his presence powerfully conjured. Sitting unobtrusively in a club, he would eavesdrop on snatches of conversation. Among the small but interconnected group of London bigwigs were men who knew someone – a friend, or at least a friend of a friend – from whom the Valet had stolen. In analysing these thefts the police let slip information about him. Eventually, almost everyone who mattered socially was aware of the Valet's mysterious existence.

Crime was the staple diet of the Victorian news journalist. With their microscopic print and cramped columns, the newspapers regularly covered the loss of jewels. The less spectacular accounts were wedged at the bottom of an inside page of dense black text and comprised nothing more than the skinny bones of basic detail: place, time and the identity of the victim. 'Police are investigating,' each piece routinely reported. Logically these investigations began with the Valet, always the prime suspect. He stupefied his victims and the police alike. As the author and criminologist Anthony L. Ellis made clear: 'He was a thief of rare order, a specialist, a master in the light-fingered art and the prince of pickpockets with a rodent-like facility for concealment and cunning . . . many brilliant coups were attributed to him.' Recognising the Valet as the culprit was one thing; capturing him was another. 'Wherever he was seen, he was shepherded by the police as assiduously as the little lamb shepherded Mary,' added Ellis. 'They shadowed him, suspected him, sought to associate him with certain notorious robberies – but the furtive creature was so rarely where he was expected to be.' It explains the police's preoccupation, bordering on the obsessional, with the Valet. It explains why – in the crowded decade before his most audacious crime – a score and more of unsolved thefts were erroneously marked down as his work. And it explains why rumour and myth swirled around him, filling the vacuum where hard facts ought to have been. At the time, the Valet bathed in his black stardom, which brought prestige and a sense of achievement.

He had no desire to conform to society's norms and could not comprehend why others tolerated a humdrum existence – the depressing cycle, as he saw it, of work and bills and filial responsibilities. He was an epicurean, out of place in a starchy, obedient era dominated by the work ethic. For him, the adage 'Travel light, travel fast' was paramount. He drifted, unchecked, in a peripatetic existence of pure enjoyment – the adrenalin thrill of jewel-taking and the nocturnal hedonism of its reward. During the 1890s, Scotland Yard's most experienced officers sought him. But, apart from two short spells in London prisons, plus a slightly longer one in Monte Carlo's, he fought the law and won. As a 'pro', aware of the risks, he stoically accepted jail as an occupational hazard. On each occasion he came out of his cell and altered his appearance, shaving off his moustache or growing a full beard, letting his sideburns become bushy whiskers or putting on a pair of spectacles – plain glass masquerading as magnified lenses. He would then carry on exactly as before, as if his 'going away' had been a holiday. He saw no reason why anything should ever change.

But a whole life can be defined in a solitary, wrenching act. So it proved for the Valet. His decisive moment came on 17 October 1898 – shortly before noon in Paris, amid the steam, smoke and smuts of the Gare du Nord station. There, as a result of a fateful entwinement and two simple mistakes, he would never be the same man again.

The first mistake was to fall in love. His second mistake was to let that love warp his judgement.

It's said that we regret most of all the things we don't do. But with the 20/20 vision that hindsight brings, the Valet understood that what he accomplished with his own brilliance at the Gare du Nord – a theft regarded at the time by Scotland Yard as 'one of the classics of crime' – was in retrospect a display of pure folly: a boneheaded show of hubris designed to prove a hollow point to a woman he wanted to marry and feared losing for ever.

The Valet regretted his foolishness, and offered in mitigation the excuse of the helpless romantic – that he was 'in love', which made him 'mad' and prone 'to do anything'. In the heat of this madness the best of intentions led to the worst possible consequences: he became entangled in a roaring melodrama combining high life and low life and a criminal chase on both sides of the Channel. At its end were absurd twists that would have been dismissed as too fanciful and coincidental had any Victorian novelist dared invent them. Even now, with the case and the conviction no more than fading and forgotten newsprint, the disparate characters it drew temporarily together seem preposterously pre-arranged, like actors preparing for a sixpenny entertainment in the West End:

Gaiety Girl actress, Maude Richardson, described as 'a mysterious woman with a past'.

The three-times-married Dowager Duchess of Sutherland, an adulteress and possible murderess – or accessory to a murder – who once served a sentence at Holloway Prison.

Her husband Sir Albert Rollit, a Member of Parliament.

Walter Dew, a policeman involved in the hunt for Jack the Ripper, who would later capture the wife murderer Dr Hawley Harvey Crippen.

Monsieur Henri de Blowitz, Paris correspondent of *The Times*.

Annie Gleason, one of the most infamous of America's female confidence tricksters.

Each had their entrances and their exits in a story the sensationalist press devoured whole and turned into popular entertainment around the world. At its bright centre was the transfixing love story between the jewel thief and the Gaiety Girl.

Maude was tall and long-legged, blonde and shapely, and always

MISS MAUDE RICHARDSON.
COPYRIGHT
Barraud 263 Oxford St London

Maude Richardson, dressed for the stage: Harry the Valet revelled in her 'great beauty' and 'sweet roughish face'.

classily dressed. The Valet was smitten instantly. He spoke of her 'great beauty' and 'sweet roughish face' and confessed: 'I was so deeply in love . . . I would have done anything to be able to marry her.' To convey that message, most men buy a ring or send wrapped flowers. The Valet chose instead to steal from the Dowager Duchess with a broad-daylight sleight of hand. In an eye-blink he swept into her railway carriage, and then out again, carrying £25,000 to £30,000 worth of gems.

Today, the jewels would be worth £2 million.

News of it spread, like a lit fuse, from one continent to the next.

The headlines focused on a manhunt unprecedented in intensity and scope to apprehend a jewel thief. The crime was so audaciously accomplished, so precise and planned, that police were convinced that no one man could be solely responsible for it; a gang of organised thieves – four-strong – was sought. With rare under-statement – for he seldom undersold either himself or his cases – Chief Inspector Dew recalled it as 'a tremendous sensation'.

All this, for a woman's heart.

Near the end of his life, after thirty darkly harrowing years brooding on it, the Valet said: 'This famous single-handed coup, about which volumes have been written, and which almost every well-known jewel robber in London has claimed falsely to have had a hand in, was one of the unluckiest achievements of my career.' It led to betrayal, bitter regret and recrimination. For the Valet, there was life *before* the Gare du Nord theft and life *after* it. But those two lives were quite different.

Long after the trial, one question remained unanswered about Harry the Valet.

Who was he?

The moniker was well known. The man to whom it belonged was a stranger. No one knew when he was born or grew up. No one knew who his parents had been, or what had turned a clearly educated and once respectable son into a thief. No one even knew the full amount of the jewels he had taken. And no one was aware – least of all Scotland Yard – of his real name. He became a magnet for all manner of speculation and fabrication. One rumour said he had moved to the South of France to live on the profits of his crimes. Another claimed he'd emigrated to Australia.

The Valet regarded his constant sparring with the police as a casual 'game of blind man's buff'. But then he was always bluffing – or trying to bluff – everyone he ever met for reasons of self-protection. As a pickpocket and plunderer of jewels, he carried no identification. 'Advertisement,' he believed, 'is a fatal thing in crime.' He was forever dusting over his tracks, constantly alive to the sound of footsteps behind him. He left nothing on his travels – not even a match-book – that might trace him. He disposed immediately of receipts, business cards or handbills he'd been given so as to offer no clue, however scant, to where he had been or – more importantly – where he might be going. He wanted no one to map his movements and find too strong a pattern in them. He told filigree lies about himself. As if reading off pat from script, he could provide more than a dozen coherent but markedly different variations of his upbringing, his profession and his family – weaving together one dubious tale with another to create a plausible, but completely false, tapestry of his life.

He came from Sussex. He was born in the West Country. He was really a man of Kent. He'd never married. He was a widower. His wife was living overseas. He was a clerk. He was a gentleman of property. He was a solicitor who had been left a huge sum of money by a distant, ageing relative and had gratefully retired on it. He lived in Park Lane. He had a house 'in the country'. He had a home in France. He had a son but no daughter. He had a daughter but no son. Or he had no children at all.

He shuffled these scenarios to suit his purposes the way a card sharp shuffles the pack. And who knew – or could possibly find out – whether there was a bright stitch of truth in any of them?

The pseudonyms he used were important, not only in allowing him to move undetected from one place to another, but also – and more crucially – in covering up his true identity in the census records. He fiercely protected his real name, guarding it neurotically and almost daring anyone to discover it, like Rumpelstiltskin in the Grimm Brothers' fairy-story. As his parents died, and as he distanced himself from the friends of his youth, the Valet's past became blurred to almost everyone around him.

His birth name was the refuge he could rely on if there was nowhere else to turn. He could shelter behind it.

The vastness of London concealed him, protecting his identity. 'There is no place so safe if you intend to go into hiding,' he said, knowing it was difficult to find someone who didn't want to be found among its streets and identical back alleys, the discreet, modest rows of semi-detached homes and flats and anonymous, crowded boarding houses. It was harder still to locate the Valet when he possessed enough money to hop from one expensive hotel to another or to rent a house at will and pay for it in cash. Or to call in a long-ago favour and take temporary accommodation with a fellow thief. With bolt-holes all around the capital, he made Scotland Yard dance like finger-puppets in pursuit of him. What the police sought was a shadow: a man who wasn't really there.

He broke cover only when the 'Life Story of a Super-Crook' appeared almost three decades after the Dowager Duchess lost her jewels. The *Weekly News* satisfied its readership with quirkiness, gossip, handy hints and mild titillation and also specialised in human interest drama and first-person accounts of crime and criminals. It trumpeted the Valet's account as 'a gripping story of his ups and downs'. The serialisation ran for six weeks from late March to early May in 1926. At last – aged nearly 75 – the Valet decided to illuminate the dark corners of his life. The *Weekly News* paid him to tell all – including his real identity.

The photograph accompanying these articles makes him appear unprepossessing; the sort of benign ancient gent who, as a boy, could remember hearing Dickens read on his farewell tour, or speak wistfully about Victoria's Diamond Jubilee, the demise of the horse-drawn carriage and clip-clop hansom cabs, or long for the way London used to be before 'over-population' made it heave with people and 'motorised vehicles'. He doesn't look as though he once dressed foppishly in the finest of English tailoring. He doesn't look as though his reactions were fast enough to snatch a

Harry the Valet, recalling the man he'd once been – one of the most notorious jewel thieves in Europe.

jewel case and then vanish completely, like a smoke-and-mirrors illusionist. And he doesn't look as though he became one of the most hunted men in Europe after stealing from a dowager duchess to win a Gaiety Girl's heart.

The story was everything the *Weekly News* hoped it would be. The Valet started his account in a strangely oblique way, writing about himself in the third person as if detached from his own existence or chronicling someone else's. 'There are few people, unfortunately for your humble servant,' he said, 'who have not heard of Harry the Valet, the man who achieved a world-wide reputation.' What followed was absorbing and revelatory. It covered his early life, his decision to turn to crime and remain with it, his triumphs and disasters in shadowing the aristocracy, his swooning courtship of Maude, his admiring pen-portraits of the policemen who spent so much energy chasing him and his love of Paris, Monte Carlo and London, which was especially heartfelt because, as he explained: 'I am Cockney, having been born within the sound of Bow Bells.' And then came his chief confession.

'My real name is Henry Thomas,' he said, giving himself up to Scotland Yard at last.

There was just one problem. No one asked whether he was telling the truth.

Chapter 1

'Have you ever seen a policeman with brains?'

Harry the Valet adored London, and saw it as a Palace of Varieties in which he could perform. He loved the city's steepled forest of churches and the high dome of St Paul's Cathedral. He loved the ceaseless throb and thrum of voices across the cobbled streets, the scrape of cartwheels and the rhythmic drum of horses' hooves. He loved the wrinkled wake of the Thames, which constantly moved like the pulse of a heart, and the traffic of boats, barges and steamers on the dark water. And he loved the low blaze of the sun that gave a coppery, russet glow to the morning sky, and the dense, pea-soup smogs and icy fogs that enabled him to materialise and dematerialise as if he possessed a touch of the supernatural. The London fog was so bad that in the late 1880s George Gissing wrote in his diary about a muddy 'black' January, a 'fog at noon', which he claimed refused to clear for four days. At the end of the same month he said: 'Must be several weeks since there was a single gleam of sunlight'. Many more identical weeks had come before it, and also followed this one – grimly bleak for everyone else, but perfect for a thief such as the Valet, who taught himself to navigate blind the capital's obscure thin passageways and pokey alleys, as well as its familiarly broad thoroughfares. He walked them again and again, gathering London in by sight until its various routes and short cuts – his valuable way of escape after a heist – were committed to memory.

The Valet studied London the way an artist studies a landscape through a grid – squinting at and sizing up the minute detail of each small square. In the end his skill for observation, and the talent to completely absorb what he saw, enabled him to view London as if he were soaring above it, staring directly down on its blue-tinted roofs, at the cross-hatching of mazy lanes, capillary paths and the connecting arteries of major roads. In his mind he could visualise its look and layout like an unfolded map spread across a table.

The London into which he was born in the early 1850s, and which flourished in the late decades of the nineteenth century, was what Benjamin Disraeli called the 'modern Babylon'. But the faster the city moved – noise and clutter and non-stop entertainments – the more the Valet relished it. Hanging in the thick air was the stench of horse dung and soot and the scent of tobacco smoke, which floated in billowy, breaking clouds. These mingled with the wafting smell of burning charcoal from stalls selling tea and coffee at a halfpenny a cup, and the sizzle of cooked food – roast beef and ham, fried eggs, potatoes sold in brown paper bags, hot penny pies of beef and mutton, eel and veal. The streets teemed with people who craved attention from shoppers and browsers alike: the boardmen, decorated with huge signs advertising everything from a newly opened haberdashery store to a miracle cure for backache; the shoeblack – his nails never clean – toting his rough wooden box of polish and brushes; the dung sweeper with his stinking cart and huge iron shovel; the pavement entertainers such as jugglers, pebble swallowers, out-of-tune hurdy-gurdy players, screeching fiddlers, and sopranos sounding like cats wailing; the newspaper sellers unintelligibly yelling the latest headlines in their own guttural, pared-down language and accepting coppers with outstretched, ink-stained fingers; the petty traders peddling bootlaces or Lucifer matches; the flower 'girls' holding long wicker baskets and dressed in tatty shawls and bedraggled bonnets; and the animal handlers with talkative parrots and docile rabbits, yapping dogs and monkeys in cages.

The very poor could not afford a shilling a week for rent, let alone for food, so there were the lost souls of beggars and hawkers too: the pretend starving or sham former workers, the broken-down or burnt-out tradesmen, the shipwrecked mariners or blown-up miners and what the Victorians delicately referred to as 'the bodily afflicted', who were either genuine or pretending to be maimed or paralysed. The fakers wrapped themselves in soiled bandages, as if the hospital had discharged them just an hour earlier. The emaciated and the famished chalked the words 'I am starving' on to the uneven ground in front of them. Past this human circus came the clatter and rattle of the omnibuses, the glistening hansom cabs, the groomed saddle horses and drays, the chaises and broughams. The London that the Valet came to know so intimately was exactly as Shelley captured it in one of his later poems, 'Letter to Maria Gisborne':

> London, that great sea, whose ebb and flow
> At once is deaf and loud, and on the shore
> Vomits its wrecks, and still howls on for more.
> Yet in its depth what treasures!

The Valet understood what Shelley meant with his deliberate placing of the exclamation mark. In this city vast wealth and immense luxury was juxtaposed with obscene poverty, squalor and deprivation. But there was something viscerally thrilling about being a part of it. The Valet looked around him and knew he was locked into a ceaseless competition for survival. The workhouse was but a single slip or misjudgement away for a population perpetually swelling as the steam train replaced the barge, as new homes – six million of them during Queen Victoria's reign – were rapidly built, as the country-dwellers fled from the fields and abandoned near-derelict cottages and as the modern city took shape in the age of the machine.

The Valet didn't want to be one of the low-wage sweats or even a starchy, middle-class Victorian, emotionally and physically constrained – constantly worrying about illnesses and disease or his unfulfilled desires, and fretting over what was left unsaid because of polite but prudish social protocol. He set out to unhook himself from what he regarded as the anchor of suburban respectability. As soon as he glimpsed the power of money, he was determined to make as much of it as possible – by whatever means and irrespective of the consequences. His father was to blame for this; though, of course, he never knew it.

'My father was a picture frame maker of Great Arthur Street in the parish of St Luke's,' said the Valet. 'When I came out into the world, he was a man in a good way of business.' He was in a good way of family too. Named William, and born in 1815 in Berkshire, Manchester or Sussex (depending on which census you believe), he was described by the Valet as being 'immersed' in his trade and 'practically self-taught'. William was the embodiment of Victorian values. He revealed a tenacious appetite for work. He doted on his workbench and his family six days a week and devoted the seventh, as the Bible ordered, to thanking God for his blessings. He believed wholeheartedly in self-improvement, the mantra that 'You can learn something new every day.' By the time the Valet was born – records of that period are scrambled to the extent that the date is given as 1852, 1853, 1854 *and* 1855 – his father had already made sufficient money to buy a number of properties besides his own. The Valet was the youngest of five children. His brother, called William in honour of his father, was born in 1838. There were three sisters: Charlotte (1842), Maria (1846) and Mary Ann (1849). His mother, Mary, was five years younger than her husband and also described in the 1861 census as a picture-frame maker. A 16-year-old niece – another Charlotte – worked as the family's servant.

The Valet insisted that he and his brothers and sisters 'lived humbly'. He added: 'In those days tradesmen remained in unpretentious houses above their premises, and refused in the heyday of success to be lured to Victorian suburban life despite making a fortune. You would find them sticking to business and scorning a chance to ape their betters.' He cited his father as a prime example. He had, however, entered a thriving and prosperous profession. For this was a period of high aspiration, and the home – or 'home sweet home', as the saccharine song celebrated it – represented far more than a roof and a front door, a bed and a fireplace. It became a showroom to display the fruits of the head of the household's labour. His status was proudly reflected in all the things he owned – and there were a lot of them. Minimalism was not a Victorian trait. The average house was stuffed with clutter: platoons of ornaments and elaborate pots for vast plants, the leaves overflowing like tentacles. Fabric stretched across the chairs and sofas – and the wallpaper too – was decorated with what *Cassell's Household Guide* of the day referred to as: 'The regular and close recurrence of stripes, circles and other geo-metrical forms, which bewilder the sight as if the pattern were in motion'. There was barely space to move. Sturdy mahogany tables, sideboards, a writing desk and piano turned the rooms into obstacle courses. Polish and wax were always in use, choking the air like a stuffy perfume.

A bonus for the Valet's father was that the floral-covered walls – usually a fashionably deep crimson, green or gold – were smothered in reproduction prints and formal family photographs in black and white or sepia. The paintings were frequently cosy and soppy images with an implicitly stern moral message attached to them, such as the value of loyalty and friendship and the protection of home and hearth. But, whatever the dubious artistic merit of the pictures, the fact is that dozens – often hundreds of them – dominated the house. And each needed a frame. 'My father,' said the Valet 'started his business in the days when cumbrous etching and the ponderous oil painting demanded the heaviest and costliest of gold frames, which were the acme of respectability.' He worked slavishly from dawn to starry night to meet what the Valet remembered as 'the steady demands of his West End patrons'.

The father let his son tag along with him to the expensive homes of his customers, and innocently set in motion his craving for the upper-crust existence. The Valet was enviously wide-eyed at the sweep and curve of marble staircases, Doric columns and spacious entrance halls. He walked through mirrored rooms decorated with silks and velvets and admired the clusters of servants. He wanted to be exactly like the aristocracy or the most profitable businessmen, who smoked cigars and drank fine brandy three fingers at a time and also maintained country estates for hunting, shooting and fishing. Some earned £10,000 to £30,000 per year. As a boy, the Valet accepted that neither birthright nor breeding would ever give him a real start in life. He would never achieve financial parity – the average wage by the 1860s was less than £50 per year – on the salary of a picture framer or a craftsman. Without a seismic shift in his fortune or the unexpected acquisition of one, he was destined to provide a service for others rather than employ servants of his own. His father knew it too, and sought a different path for him. He thought books were the answer and became sure that reading would make a man of his son. Deprived of a grand education himself, he wanted his last-born to read extensively and become a scholar.

Whether knowledge was dispensed at home or in school, education did not come cheaply; a hardback novel or play – Shakespeare, Dickens, Trollope – could cost as much as a set of decent clothes. Yet the father invested in books for the son's well-being, encouraged him to read newspapers and periodicals and also instructed him in diction and deportment. 'I am going to send you to college or to France,' he said. 'See that you stick to your lessons and do nothing that would bring disgrace.' In less than ten years his father's words returned to the Valet as he sat in the silence of a prison cell in Pentonville.

Sophisticated analysis is not required to trace the root cause of his criminality or why it became habit-forming. His father never lived to propel the son into society, and turn him into a bona fide gentleman. Before his eleventh birthday, the Valet learnt of his father's death. The curtains were drawn. The house in Great Arthur Street was draped in funereal black. 'He died as a result of a rupture of the heart through overstrain,' said the Valet, who would subsequently view it as irrefutable proof that the motto about hard work killing no one was emphatically false. If he needed an excuse to plunder the pockets of the wealthy and stalk London's streets for opportunist pickings, the sight of his father's coffin provided it. Here was a man who'd done everything Victorian moralists preached. He'd worked and worshipped, provided for and protected his family, acted humanely and shown humility towards others. His reward was an early grave.

With his father gone, and his mother forced to maintain the family firm as best she could, the Valet found he had licence to roam. Why bother with the chalky aroma of the classroom when the world beyond it was within his grasp? He admitted: 'I had already acquired the fondness for the companionship of boys older than myself. I promptly left school, a fact which I carefully kept from my mother for many weeks.' Swallowed by grief, confused by the quotidian tasks of meeting orders and balancing the accounts and unable to manage or improve on the contacts book her husband had left, the Valet's mother was too distracted by her own difficulties to notice the waywardness of her son. Within twelve months, one property after another was sold to pay off debts, her clientele had dwindled and the workshop accompanying the shop was empty and redundant. Before Fate intervened – taking his father prematurely and making his mother suffer intolerably – his parents had told him that sacrifice was something he would have to accept as a necessary part of making his way in the world. The Valet now regarded this as over-sentimental nonsense. He began to live by his own rules. Simply to survive you had to be cynical and streetwise. To live well you had to be self-reliant and self-indulgent. But to really prosper you had to be detached and dispassionate in 'business', unafraid of reaching out and taking whatever you saw and wanted. There are seminal moments – seen as such only in restrospect – that determine not just the direction of a life, but also the way it is lived. Like a fork in a road, you choose to go one way or the other. The Valet's criminality began like this, almost innocently. With his mother's back turned, he stole a sovereign surreptitiously – but calculatingly – from the till of her shop. From that moment, the Valet could not stop stealing. From that sovereign, a whole career grew.

On the crowded pavements of Victorian England it was commonplace to buy racing tips in brown sealed envelopes from self-proclaimed experts in chequered suits, who claimed to know all the mysteries and vagaries of the turf. They attracted punters by shouting the day's runners and riders from the back of stationary carts. Devoted racing men gathered around them, listening to the well-rehearsed patter and waving rolled-up copies of the *Sportsman*, the *Sporting Life*, the *Sporting Chronicle* or the *Sporting Times*, the soft pink pages of which also contained gratuitously scurrilous gossip about prominent society figures. The Valet didn't need the vociferous tipsters, or the guidance of racing's most accomplished on-the-course reporters, to tell him what to back. 'St Luke's was the haunt of racing men,' he explained, suggesting that the talk in every bar and pub and on every street corner became a flow of stories about horses and jockeys. He found gamblers were like fishermen. They dwelt on the big win that got away.

The Valet's benefactor, Abraham Mitchell, taught him to understand the finer points of betting and form and the state of the tracks. He showed him how to read the elaborate gestures and frenetic, quick signals of the bookmakers, as bewildering as a foreign language. There was also Mitchell's indispensable guide about how to differentiate between a bred horse and a panting nag. He was a professor of the course, and made a legitimate portion of his income from buying and selling horses. Born in St Luke's, Mitchell travelled itinerantly, from the West Country to Hampshire, before returning to London. Already in his greying fifties, the Valet regarded him as a second father, Mitchell was capable of providing alternative schooling to someone ambitious, impressionable and willing to learn. The curriculum he offered was relevant to his talents and needs, and the kudos of sharing a yellow-wheeled gig and tugging at the Irish Prince's reins was preferable to writing down French verbs or listing kings and queens of England in order of succession. Mitchell seemed more alive than his father had ever been, unconcerned with passing fussy social judgements and criminally promiscuous without ever being aggressive about it. He stole with a smile. He betted with abandon. Well armed with his 'inside' racing information, the Valet lacked just one thing to turn him into a genuine racegoer: enough cash with which to bet. His mother allowed him to spend no more than sixpence a week. 'That was no good for the bookmakers,' he said.

He was given a tip, which he claimed – slipping into the parlance of the ever-optimistic loser – rated as a 'dead cert'. The horse, called Flutellin, was running at the Epsom spring meeting. 'The only difficulty was money,' said the Valet, stony broke. 'Suddenly a bright idea came into my head. Why not borrow a sovereign, put it on the horse and pay the money back when it won? The idea seemed such an excellent one and so innocent that I scarcely gave it a second thought.' There was just one flaw in his plan. Flutellin 'forgot to run well that day', he said. It trotted home with the stragglers. 'Of course,' said the Valet, 'I was in a dreadful stew.' If his mother discovered the loss, he feared exposure as a thief. He imagined himself thrown out of the house. 'For days I worried and fretted. When my mother looked at me, I felt sure she was watching me and waiting for me to confess, and two or three times I was at the point of telling her all about it.' But he never did. Either blissfully unaware of her son's infidelity, or regarding it as an isolated incident most sensibly ignored, she said nothing. Her silence made the Valet bolder and turned him into what criminal slang describes as a 'till frisker'. The guilt which had threatened to engulf him soon passed.

Thinking he could win back his losses, the Valet took two postal orders worth fifteen shillings from the till. 'That day,' he said, 'marked the commencement of my career as a criminal.' A depressing but inevitable sequence had begun. 'Whenever I lost I stole more money from the till with the easy excuse that, after all, my mother could spare it. And whenever I won I kept the proceeds and enjoyed myself at night.'

The Sport of Kings appealed specifically because there was a grown-up glamour about it for someone so young. In his book *The Victorian Underworld*, the author Kellow Chesney wrote: 'Nowhere could one see so much of the genteel part of society cheek by jowl with its dregs as at race meetings.' The Valet was particularly fond of the Epsom Downs. William Powell Frith captured it in his 1858 painting *Derby Day*, which he described as portraying the kaleidoscopic aspect of the crowd and modern life with a 'vengeance'. The dirt poor or poorly off – and there was a distinction between them – were able to rub along with the toffs there. As Frith demonstrated with oil on canvas, the big races at Epsom resembled a carnival: bright flags, white tents, music and picnics with strong drink. It was the grandest of days out. Wealthy racegoers wore silk top hats, frock coats and soft gloves. The women accompanying them were stylish in long, showy dresses, and twirled dainty parasols. There were impromptu sideshows of minstrels, Gypsy fortune tellers, acrobats and con men who encouraged the gullible to find the thimble, which their fast hands hid. The racing itself was almost incidental. But the surge and press of the crowd to witness it served an ulterior purpose for criminals. It was the perfect place to pick pockets. Published in the early 1870s, Routledge's *Popular Guide to London* warned tourists to the capital: 'Carry no more money about you than is necessary for the day's expenses.' Sightseers were also told to 'avoid lingering in thoroughfares'. The tone of menace and foreboding continued. 'Never enter into conversation with men who wish to show you the way . . . or invite you to take a glass of wine or play a game of skittles.' The stranger to what it christened 'the Great Metropolis' was particularly cautioned to look after his or her watch and chain and to 'take care of your pockets at the entrances (and exits) to theatres, exhibitions, churches and in the omnibuses'.

A race meeting brought together a crush of people with large amounts of money for betting. The good pickpocket could take advantage of it and slink off before the victim realised the loss. The most prolific earned £20 to £30 per meeting. There were different types of pickpockets: the prop nailer, who took pins or brooches; the thumble screwer, who stole watches; and the mobsmen or buzzers, who lifted wallets and loose cash through incredible manual dexterity. Pickpockets generally worked in teams, which allowed a trinket or a wallet to be passed like a baton so speedily that in seconds the loot was transported a safe distance from the spot where it had been taken. Wallets and purses were preferable to jewels or watches. If a watch or a gem was stolen, it had to be given immediately to a fence to be sold in case the pickpocket was caught in possession. If a wallet was stolen, the money could be removed, and the wallet itself discarded. No one could trace individual banknotes. An experienced pickpocket wore a specially made jacket with cavernous pockets, almost as deep as sacks for swag, and carried a sharp knife to lay open the pocket of his targets.

The Valet became a fingersmith, taught to pick a pocket so nimbly that eventually, at a casino table in Monte Carlo, he took £1,500 from the man sitting beside him. The man knew absolutely nothing about it. 'I continued to sit next to him,' said the Valet, and 'gamble his money away'. He could shake hands with someone and strip a loose ring from a finger without marking the flesh. His study and apprenticeship in the black art was intense; and the method of training was identical to the way in which Dickens wrote about it in *Oliver Twist* where the 'so jolly green' Oliver watches as a 'very curious and uncommon game' is played out in front of him between the Artful Dodger, Charley Bates and Fagin.

Fagin places a snuff box in one pocket of his trousers, a note-case in the other, and a watch with a guard-chain in his waistcoat. He sticks a mock-diamond pin in his shirt. He buttons his coat tightly around him and hides away his spectacle case and his handkerchief. Oliver sees him saunter up and down the room with a stick – 'in imitation of the manner in which old gentlemen walk about the streets any hour of the day'. Fagin pauses at the fireplace and then the door, as though 'staring with all his might into shop windows'. As he does so, the Artful Dodger and Bates glide and dive around him like swooping birds. Dickens then has Oliver observe: 'At such times, he would look constantly around him, for fear of thieves, and would keep slapping all his pockets in turn, to see that he hadn't lost anything . . . At last the Dodger trod upon his toes, or ran upon his boot accidentally, while Charley Bates stumbled up against him behind; and in that one moment they took from him, with the most extraordinary rapidity, snuff-box, note-case, watch-guard, chain, shirt-pin, pocket-handkerchief, even the spectacle-case. If the old gentleman felt a hand in any one of his pockets, he cried out where it was; and then the game began all over again.'

This is how the Valet learnt too – slowly and laboriously. Sometimes a coat with a bell attached to it would be hung on the wall. The novice would strive to take a silk handkerchief from it without making the bell clang. This was called cly-faking. Or, just like Fagin, a trainer such as Mitchell would put a handkerchief in his back pocket to test his pupil. As an outdoor activity, he would ferry the recruit to the market and tell him to take apples unobserved from a stall. The Valet was a fast learner. He kept his fingers soft and supple and progressed from apples to wallets, from handkerchiefs to jewellery. The money he earned was spent in jubilant sprees at the races. For a while, during his late teens, there was only drinking, betting and crime in his life – and no punishment to accompany it. He learnt in the field, making mistakes and then correcting himself. By the time Mitchell died in 1876, the Valet could have taken a tie clip from Lord Tennyson and put it back again without the Poet Laureate knowing a thing about it.

The Valet maintained that he once possessed the chance to create an honest living for himself. 'If I had stuck to that way of life,' he added 'there would have been no sensational story about Harry the Valet.' He said that he fell in love with the daughter of a respectable builder who lived in St John's Wood. Her name was Mary. She was on friendly terms with his mother, he added. His father and hers had attended the same Freemasons' lodge. The account the Valet gave ran like this: he was 21; Mary was 18. He regarded her as 'very pretty' and insisted: 'I had always had a certain admiration for her.' He called her a 'mere child' who 'knew nothing of the other side of my character'.

He said he was walking along Great Arthur Street and met her coming the other way. 'In those days it was not considered fast or wrong for a respectable tradesman's daughter to take a glass of port with a young man,' he explained. He took her to the Old Horseshoe pub in Tottenham Court Road and fanned out some money he'd recently won at Epsom. She was so winsome and charming that, the Valet claimed: 'For the first time in my life I began to have doubts about the kind of life I had been living. By Jove, I thought to myself, here is the chance of a lifetime.' He said he asked Mary to marry him, telling her, 'You know I have always admired you, and now that I have saved a bit of money – enough to settle down comfortably. I would make you a good husband if you would accept me.'

According to the Valet, the proposal arrived so unexpectedly that she had no idea how to reply.

'Why not say that you love me, Mary?' he asked.

'How can I when I have never thought about it?' she responded.

The Valet answered one question with another. 'Suppose I take you home now and see what your father says about it?'

The father was 'a practical man not inclined to throw his daughter away on the first man who came along'. The Valet said he received his blessing with one proviso: that he devoted himself to the picture-framing business. The wedding took place in St Luke's Church and the husband and wife subsequently lived with the Valet's mother above the premises. 'For three months while I was courting Mary, I stuck to the shop. For another two months we lived very happily together.' Then, he said, 'married life began to pall a little'.

There were soon rows. He said his friends 'chaffed me a good deal about my married life, which kept me at home at nights and so worked on my mind that in a very short time I had forgotten all my good resolutions and was drinking and betting as heavily as before'. He remembered a 'disconsolate' and weeping Mary telling him: 'If you go on like this I am sure something dreadful will happen. The people who are keeping you out cannot be any good for you. You promised me that you would never stay out late like other men do.' He replied: 'Stuff and nonsense, girl. A man must have friends and it is a mistake when a wife tries to interfere in this way. It will only lead to trouble, so you had better leave me alone.' The Valet added: 'Time and again I came home in the early hours of the morning after a night's merriment, turned a deaf ear to her pleading, and was so blind to my own foolishness and wickedness that I did not see I was killing her by inches.' He labelled the marriage 'The one thing in my life that I have always regretted'.

The Valet was blunt about what he'd now become: 'A hardened little scoundrel,' he said. He colluded with scoundrels too. His friends were criminals – 'more frequently in jail than out of it'. With them he lived vicariously, simply satisfied to have enough free cash to drink heavily and dress fancily, and to bet whenever the chance arose. Nothing was ever saved. As he put it: 'Some days I was lucky, and other days broke.'

A horse called Fulminitas, again running at Epsom, made him a tidy sum. He backed it with £50 at 100/7 – and won £750. 'It was more ready-money than I had ever won in my life,' he said. The Valet's head became giddy with his surprise success. He lost his sense of proportion, flinging cash around in a ticker-tape parade of excess. At one end of the social scale he frequented swish clubs and indulged in lavish dinners with candlelight and champagne. At the other he spent boozy lunchtimes drinking rough ale and eating whatever was served on grimy plates in a German chop house in the Seven Dials. Some of his winnings were wantonly squandered on horses which, unlike Fulminitas, failed to live up to their pre-race hype. He never counted exactly how much he had already spent, or how much he still had available to spend. His funds vanished at an alarming rate. 'The time came when I saw clearly that I would soon be at the end of my resources. The business was scarcely paying; what little income there was my mother required. What to do, I knew not.' Within three weeks he was broke and 'pretty desperate'.

The Valet was nursing his financial bruises when pure chance pulled him into the company of another down-on-his-luck racing man, whom he would only ever call by his nickname: Bill the Dasher. At first, he thought this meeting was one of the luckiest things to have ever happened to him. The Valet and the Dasher dissolved into self-pity, consoling one another in a beery session, cursing their ill-fortune and conveniently overlooking the self-inflicted nature of it. The Dasher tried to 'touch me for a fiver', he recalled. The conversation then went like this:

The Valet: I'm broke, Bill. Everything I've touched has gone down. My luck's dead out. I'm very sorry. You know you would have it if I had it myself. But I haven't a bean and I don't know where to get one.

The Dasher: I say, have you ever tried to do anything on the crook?

The Valet: Not me. I don't think I'd care to go as far as that. It isn't a very safe game.

The Dasher: Dead safe to a man like you. What I always says is the fellows that get pinched are the mugs that deserved to get pinched. Have you ever seen a cop with brains?

The Valet: Never studied them much.

The Dasher: Well, you can take it from me that they haven't any. Only policemen in plain clothes with an education.

Now a fellow like you with brains . . . I've known you a long time, and I know – why bless my soul – you could beat 'em, whack 'em hollow every time. Why Harry, my boy, you'd make your fortune with a bloke like me to advise you.

The transparent fib was the Valet's claim never to have done anything 'on the crook' before, as if he were a paragon of honesty and virtue. He needn't have been so prim. The Dasher's question was a superfluous tease. For he knew the vague outline of the Valet's pickpocketing past. What he needed to find out was whether the Valet would own up to it, thus making him available for hire, or whether he would dissemble, leaving the Dasher to resort to greater powers of persuasion. He knew the Valet was a fast learner. He knew he was quick on his feet too. He recognised him, at best, as a potential partner or, at worst, an ally whom he could usefully mould.

All was vanity with the Valet. The blandishments of the Dasher made the recipient a willing sop. He conceded: 'There is nothing like flattery to turn a man's brain, especially if that man thinks a good deal of himself.' The Dasher talked on, almost without pause, about the 'clever things he'd done to baffle the police', whom he continued to portray as slow of mind and foot. He was a case hand – an innocent-sounding term for someone who sneaks luggage away from its owner at railway stations and boat docks. 'The police are so stupid,' said the Dasher, warming to his theme and sensing he was close to converting the Valet to his cause. 'Once, when I was working at King's Cross, I walked up to a policeman who was standing at the van of the Scotch Express and, handing him a portmanteau I had picked up, I asked him to put it on a hansom for me, which he did like a lamb.'

'You don't say so,' said the Valet, a captive audience by now.

The Dasher discussed the simplicity of his modus operandi and his previous successes. The Valet ought to have made the obvious point. If the Dasher was as competent as he claimed, why had he originally tried to borrow money from him? The Dasher's soft soap continued: 'If you and me were to work together . . . why, a smart looking bloke like you could get away with a jewel case as easy as winking.' Having enticed the Valet into his scheme – a classic spider, fly and web scenario – the Dasher made certain there was no possibility of hesitant second thoughts. He arranged for the two of them to work in tandem less than six hours later. The men went to King's Cross to wait for the continental train. Under the Dasher's careful instruction the Valet simply walked up to where a porter had placed several cases on a hand-barrow and snatched one up and walked quickly away. He took the case to the Dasher, like a dog bringing a ball back to its master. 'He was hugely delighted at my success,' he said.

The Dasher called for a hansom cab and told the driver to take them to a pub in Aldgate, where the case was opened in a private room. 'It was evidently the property of a man and wife,' said the Valet. Inside was a ruby necklace, a pair of coral and gold earrings, a number of dress rings and a handsome gold hunter watch. 'The watch,' said the Valet, 'attracted my fancy.'

'I've always wanted a watch like that,' he told the Dasher. 'If you don't mind, I think I'll keep it.' A grizzled pro like the Dasher wasn't impressed with such a carefree, almost cocky attitude or the Valet's apparent belief that he could do what he wanted with the loot. 'Don't be a fool,' he said, almost begging the Valet to trust him. 'You don't want to stick to anything that would give you away if it was found on you'. The Valet frowned, reluctant to admit that his new accomplice was right.

'But who's going to find it?' he asked.

'The cops to be sure,' replied the Dasher. 'If you have a tumble. Besides, we're going halves on the deal.'

The Valet interrupted: 'Who said we were going halves?' he asked, irritably.

'It's the rule of the game,' added the Dasher, slapping him down, 'and there's no good getting nasty. I'm only telling you for your own benefit.'

Dazzled by the glint of the watch, the Valet was stubbornly unrepentant in his decision to cling on to it. It felt pleasantly heavy in his hand. It was a smart-looking timepiece, which he thought would make him look distinguished in the Seven Dials restaurant or standing by the rail at Epsom. He imagined stringing its barley-twist chain across his waistcoat and lifting it out of his pocket, depressing the catch and opening up the cover to reveal its white frame with neat Roman numerals. 'I don't care what you say. I've always wanted a watch like this, and I'm going to keep it,' he said flatly. The Dasher and the Valet raised £80 from the sale of the jewellery. It was bought by a fence whose office was a back parlour which opened off a small chandler's shop in Brick Lane. The Dasher was 'very upset' at the junior partner's obstinate refusal to part with the watch. He sensed the worst. 'But, seeing he could do nothing with me, he consented to let me keep it,' said the Valet.

With the prize in his pocket, he dismissed the Dasher's concern for his well-being as over-protective nannying. The Valet thought he knew best.

It was a grievous mistake.

Patterns recur in life. Harry the Valet's foolhardy crush on the watch, and the status which he believed ownership of it would bring, emphasised his vulnerability to bright things, as if confirming him as a magpie who could never resist sparkle and glitter. Money, precious stones and the Valet, however, were soon parted – and in predictable ways too, revealing his insatiable desire for luxury and the maelstrom of London's night life. He pitched himself into it with insouciance, gadding about the West End theatres and variety shows, eating five-course lunches and promenading in new clothes.

There was a charitable side to the Valet's nature too; a naive, over-generous streak that always led him back to poverty's door. He shared his cut of £40 among associates and total strangers alike. 'I entertained all my friends to champagne and lent a sovereign to anyone who asked for it,' he said. He behaved as though he had an inexhaustible supply of money or could replenish it whenever he liked. The inevitable fall followed. 'At the end,' he said, 'I was no better off.'

Scraping the lining of his pockets for any stray coin he could find, the impecunious Valet realised he could only maintain the lifestyle to which he'd become accustomed by finding another jewel case to steal. He set off without the Dasher. Charing Cross proved barren ground. So did Paddington. The porters and guards were gimlet-eyed, the owners of cases proved watchful of their possessions and uniformed police were spread across the platforms, as if expecting him. He had barely enough money left to take a hansom cab home. The solution to his dire straits was straight-forward simply because no other short-term option existed: he would pawn the watch he'd fought so doggedly to prevent the Dasher from selling. With reluctance, as if being dragged there, he went to the broker's. 'I had no difficulty in getting a loan of twenty pounds on it,' he said, indulging immediately in a last round of champagne and hospitality with the proceeds, as though saying a fond farewell to prosperity for the time being. The Valet thought nothing more of it. When the wheel of good luck turned his way again, he planned to return to the pawnshop and reclaim his most treasured possession. Just 48 hours later, there was a knock on his front door. A man was lingering on the doorstep. 'Are you Henry Thomas?' he asked.

'That's me,' said the Valet. 'What can I do for you?'

'You can give me some information. I understand you pledged a gold watch?'

The Valet felt his heart lurch. He stammered a reply. 'Er – no. I didn't pawn any watch; I never had a gold watch to pawn.'

'Are you sure? I must warn you that I am Sergeant Record of Bow Street, and I have information that . . .'

The sergeant's words drifted away from him; the Valet was too shocked to absorb what came next. 'In an instant I saw how foolish I had been to deny pawning the watch, as I had been idiot enough to give my own name and in my trepidation not to speak with cunning,' he said. He fumbled for an excuse, an alibi, a way out of the corner he had so crassly backed into. 'I remember it now,' he said to the sergeant, as though he was an amnesic whose memory had just returned. 'It was a watch. I bought it from a man in a restaurant.'

The sergeant's response was calculated. 'You do admit pawning it?' he asked coldly.

The Valet nodded, already regretting the fictitious figure that he had created in haste. The sergeant paused for effect. 'I don't want to make it hard for you,' he said, 'and if your story is true I may be able to help you find this man. But if you are lying and you are found out it will go very badly for you.'

The Valet could do nothing but plead his innocence. With each word, he condemned himself. 'I am not lying,' he said, deluding himself that the denial carried conviction. He made his parlous position worse still by adding: 'I do not believe I could recognise the man if I met him again.' The sergeant took a step closer. In measured tones, he said, 'I am afraid that will not wash.'

The Valet was charged with unlawful possession and taken to the Bow Street cells. He called it a 'night of terror I will never forget' – the slam of the metal door, the rattle of keys, the pounding of boots on bare stone floors and the nightmarish shrieks of other prisoners scared him beyond belief. That fear manifested itself in sweats and shakes. The Valet spoke in a trembling voice to his jailer. 'What should I do?' he asked. The jailer passed on the same advice he gave to hundreds of other first-timers exactly like the Valet. 'Tell the truth,' he said.

In the morning the stunned accused stood up when the charge was read, fingers gripping the lip of the dock in a token effort to conceal his nerves. He pleaded guilty in a thin, reedy voice that hardly filled the courtroom. 'With a sort of dare-devil stoicism,' he said, 'I awaited the decision. While still waiting I felt a tap on my shoulder.'

'This way,' said the jailer, pointing at the door leading to the cells.

The Valet followed him meekly, his head bowed, oblivious to where he was being taken. The acoustics in the court were so poor that he had not heard the length of his sentence; nor had he realised it had been delivered.

'What's happened?' he asked the jailer. 'Am I to get off?'

The jailer shook his head. 'What do you think?' he said, with a knowing smile. 'You've got four months. Consider yourself lucky. You'd have got seven years at the Old Bailey.'

Whenever the Valet looked back on the confusion he experienced in court, and the grim realisation of what lay ahead, he physically shrivelled, as if protecting himself against a blow. 'It was a broken man who stepped into the Black Maria,' he said. The van carried him to Pentonville, where 'my whole life flashed before me on the way to the cell. I saw my grey-haired mother. What a fool I had been. What an utter mess I had made of my life.' In the isolation of his cell he thought of what his father had once told him: 'Do nothing that would bring disgrace.'

The sight of Pentonville became engraved on his mind. He stared out of the window on the way there, gazing longingly at newly built suburban homes with their formulaic strips of garden. An ordinary, modest life now didn't seem so awful after all. The jail loomed in front of him, formidably dark and hulking. He saw the wall which encircled it, the postage stamp windows of the cells, the black metal portcullis jutting from a porch and archway. A small square clock tower rose just behind it. It was a dim, brooding place.

The Valet was bundled out of the van like a sack. He stood in the courtyard with the other new inmates before climbing one flight of broad steps to face a glass door. The frock-coated warden was waiting, his clutch of keys hidden in a shiny box and fastened to his belt with a wide leather strap. The Valet was marched into the hall where he began to take in his surroundings. From the central point four long corridors diverged, like the spokes of a half-wheel. Cells were compressed into three tight tiers, which were reachable across an iron bridge. To get on to the bridge the prisoners had to scale an iron ladder. The author Henry Mayhew once watched all the doors swing open simultaneously and likened the sight of inmates bursting out of them to 'bees pouring from the countless cells of a hive'.

When it was opened in 1842, Pentonville – called 'The Model' because more than fifty other prisons were based on its design – operated what were called separate and silent disciplines. The separate kept the prisoners apart, confining each to his cell which became a workshop by day and a bedroom by night. A prisoner could only be identified by his number. The silent forbade one prisoner to communicate with another by word, sign or gesture. He could speak to warders or instructors – but only as often 'as is compatible with judicious economy'. Leaving the quarantine of their cells, the prisoners wore a brown Scotch cap, the peak large enough to be tugged to the chin as though it were a mask. There were holes cut for eyes, which to the then Surveyor-General of Prisons, Sir Joshua Jebb, became 'phosphoric lights shining through the sockets of the skull'. He added that the prisoners had a 'half-spectral look . . . some wandering soul rather than a human being'. For exercise, a short drill – lasting almost two hours – forced prisoners to stand on three sides of the prison yard and pass a cannonball to one another after fetching it from a pyramid stack.

Pentonville's policy of extreme discipline had scarcely softened by the time the Valet experienced it in the mid-1870s. He was stripped of personal possessions and keepsakes. Wearing what he called his 'broad arrowed suit', he was taken to a scrupulously clean but gloomy cell – number B4. The cell was 13 feet long and 7 feet wide and contained only a plank bed, a water-closet pan with a cast-iron top and a metal basin for washing. Set into the door was a Cyclops-like eyelet, which the warders slid open to spy on him. The arched ceiling of the cell reached 9 feet at its highest point and 18-inch-thick walls deadened the acoustics. The still silence was worse than any eerie echo. In the abysmal darkness of the cell he felt emptiness and panic. 'To describe my first night at Pentonville would be beyond my power,' he said. 'I could not go to sleep. The silence nearly drove me mad. The shame of my position and my grief made me want to commit suicide. It was with relief that I saw the first light of early dawn creeping through my cell window, and rose from my bed to see the stars still shining coldly in the silver-grey sky of the morning. Strange and almost fearful was the silence of the prison at that hour.'

Blue light still enveloped the jail, funnelling through the solitary window of his cell, when the clock tower chimed and his breakfast of ten ounces of bread and a cup of cocoa arrived. The main dish was porridge – a food he could never eat again without thinking of Pentonville. Prisoners there regularly suffered dyspepsia and constipation, and mental disorders too. With pride and all too obvious glee, which suggested that the meals were tantamount to warm slop, the cook took it as a matter of personal achievement that 'There are few persons who can hold out against short commons. The belly can tame every man. It hurts him more than any cat that could be laid across his back.'

The Valet knew he was right. He was docile and obedient, with enough drive only to will the weeks to pass with as little physical and mental pain as possible. Talking to other prisoners was a difficult process. In the yard, he learnt the art of ventriloquism so he could carry on whispered and abbreviated conversations without the knowledge of the warders. Under the eye of the clock, each day was regimented: exercise at eight and then a variety of tasks, including sack-sewing, boot-making, basic tailoring or oakum-picking, until twelve. Lunch was a pint of soup with lumps of meat and boiled potatoes. 'For four months,' remembered the Valet, 'one day was like another. I toiled laboriously at my task until each dinner hour.' His fingers became hard and calloused through clumsy sewing, the needle repeatedly pricking his fingers and drawing spots of blood.

At the end of his sentence, the Valet walked alone out of the portcullis gates with nothing except bad memories. He confessed that his short incarceration – sixteen weeks of tedium, repetition and horror – ought 'to have strengthened my resolution to go straight'. But spiked by what he saw as the injustice and inhumanity of his treatment, the Valet decided to take his revenge. Instead of fashioning a new life, he went instantly back to his old one.

Chapter 2

The Garden of a thousand diamonds

'Rare gems have that strange uncanny fascination for all who are in the habit of handling them,' said Harry the Valet, articulating in the plainest terms how – and why – his obsession grew so quickly. He went further: 'They have the power to hypnotise,' he said, as if that sentence alone was sufficient explanation for his feverish pursuit of diamonds and rubies, emeralds and sapphires. These jewels entranced him to the extent that his waking thoughts were dominated by ways in which to procure them. The next theft was always uppermost in his mind. He became preoccupied with their cut and look, their colour and dazzle. He would roll them between his fingers, feeling the hard, solid points or caressing the smooth, rubbed curves. He liked to sit a diamond in the shallow well of his hand, tilting his palm so the light broke and fractured over it, like a wash of clear water. The sparkle of the stone stayed on his retina long after he viewed it.

The Valet never lost his fascination with stones. If a pendant, bracelet or ring came into his ken, he found it impossible to look away. He always wanted to possess the dainty jewel embedded within or around it. He would wait – hovering close by without being conspicuous – until, like a hawk descending on unsuspecting prey, the right moment came along and he took it in a sudden, elegant dip.

So it was that less than three hours after he left his Pentonville cell, stripped off his prison garments and dressed in his civilian suit, now fusty and cold from storage, he was a thief again.

It happened like this.

The Valet strongly believed that his sentence was 'cruel and perverted' in relation to the meagreness of the crime. To be locked up so long – and in such vile conditions – for nothing but a 'trumpery' gold watch was a sign that society itself was institutionally corrupt and lacked any sense of fairness or decency. In his splenetic fury, he saw no irony in the fact that he was a criminal – legitimately caught and properly tried in court – and complained acidly about the cold hand of justice. He no longer blamed himself for stealing the watch in the first place or for getting caught through his own absurd greed and stupidity. The police, the courts, the judge and even the warder, who had been so curt and sardonic, were even more culpable. They were dunces in a confederacy against him. Each had dealt with him as though he belonged to London's detritus, which could be swept up and binned in filthy places such as Pentonville. He was no longer afraid of the callousness of prison, or the miseries and deliberately dull, dehumanising routine of another stretch inside one. Pentonville had not crushed him. On the contrary, he had endured and survived it intact. He had not only emerged unbroken, but was stronger and more determined as a consequence of his experience. He wouldn't bother again with mere trinkets, such as the odd watch. He wouldn't again let himself be caught – especially by patronising policemen who thought themselves so bloody superior. And he wouldn't again allow anyone to treat him with such disregard and ill-respect. If society had already decided he was a thief – and had labelled him as one too – he would become the best of them. He would make it worth his while to steal. In his anger and resentment, the Valet told himself that each strand of his self-justifying argument constituted perfectly rational and calmly logical thought.

The chaplain of Pentonville was the Reverend Joseph Kingsmill, a pious thinker and writer as well as a respected if windy theologian. He subscribed wholeheartedly to the idea that rigorous, unflinching punishment was necessary to straighten out crooked timber such as the Valet. Prison, he said, 'allowed the mind to contemplate the deed' and character reform would surely follow in a Damascene conversion. Eventually the prisoner would see the waste and futility of his criminal ways. This was the theory he passionately advanced to the Valet, preaching to a one-man congregation, as soon as he arrived in the jail. On his release, the Reverend's simplistic but well-meaning words had the same effect as dropping a lighted match into a box of rockets. The Valet had scores to settle. He said he was 'resentful of everyone' and had become 'the foe of constituted society'. He made the decision to 'revenge myself on them and their system'. The Reverend Kingsmill's belief in the transforming powers of prison were about to be disproved.

The Valet always claimed Kingsmill's words were nonsense because of one fact. At Great Arthur Street, he said, he found his mother sitting by the parlour fire. 'She looked at me sadly, and rose to greet me and said "Well, my son, you have come home." Then she told me in hushed tones that my wife Mary had died.' The Valet continued: 'The shock was terrible. When I realised the truth I sat down trembling in every limb and covered my face with my hands, while my mother strove to comfort me. She told me how peaceful Mary's end had been, and, like a poor fool, I believed her well-meant words, not knowing, as I knew later when I met her father that she had died of a broken heart. She passed away with my name on her lips.'

If the Valet's first thought was for Mary, his second was for hard cash. 'Money I must have,' he told himself. 'Money for drink to bring forgetfulness. Money to set me on my feet after the unfruitful months in jail.' He headed immediately for Paddington station to wait for the noon express from Manchester in the expectation of finding something to steal. 'Bill the Dasher told me that the best time to get away with a case was the minute the train actually stopped at the platform,' he said. Conscious of the advice, he prepared to strike as soon as its doors swung open. When the train arrived punctually, the Valet walked 'leisurely' along the platform, his eyes searchlight-bright. He began to peer through the grimy carriage windows in the hope of finding a grand lady or a grand lady's maid, who was likely to have brought a jewel case with her. In one carriage he saw a neat, fashionable and pert woman. He lurked behind a porter, who politely twisted the handle of the carriage and allowed her to step out backwards. She was clutching a tied box in each hand and carefully watching two other packages, which remained on her seat. She placed her boxes on to the concrete platform and went back into the carriage to reclaim the rest of her luggage. 'This was my opportunity,' said the Valet. 'The crowd was pressing around from the other carriages; porters running hither and thither; friends greeting family; everyone pushing and hustling and bustling.' No one noticed the Valet. Casually, as if he might have dropped it in the first place and was now retrieving his own belongings, he bent down and picked up the nearest box with a handle. One moment he was there. The next he had gone – along the platform, through the barrier with a tip of his hat and out of the station. At full pelt, afraid of being tracked, he ran through the streets without hesitation and without looking back. He found a pub and persuaded the landlord to lead him to a secluded corner of it before levering open the case. 'Believe me, I could scarcely credit the evidence of my own eyes when, after throwing out several articles of ladies' apparel, I came upon a jewel-case,' said the Valet. Concealed within the well-folded clothes he found what he would forever rate as: 'Some of the most beautiful bits of jewellery it has ever been my lot to handle'.

One brooch was in the shape of a cross and comprised an emerald of 56 carats, another of 24 and a third of 15. Around it were set smaller stones of rubies and sapphires. The brooch was unique in that it could be taken to pieces so the wearer was able to turn part of it into a pair of earrings. The jewellery had clearly been made specifically for the owner. It was, said the Valet breathlessly, a 'marvellous *objet d'art* . . . the thing was so wonderful that it must have been designed and wrought by some very clever craftsman in Rome or Florence, where there are still artists of the old school. It must have belonged to a very wealthy woman.'

The Valet was reluctant to pick the brooch apart. 'I would have liked to have sold the cross complete to some dealer,' he said. His dreadful mistake over the gold watch nonetheless persuaded him to take a pair of tweezers and lift out the emeralds and the rubies. He dropped them into a small cardboard box lined with cotton wool. 'No doubt the owner of the cross was crying her pretty eyes out,' he said. She would have cried harder tears if she'd seen what the Valet did next. He smashed her cross into several pieces so it could never be identified. The excuse he gave was self-preservation. 'I had to stifle my finer feelings and do what any ordinary crook would do.'

Without contemplating too deeply the act of vandalism he had just performed, the Valet travelled to Brick Lane where Bill the Dasher had first taken him. The fence, stroking a long white beard, greeted him like the Prodigal Son.

'You have come to see me again,' he said expansively. 'What have you got to show me?'

The Valet shook the fence's hand. 'Something good,' he replied. 'I hope you will deal straight with me.'

The fence took umbrage at the implication that he might be about to pick the pocket of his newest customer. He gave the Valet a hard, accusing stare. 'You must not talk like that. I am always honest,' he said. As the Valet handed over the stones, he registered the fence's untrammelled pleasure at receiving them. 'I saw the old man's eyes glisten,' he said. 'He was so excited that it was like a play to watch him.' The fence was appalled at the Valet's destruction of the cross. 'What have you done?' he asked, inspecting the once perfect cross with a furrowed brow. 'Why have you broken it?'

'It was safer,' said the Valet defensively. 'You can't sell a thing like that anywhere. There can't be two like it.' The fence was unimpressed. 'What foolishness,' he said in a snappy rebuke. 'Young man, you have done wrong. You think you know your business. I could have sold it to my friends in Amsterdam for more money as it was.' The Valet dismissed his criticism with the retort 'what's done can't be undone' and then began to haggle over the price for the stones and the other bangles, bracelets and rings. There was an exchange of shadow-boxing. 'Knowing well I was a mere beginner,' said the Valet, 'the fence started off at £1,500, which was sufficient to tell me that the articles were worth three times that.' The Valet shook his head and told him: 'Look here. These things are worth £5,000 to £6,000 and if you want to do business in future with me let me have £3,000 and it's a deal.' The fence's shoulders visibly sagged, and his face fell into a grimace. To the Valet, 'the old man looked as though I had stabbed him in the heart'. There was a pause before the fence said: 'Three thousand pounds? But it is foolishness. I have not got the money, and it is not easy to sell stuff – there is a risk—' The Valet cut him off before the sentence was finished. 'There is a risk in pinching it too. I am not in the mood to haggle. Either you give me what I want or I go elsewhere.' The temperature in the room fell. The fence became harassed, as if afraid that the Valet would scoop up the jewellery and carry out his threat to take it to a more receptive and less complaining rival. 'There is no need to talk like that,' he said with agitation. 'Just to be friends with you I will give you two thousand.'

The fence had called the Valet's bluff. And the Valet, in calculating his limited room for manoeuvre, decided to fold. He was almost destitute. He knew few other fences – certainly no one else who was as experienced or had as many contacts in London or abroad as his new friend in Brick Lane. And he didn't want to traipse around the capital with thousands of pounds' worth of stolen jewellery hidden in his jacket. So he agreed to the fence's price, consoling himself with this fact: 'It was a lot of money to a man who had only just come out of jail.' In the underworld, a brief nod and a sly wink counted as a deal done. A handshake, which the Valet and the fence now traded, was like a signed contract, which could not be broken. The Valet was flush again. But this was only the start for him. As though he was a stockbroker, fixated on the market, he talked about growing his wealth to make himself independent. He told the fence: 'I admit I don't know much about this game, but before long I am going to know as much as you.'

In his own way the Valet was a genius. Exactly as he predicted, the novice was soon an expert, who knew as much as – if not more than – the cutters and merchants of Hatton Garden, let alone the fence in Brick Lane.

With commendable application, the Valet taught himself to appreciate jewels and not merely to steal them. The knowledge it took others half a lifetime to learn, he managed to absorb within a handful of years. He came to discern by sight and touch the origins of the gems in his possession. He read the telltale pattern of each cut, which was like knowing instantly the identity of an artist from the style of his painting rather than the scribbled black signature in the bottom corner of the canvas. And he became savvy enough to estimate the true value of a stone, which meant he could fully exploit it on the street. The fences of London could never again hoodwink or compromise him about the price of his haul. The Valet acquired both a connoisseur's eye for gems and a deft, sinuous reach with which to take them. This was no trade for the clumsy or the heavy-handed, and his nonchalance belied the complexity of the very action itself – the timing behind the decision to strike and the steely nerve to complete it. His hand–eye co-ordination was stupendous, and made theft seem blissfully simple. It was as if, too, he had been blessed with panoramic vision, a spatial awareness that enabled him to freeze-frame in his mind the precise position of anyone who might witness the theft, move to prevent it or be an obstacle to his escape afterwards. He proved so adept that to plot his progress around the capital would have required a map the size of a ballroom and battalions of pins or coloured flags to mark each success. He moved across the landscape like the Great Fire. Most of these thefts went unreported – often to protect the victim from embarrassment – and others went unsolved. The police attributed them nonetheless to the Valet, who was soon a thief of repute to Scotland Yard and among other criminals.

Patience and minute detail mattered to him. The actual theft of a case would be quickly achieved, but the planning of it was painstaking and seldom rushed or done on the spur of the moment. For early on the Valet understood that predatory instinct had to be harnessed to two things: essential background information about the places he was hunting and an intimate insight into those being hunted. The geography came first. At first, he followed the rules Bill the Dasher set down for him. He concentrated on railway stations. The Valet was essentially a north of the Thames man, focusing on the terrain he already knew well: St Pancras, King's Cross and Euston stations. He frequently switched to Liverpool Street or to that 'aisled cathedral in a cutting', Paddington, which became his favourite because 'I took tens of thousands of pounds from there'. He could slalom between its pillars, evading detection or capture. Later he tried Victoria, where after a lift he could walk pleasantly through St James's Park and admire the architecture of Buckingham Palace. Charing Cross became fertile ground too. From there he would head, as though just another ordinary shopper or sightseer, along the Strand. Only rarely did he cross the river to Waterloo. The three closest bridges – Westminster, Blackfriars and Waterloo itself – could be blocked off by the police too easily.

His stations of choice were generally cloaked in a Gothic darkness, illuminated by thin smears of light. They were congested with eager, anxious travellers who had nothing on their minds except catching a train on time and the excitement of a journey to come. The poor were able to take trips cheaply, which swelled the already packed platforms. With the overworked porters straining to meet the demands of passengers and always angling for a tip, the Valet could blend into this tableau without arousing attention. Each theft was nonetheless meticulously thought out. He memorised the railway timetables, his mind becoming a matrix of arrivals and departures which he could summon on demand and at speed. Every one of these operations was a sting, a piece of theatrical flimflam based on his own flamboyant sense of self and rooted in the fundamental flaws of human nature. For the porters were working class. They knew their place. With the wealth from his first big haul, the Valet was able to dress as though he belonged to the upper classes. In an age of deference he knew his fancy clothes would intimidate them: 'The crooks of that day had not awakened to the importance of disguise. There were few of the Raffles type, like myself. Who was likely to interfere with – or question – a gentlemanly-looking fellow?'

To endorse the point, there was no interference at all when he spied on one particular bejewelled woman and her maid. Lady

Eugenie Brett, wife of the then Lord Justice Brett – later to become Master of the Rolls and the 1st Viscount of Esher – was heading to her country estate in Surrey for the weekend. She was carrying gems worth £1,200, and gave the case to her maid before sending her to the ticket booth. The maid was idiotic enough to go to the window but leave the case on the ledge beside her. By the time she realised it was gone, the Valet was already transporting the jewels abroad. Given the position and reputation of her husband, he thought it safer to fence them in Amsterdam. The ticket collector saw him pass the barrier without arousing 'any suspicion of theft', remembering him only as 'just another smart gent'.

As railway crime increased, the porters and the police became more vigilant in trying to counter it. It became harder to part the likes of Lady Brett from her jewels. The Valet's natural habitat became instead Hatton Garden, the place of a thousand diamonds. The number of merchants and the amount of business done there made it more lucrative. 'Of course,' he said before using the slang of the criminal world, 'it was one of my haunts, and a Tom Tiddler ground for everyone of my kidney who was anxious for a likely job to tackle.' He drew a vivid portrait of the Garden, which made it appear a brick and glass version of Epsom racetrack:

> It is a wide street, where hundreds of men of all nationalities and all grades of morality meet to transact their business. They do not use the adjoining offices because they are not safe. A sandbag on the head, a sudden rush up the stairs, might easily result in several thousands of pounds changing hands in a few seconds, so they meet – Greeks, Russians, Poles, Frenchmen and Dutchmen – a mostly gesticulating and jabbering crew – to show their precious jewels to one another on the pavement stones, their backs to the wall and their eyes glancing suspiciously at all who approach them.

Always anticipating trouble, the Valet compiled an A to Z of jewellers and merchants, studying and pursuing them like a lepidopterist chasing butterflies. He gathered encyclopaedic intelligence on each target: where he liked to drink; what he liked to eat and which restaurants he preferred; the name of his tailor; the route he walked to and from his shop. The writer Anthony Ellis said of the Valet: 'He knew them all by sight, the big and the little, the honest and the dubious who did not inquire too closely into the origins of the gems they bought.'

The criminologist Major Arthur Griffiths, a former HM Inspector of Prisons, was explicit about the constant strain of dealing in jewellery. 'Every London jeweller has to defend his stock at the point of a sword; he is liable to daily attack,' he wrote. Security meant putting up thick curtains in shop windows to prevent thieves from watching the transactions inside. It meant hanging huge mirrors near the counters. 'They can then tell at a glance from where they stand what is going on around, while the evilly disposed are unconsciously betrayed,' added Griffiths. A secret spring was also installed under the counter, which automatically locked the front door to prevent a thief from escaping. Some thieves would digest the jewels raw, as if taking a tablet. 'This ingenious person is afflicted with a terrible cough,' wrote Griffiths, 'and every time he puts up his handkerchief in a paroxysm of coughing he swallows several stones.'

Another ploy was to politely ask the jeweller to spread stones over the counter for inspection. A well-dressed gentleman would look at them intently and then promise to return the following morning with his wife, who he insisted was responsible for making the final selection herself. He would reappear alone the next day, claiming his wife was sick. Again, the stones would be laid on the counter on his behalf. He would select those he wanted and leave them to be made into a brooch, ring or pendant. But one stone would already be obviously missing. As the jeweller began to search for it, and question the probity of his customer, the gentleman would graciously allow himself to be searched. Of course, nothing would be found. The jeweller would offer a fulsome apology for his effrontery in suspecting the buyer. Within a few minutes the next customer would appear, leaving an almost worthless piece of jewellery to be repaired. But he would depart with the stone the jeweller had just lost. For the first man had embedded it in a lump of soft wax, which he had previously stuck to the underside of the counter. His partner would take the stone from it without being suspected. The Valet was more subtle in his approach.

An uncut diamond resembled a puddle-grey pebble. Often merchants carried them in modest folded packets – oblong, white paper parcels similar to those that chemists used for made-up powders. The Valet would steal directly from the pockets of these men or their customers, beginning his raids on the stroke of noon or in a two-hour window after it when the Garden was at its busiest. He liked to follow his quarry at a safe distance into a shop or to wedge himself alongside them in the crush of a restaurant, where an accidental collision might occur. The Valet would reproach himself for his maladroit stumbling before promising to 'look where I am going next time'. The merchant whose wallet had gone would tell this well-dressed gent to think nothing of it. Only later, sitting in a restaurant and about to pay his bill, would the unfortunate man discover that something was missing.

He was always on the lookout, too, for the careless buyer who might leave a new purchase in a cab or carriage. By way of self-justification, the Valet said that 'To hold up a man was dangerous because a shout for help, and in a second the whole market would be on one's heels. To wait until nightfall to break into a safe was a cracksman's job, and real jewel thieves have their personal pride, and do not care to soil their hands by crude burglary.' He was not 'crude'. He would not 'soil his hands'. He had his 'personal pride'.

This pride meant that he was one of the planners – but not the perpetrator – of the £30,000 to £40,000 raid on the post office at St Martin's-le-Grand near St Paul's in November 1881. No one was ever caught for the crime. No one ever knew – at least definitely – how the robbery took place. The Valet was able to say with relish: 'It stands in the pigeon holes of the Yard as an unsolved crime. One of the most daring ever.'

The theft was carried out after criminals realised that some merchants and buyers preferred to deal by post rather than openly on the street. The mastermind was Adam Worth, who Sir Robert Anderson, the one-time Head of Criminal Investigations at Scotland Yard called 'the Napoleon of the criminal world'. Anderson added that 'None other could hold a candle to him.'

Adam Worth, cunning enough to mastermind a series of particularly daring crimes and clever enough to side-step those in pursuit of him.

Worth once claimed to have earned nearly £70,000 in each of three successive years.

According to one account – by the writer C. L. McCluer Stevens – Worth, a 'tall, clean-shaven man', went into the post office around 5 p.m. Outside the streets were dark and the fog was impenetrably thick. Worth innocently asked for a shilling's worth of stamps. Behind him came a messenger with 'golden, curly hair' beneath a uniform cap – actually a female member of Worth's gang disguised as a man. She ran into the basement and turned off the gas, which extinguished the lights. With darkness came chaos. The chief clerk, whose instinct told him it was a robbery, tried to get hold of the registered mailbags, which were on iron hooks behind the counter. Worth got there first, vaulting over the counter in one smooth move. With a bag over each shoulder he got away to a waiting cab. The Valet offered more details about it than ever before.

'For weeks,' he said, 'several of the cleverest diamond robbers in London shadowed the place to find out how the land lay. Each was picked for his job and we chose an array of characters: there was the workman type who was able to find out how the van-drivers received the mail, another who knew how the sorters worked and where, the Raffles-type [like the Valet] who was able to get into the office itself and find out about the internal arrangements.'

A timetable was made of incoming letters, which examined the procedures of sorting and sealing and handing over to the van man. A scale blueprint was drawn up to mark each room and passageway.

'It was a fine plan,' said the Valet, 'as neatly and as accurately drawn as if by an architect.' But, he added: 'The secret of the whole business was that all of the members of the gang were not *outside* St Martin's-le-Grand.' For, he said: 'It was considered that it would be courting failure to attempt to bring it off without having at least one confederate inside.'

The Valet described the sorting room – long benches where

men in overalls stamped mail with the government's leaden wax. In the streets horse-drawn vans waited to take the full sacks. When the gas was turned off, he added, there was a 'rush of feet and muffled sounds of bags being pulled along the floor'. The postal workers took no notice: 'They still stand where they were standing when the lights were doused.' said the Valet.

The gang escaped through a side door into a cab, which as the Valet disclosed, 'was not constructed exactly to the pattern with the Government coat of arms on it'. Vans in need of repair or service, he explained, were often replaced by an ordinary one. The impostor holding the driver's reins, however, wore the red cap of the postal service. The gang rode off in the van and unloaded it in a disused builders' merchant's off the Old Kent Road – less than three miles south of the Thames. A few hours later the empty cab was found north of the river in Euston Road.

'Myself,' said the Valet, 'I was not in town.'

He was in Russia, where he met the French actress Sarah Bernhardt, who was performing in Dumas's four-handkerchief weepie, *La Dame aux Camélias*. Bernhardt was then 37: still skeletally thin, still christened 'The Divine Sarah' with her sultry eyes, oval face and mop of black curls; and still dominating the stage and the showbiz gossip. From her theatrical contracts she could demand and receive 100,000 francs for expenses alone before agreeing to take a part. What became a three-month tour of Russia followed a similarly exhausting trek around America. In Odessa, however, she was verbally abused by an anti-Semitic mob; she threw fake jewellery at them, inflaming the locals further, and needed a ten-strong Cossack guard to protect her.

In St Petersburg Bernhardt mistook one of the Valet's associates, also linked to the post office raid, for a stockbroker. Trustingly she let the two of them show her around the city. The actress even allowed them to carry her jewels.

For once, the Valet sensibly resisted the temptation to steal them.

Chapter 3

The woman in the black and white poster

All serious daring starts from within. Some would say that the Valet possessed too much of it. He was a pleasure-seeker for whom the railway stations, the hotels and the clubs, and jewellery shops of The Garden were an interlinked carousel on which he could ride without paying. He stole because he enjoyed it, and he seldom invested or kept aside any of the money he made from his crimes; not only because he was a compulsive spendthrift and addicted gambler, but also because he felt he would always make more opportunities than he found. He never concerned himself over-much with the distant scene. He lived for each hectic, rousing day, and planned only as far ahead as his next coup. To continue to fashion his life around smart clothes, fine wines and entertainment, he simply had to steal to raise the necessary funds. When these dwindled, he would steal again. 'I made a fortune by crime,' he boasted before immediately emphasising his profligacy: 'And I spent it as fast as I got it.' The Valet reckoned he would never be poor for long. Nor did he think Scotland Yard would ever catch him. Even if he committed an error, through uncharacteristically shoddy planning or complacency, he believed any prison sentence would be moderate and survivable. The Valet also knew this: his use of aliases meant previous convictions would not appear on his record until the police began to recognise him by sight rather than reputation.

The thought of abandoning crime never occurred to him. It was the *only* way to live. The one-time juvenile till-frisker, apple stealer and apprentice pickpocket was flourishing. The 1880s swept by, taking him from one jewel case to another and from one wallet or fat pocketbook to the entire contents of a drawer in a hotel bedroom. He was untouchable, and each job urged him on to the next in an unbroken sequence of success.

The actual theft for him was a battle of wits and he always went into it fully armed. For the Valet really did believe that all the world's a stage. But to strut across it took enormous guile, and so did persuading the rich that he was unquestionably one of them – a highfalutin man about town. Like the art forger, who needed to know which varnish, paper and pigment were appropriate for his framed fraud, the Valet had to achieve the required verisimilitude too. Steadily he worked on his accent, shaving down and smoothing off its blunter edges, and refined his behaviour, which became courtly.

One of the attractions of the profession as he practised it was dressing up for an occasion – the theatre, a drinks party or reception, the opening of a new restaurant, where he could convincingly pretend he'd been asked to attend without producing a printed invitation. Preparation for the chase became as important to him as the catch itself. Chief Inspector Walter Dew gave one reason why the Valet's credentials were hardly ever challenged. Dew talked about the 'wonderful' clothes he assembled – the best suits, the softest shirts, an entire rack of shoes. 'Good clothes were part of his stock in trade. He loved nothing better than to live extravagantly and dress in the height of fashion,' he said. The Valet wasn't as flamboyant as Beau Brummell. He didn't dress as flashily as Oscar Wilde. But his love of the fit and feel of fabric, as well as the need to be convincing, made him fastidious about his appearance. He liked to admire himself in the mirror and was always ready to assume a part, as if criminality was a costume drama.

Clothes were one of the reasons he became so attached to the grouse-shooting season in Scotland, which spanned the Glorious Twelfth of August to mid-December. He called the Glorious Twelfth itself 'The one day of the year I looked forward to'. It was as if a starting pistol for crime had been fired across the dog days of summer. He expressed his passion for the grouse as though he was born on the moors wearing a tweed suit and carrying a shooting stick. 'I must say,' he claimed, 'that I always thoroughly enjoyed my season in Bonnie Scotland.' He didn't mean the visual splendour of the cadmium yellow and purple shaded countryside or the high, jagged lines of the pale blue Scottish mountains. He explained it in another way: 'You can picture me, at Euston Station, dressed in immaculate tweeds with my guns and servant walking up and down the platform ostensibly looking for a comfortable corner in a first-class for Perth, but really keeping my weather eye open for a well-filled jewel case to purloin with that ease and skill which invariably characterised my work of the period.' While others were distracted – 'thinking more about the little brown birds than their luggage,' he observed – the Valet went to work. He found it easier than shooting grouse out of leaden skies. 'I used to get away with as many as three or four boxes a night on the tenth or eleventh,' he said. 'And en route I would perhaps capture another one or two, and would then go to Edinburgh or Glasgow and pull off another big coup in either of these cities. The thing was so dead easy.'

In passing himself off as a grouse hunter, the Valet was so assured that he tagged along to country house weekends and shared in the hospitality. The malt whisky was a particular attraction. 'When I speak of enjoying the shooting,' he said, 'I am not merely dealing in figurative language. On more than one occasion, along with one or two of my friends, I shot over the Scottish moors without anyone being any the wiser or attempting to stop me.' The Valet would lodge at a hotel in Perthshire, where a number of shootings were taking place simultaneously. He would then mingle with a specific party, each member of which thought he was a friend or associate of someone else. There was safety in numbers, he decided. 'On the morning when we wanted to enjoy a bit of sport we simply sallied forth with our guns and took up a position at some considerable distance – say, around the side of a large hill – away from the main body. All the time the birds were being driven we kept a discreet distance, so that if any of the keepers chanced upon us they would imagine we were stragglers from the main body, or so that it could be explained to them if awkward questions were asked that, not knowing the geography, we had strayed from the adjoining pack'. The Valet was proud of the fact that he was never caught.

Bagging the odd grouse was one thing. But the main prize was always jewels and in October 1889 he took a case belonging to one of the country's best-known and most loved singers and actresses, Florence St John. She was then 34 and among the most prominent figures on the London stage; someone whose presence in a theatre guaranteed full houses. *The Times* talked lyrically of her 'burlesque talents'; the *Daily News* spoke of her 'vivacity and grace'. She performed in light operas, music hall and the occasional comic play. St John was a dainty thing – black hair piled up in corkscrew curls and ringlets, a minuscule mouth with thin lips, and a small nose. She was pictured regularly on cigarette cards and posters, advertising the Gaiety Theatre, which paid her £3,500 per year. With other engagements her annual income was £5,000. A fabulous wage, indeed, for someone born so humbly as Margaret Florence Greig, one of six children of parents who ran a run-down boarding house and a small shop in Devon. The Valet, a star-struck theatregoer, first saw and admired her from a seat in the stalls of the Strand in 1887. She was cast as Madame Favart. He saw her again as Olivette, which, he said, 'firmly established her as a public favourite'. She proved unforgettable as Marguerite in Offenbach's *Faust up to Date*, which toured America. There was even a song written in her honour there:

> Oh, tell me why should Miss St John
> Pronounce her name as *Sin Jin*?
> It would be better, two to one
> I've heard a hundred people say
> To substitute the hard g for j
> For then she would be *singin'*

Florence St John, who made theatre audiences swoon and compelled would-be suitors to trail across London after her.

Her friends called her Jack or Johnny. She was already four-times married (and a fifth husband would follow) by the time the Valet became tenuously acquainted with her. St John was first married in 1869, aged 14, to a 22-year-old sailor. The brief union was broken by both sets of horrified parents. In 1872 she became the wife of pianist and conductor St Alfred St John, who died in 1875. Next, at the end of 1876, she wed the baritone Lithgow James, divorcing him three years later. Her fourth beau was the French actor Claude Marius Duplany. Fame brought her everything but marital harmony; she left Duplany in 1888. Shortly before running into the Valet, St John was embroiled in a messy and highly publicised libel action. The court heard how 'a most malicious and foul' story, printed in a publication called the *Wasp*, had accused her of gross immorality based, purely it seems, on her string of marriages. The editor cum proprietor was subsequently fined £50 and his allegations dismissed as 'foolish chaff'. But, as well as stirring prurient curiosity the court case aroused the reading public's insatiable interest because of an interview St John gave to accompany it. She provided an intimate insight into her physical and mental state, discussing bouts of ill health and the pressure of fulfilling the expectations of her adoring audiences. 'One of my lungs has gone and I suffer tortures with my nervousness,' she admitted. The Valet found her in a vulnerable state. For in the year St John lost her jewels, she also fainted during one performance and ran into stage equipment, spraining her wrist, during another. She was a muddled mess: full of self-doubt, unable to sleep or relax and struggling to concentrate on her singing. Her run of bad luck was about to continue.

Normally the Valet preferred to work alone. He found associates bothersome. 'My experience was that confederates sometimes get in the way or talk too openly afterwards and menace one's precious liberty,' he argued. The Valet had also experienced a frighteningly close shave with an 'avaricious American', who had just been released from a French jail. After the Valet had taken a jewel case from a woman passenger before leaving the Gare de Lyon his American friend followed her into the buffet car and picked her pocket before returning to the carriage which the Valet was occupying. The woman's maid went through the train, identified the American and alerted the stationmaster. Guards uncoupled the front and back of the carriage at Avignon and left it stranded there. 'If I had not had plenty of money to brief a lawyer, I would undoubtedly have been sent to jail,' said the Valet.

But in Scotland he took an assistant for expediency's sake. In his *Weekly News* autobiography, the Valet frustratingly called him 'Ernie S——', the surname removed to protect his anonymity. Ernie had guarded the Valet from police prying; in return the Valet guarded Ernie from the law's later scrunity. Ernie was indispensable. The Valet could not travel alone because he'd be the only grouse shooter doing so and would consequently give himself away. The logistics of the charade – various pieces of hunting tackle which had to be toted to Perth – also obliged him to hire Ernie to act as his servant in the way that Bunny Manders fetched and carried for Raffles. The Valet travelled in the oak-panelled splendour of first class; Ernie bunked down with the unwashed and the other gentlemen's gentlemen in third. True to type, even before the train headed north of the border, the Valet had chalked up his first triumph at Euston. 'I succeeded in lifting a box from amidst luggage in the central hall,' he said. The jewels were the property of a wealthy American. The Valet gave the box to Ernie, who smartly took it to a pub on the Euston Road, emptied and sorted the contents and collected £100 from a fence. All this happened within one hour. On his arrival in Perth, during the dark early hours, the Valet was wide awake to the possibility of another good haul. 'Everyone else,' he said, 'was half asleep. I had no difficulty getting a jewel case belonging to some unknown lady, and with this in my possession I jumped into the first train for Edinburgh.' Leaving Ernie behind, the Valet found an empty compartment and changed into a lounge suit. 'I made the transformation from a sportsman to a man who might easily have been mistaken for a legal gentleman up in Edinburgh to consult with a client.' The jewels were worth £350 and he hid them in his pocket and discarded the box, leaving it under the seat in the carriage. 'With dozens of similar cases lying about the platforms of Perth awaiting owners, none of the officials would ever dream it had been anything but mislaid and would not think of wiring to Edinburgh about it,' he explained.

The Valet had already eaten a sumptuous breakfast in the Caledonian Hotel when a tired, forlorn-looking Ernie staggered into Waverley station with the guns and the rest of the luggage. This contained nothing but a change of clothes and a few house bricks, added in case a porter noticed anything awry if he picked up one of the cases and found it to be feather-light. By now, said the Valet, 'I was quite satisfied with the success of my trip'. But if there was a chance of sneaking in yet another job, the Valet could never resist it. He was like a fox who simply could not refuse one more chicken for lunch.

When he saw a theatrical poster advertising St John's arrival at the Theatre Royal, he said: 'I suddenly decided to delay my departure south'. He was vague about the title of her performance, unable to recall whether it was 'Nell Gwynne or My Milliner's Bill or Mrs Parker Jennings in Jack Straw' (it was actually Madame Favart). But he didn't care. 'The name of this brilliant actress conjured up memories,' he said. 'A very beautiful and talented woman who took London by storm. I never missed a first night when she appeared. On these and other occasions, while I would not say that they detracted from my interest in her splendid acting or in the drama itself, I always admired the sparkling gems which she wore.' Ernie was unenthusiastic about the proposal.

'They won't arrive until tomorrow,' he said of the theatre group.

'We've got a lot of stuff on us, and Edinburgh isn't London.'

'We can easily sell the stuff in Edinburgh,' insisted the Valet.

'I know,' said Ernie. 'It isn't that I'm thinking about. We've done well so far. Why risk a tumble here? You've never done a lagging in Peterhead Prison, and from what I've heard about that place I don't think you would like it.'

The Valet looked at him with contempt and said, 'I'm not going to lose a few good jewels for fear of Peterhead. If you have cold feet you can go back to London and I'll do the job myself.' Ernie came obediently to heel.

The Valet relabelled the luggage and sent it on to London. The guns were pawned in a shop in Leith. 'We'd have aroused suspicion,' he reckoned, 'if we'd sent those back early.' The two men booked into a miserable hotel behind Waverley station. The full breakfast of the Caledonian Hotel was replaced next morning with a bowl of porridge. 'I loathed it,' said the Valet, 'because it carried my mind back to my first oatmeal in Pentonville.'

He knew Edinburgh only as the occasional visitor or tourist would know it. The city was more uniform and sombre-looking than London, as if most of it was cut from a single block of stone. The curved streets of the Old Town, wrapped in chimney smoke, and the compactness of its architecture seemed to shrink the size of the sky; and yet, beneath them, the long, wide strip of Princes Street and the garden running beside it gave the place a sense of grand space. On this Sunday, which he said was 'quiet as the dead', lights burnt behind drawn curtains, another sign of the Presbyterian reserve characterised by stern conformity and serious expressions. The perpetual exuberance of London, the feeling that something was either happening or about to happen, was never evident to him in Edinburgh.

As St John's train arrived with a company of twenty or thirty artistes, the Valet and Ernie tucked themselves unobtrusively behind waiting travellers on the platform. The two men looked for patrolling policemen; there were none in sight. Accompanied by her maid, the actress wore a neat blue travelling coat and a large black picture hat. 'She was looking as charming and as beautiful as ever,' said the Valet. 'I followed her every movement until she stepped out of the carriage and on to the platform.' St John handed her jewel case to the maid, who walked in front of her towards a small square where a line of cabs waited. The maid laid the jewel case in the cab and stood aside to let St John climb in first. She signalled to the driver to move on. She didn't see either the Valet or Ernie standing, like twin compass points, on either side of the cab doors. In the three seconds between the maid's careful placing of the jewels on the seat and then her backward glance to beckon St John into the cab, the Valet stole the case. 'I simply shot an arm through the offside window with the quickness of lightning and was off before the case was missed,' he said. He and Ernie hared up the narrow stairway leading to Princes Street as if all the bats of hell were in pursuit. Of the theft, the Valet said: 'These things are done in the twinkling of an eye. You must think quickly and act quickly or the result will be failure. Really it was funny, just like the clown in harlequin at the Christmas pantomime, and often I have chuckled to myself as I recalled it.'

The Valet and Ernie darted along passageways which were unfamiliar to them and through the nooks and crannies of a city as difficult to navigate for a new arrival as the Hampton Court maze. With supreme irony, they found themselves in front of the theatre where St John would be performing. The Valet lingered, letting his eyes wander across the theatre's Doric columns, its wide pediment and arched windows and the short carved figurines perched on the roof, like ship's lookouts. The front of the cream-coloured building was streaked with soot, which ran down it like tear stains. The Valet read the colourfully lettered words on a tall advertising bill pasted on the wall near the double doors of the entrance. In its centre was a full-length, black and white photograph of St John resplendent in her ornate costume. She was smiling back at him, as if beckoning the thief into her first show. The Valet turned to Ernie. 'Bet you a fiver she isn't smiling now,' he said. 'Neither am I,' replied Ernie, nervously. 'We're too near this theatre to be comfortable. She may head straight for this place.'

With no London-bound train imminent, the Valet and Ernie searched the backstreets for a hotel or a boarding house in which to pass themselves off as commercial travellers. 'To add to our difficulty,' said the Valet, 'people seemed to have taken vacant apartment cards out of their windows. We were at a loss about what to do.' Ernie became especially afraid, expecting, as he turned each blind corner, to find a dozen policemen facing him with handcuffs and rattling shackles. 'Fate had been in our favour,' said the Valet, 'but little did we think what she had in store for us. How we got out of Edinburgh safe and sound I cannot imagine. Just pure luck! What will, must be!'

It was murky mid-afternoon and the early autumn light was beginning to fade. A figure was walking towards them, and the Valet latched on to him. As the Valet said, struggling to believe it himself, 'He turned out to be the very man we were looking for.' Did he know of a boarding house nearby? Of course, he said. In fact, he lived in it and the landlady was looking for boarders. The location in Spittal Street was just a four-minute walk from where the three of them were now standing. If the Valet and Ernie cared to accompany him, he would be glad to make the formal introductions and vouch for them. The Valet claimed he and Ernie were salesmen carrying valuable samples. The man told them he was an Indian medical student studying at the University.

'We secured two bedrooms for ourselves, and the man very kindly offered to allow us to share his sitting-room for the rest of the evening,' the Valet said. He explored the house to find somewhere to store the jewel case, which was marked with the actress's initials: *F. St. J.* Neither he nor Ernie had a wardrobe. 'There was nothing for it but to ask the man if he would mind if we locked it up in the cupboard of his sitting room,' he added. Ever polite and trusting, the medical student handed over the brass key. So, as the Edinburgh police force aimlessly scurried around in search of the actress's jewels, the thieves responsible for taking them sat in comfort beside the warmth of a coal fire. The Valet had begun to relax, slumping back in his chair and stretching out his legs before embroidering the fictional story of his travels for the benefit of the medical student. 'Everything looked rosy,' said the Valet, 'when all of sudden there was a rat-a-tat on the door and a chatter of voices which made me sit up . . . The police, I thought.' A solitary image rose up in front of the Valet's scared eyes. 'Peterhead Prison was the picture I saw,' he said. The Valet glanced anxiously at Ernie, whose face was now the colour of parchment. 'Ernie looked,' recalled the Valet, 'as though he was about to make a dash for the window and jump out.' The Valet tried to calm him. 'What's all the row?' he asked the medical student. 'Who is coming to disturb the peace of the Scottish Sabbath?'

'It's only the new lodgers,' he was reassured. 'This is one of the houses on the theatre list. I hope the girls are as pretty as the last lot. We get some very charming companies sometimes.'

A troupe of female dancers and singers arrived and stood in the hall. The Valet heard them 'chattering like magpies' and saw them 'casting inquisitive glances' towards him. The Valet was outwardly composed. Inside, however, the arrival of St John's entourage had 'knocked me to pieces . . . I gave Ernie the signal that I wanted to see him upstairs.'

'Got the wind up?' asked Ernie.

'Not exactly,' said the Valet. 'But we've got to get out of here all the same.'

Ernie took a lungful of air. 'Can you beat it? If you saw a scene like this on the stage, would you believe a word of it? Fancy walking like this into the lions' den.'

The Valet gave a measured response. 'It certainly is a striking coincidence. And for all we know every one of these girls may have heard about the loss of the sparks.' Ernie offered moral support. 'We'll get out,' he said, 'no trouble about that. But how are we going to get the jewel case out too?'

The Valet found a solution. He told Ernie to draw the medical student out of his sitting room. Any excuse would do, and Ernie announced that he needed to find the post office to enquire about his mail. As he was a stranger in a strange land, he didn't know the way. Would the medical student be gracious enough to take him? The Valet waved them off, reopened the cupboard and forced the back of the jewel case, leaving its lock intact. He put the key to the cupboard inside his pocket and forgot about it. Until he tipped the contents on to the table, St John's jewels were a mystery to him. They might have been theatrical paste. But what he found was 'a sight for the eyes':

One single-stone necklace worth £2,000
A pair of large eight to ten carat earrings valued between £300 and £400.
An array or rings and brooches, necklaces and wrist bangles.

The Valet valued the jewels at £15,000 to £20,000. The previous evening, he'd contacted a trusted fence in Leith Walk, who now agreed to hold them for a week. The Valet and Ernie fled Spittal Street, without saying goodbye to the student. They took a train to Carlisle. Again the Valet went into a first-class smoker and fell asleep; Ernie roughed it in third class, where a combination of hard seats and jerky rails made it possible to dream only in short snatches. 'It was a perfectly safe thing to do,' said the Valet of the rapid escape. 'It made it impossible for either of us to be detained:

even if we were arrested on suspicion there was nothing to connect us with the robbery.' Detectives patrolled the Edinburgh stations without spotting, let alone bothering, the Valet. He expected a 'welcome' party of police at St Pancras and got off the train tentatively. 'But if there were any Scotland Yard sleuths there,' he said, 'I can only say that I never saw them.'

A coded message was sent to the fence, and the jewels were forwarded to the Valet by parcel post in two cigar boxes. The necklace and earrings, the rings and bangles were swiftly sold and then disposed of in Hatton Garden and Antwerp. There was a twist to the story, which the Valet read about over breakfast on his arrival in London. 'The papers made a big splash of the robbery of the actress,' he said. Agency reports said that the landlady had called a locksmith to open the sitting-room cupboard (the Valet still had the key). The locksmith found St John's jewel case, and believed the jewels themselves were inside it until he examined the damaged back panels. Suspicion immediately fell, like the arc-glare of a spotlight, on the student, who, despite being an Indian, was described in the press as a 'well dressed man with broken English, speaking German'. The article said: 'He always paid weekly in advance and on the afternoon of the robbery he left the house and returned with two men, evidently English of gentlemanly appearance.'

After the discovery of St John's jewel case, the student fled and never went back to his room. The Valet speculated that he was 'terrified beyond measure' at the thought of the awful conse-quences awaiting him if he failed to prove his innocence beyond reasonable doubt. But, impaled on a spike of his own making, he knew nothing concrete about either the Valet or Ernie. He could only repeat, parrot-fashion, the fabricated lines he'd been fed and gullibly swallowed. He'd been duped and framed. Would the police believe him, or merely conclude that: (a) he'd been a willing accessory to the theft, and (b) he was withholding evidence to protect his friends? 'Putting two and two together, he saw his danger, as he had brought me to the house,' said the Valet. 'He cleared out of Edinburgh, which made it all the better for me. The landlady had not seen me long enough to provide the police with a good description. As a matter of fact, I do not think I was even suspected.' The Valet was right. He and Ernie were described blandly as between 'thirty and forty years of age' and wearing 'moustaches but no beards', which was so vague as to cover almost 35 per cent of the male population.

The loss of her jewels did not seem to affect St John on stage. The *Daily News* review of her act claimed she 'sung with her accustomed taste and power'. For the only time in his life, the Valet was not sorry to have missed her performance.

Chapter 4

Dancing the cancan with the Prince of Wales

It was five to eleven, and the lean black hands of the clock were locked together, as if in a lovers' embrace. Below them the purl and push of travellers, trainspotters and onlookers clogged each of Charing Cross's six platforms. It was almost impossible to turn in a half-circle without falling over or colliding with someone else. The bookstall and booking office were crammed with people, all of whom were in a desperate hurry. The noise was extreme – the hiss of steam and the spit of water, the high pitch of a whistle, the hard thump of cases and bags, trunks and boxes, the bark of dogs and the yelling of porters and anxious passengers being urged to 'hurry up' and 'move on' and 'mind where you're going'. Voices drifted away and were lost in the echo created by the station's impressive architecture – a vast arched roof, more than 160 feet wide and almost 100 feet high at its apex, which swallowed each word.

Three types of Londoner spilled into and filled Charing Cross. The first was the aristocratic and rich heading for the coast. A cabin was already reserved on a boat to carry them across the Channel. Another train would then ferry them further south still, enabling those who could afford it to leave behind the appalling weather of early March 1893. There was no suggestion that spring was on its way. The sky was a dirty pale grey, as if a sheet had been pulled tautly across a flat, high frame. The wind cut in from the east in prolonged, billowing gusts, making the thin trees bend and sway and whipping up huge scoopfuls of loose paper and other rubbish into the cold, dank air. It brought shower squalls too: blocks of fine, unremitting rain that soaked to the bitter bone anyone caught in it. The light was dismal, so dusky it seemed more like late afternoon than late morning. Waiting passengers peered through the open, half-moon-shaped end of the terminus. From the platforms, the city beyond the Thames looked hazy and indistinct, its buildings flickering reflections in a grimy window. Everything was leached of colour, looming out of the murk in a feeble wash of monochrome and sepia. In such gloom, the painter's palette of the Mediterranean – strong cobalt and ultramarine – was not only enticing. It was also a relief: a restorative cure to the miserable sight of London when winter's dead, clammy hand was still laid across it.

The second type at Charing Cross was the ordinary grafter, who was taking advantage of the weekend's blessed half-day or curtailed working day to travel at a penny-per-mile to see family and friends or to escape the capital for the wide fields of the country, irrespective of the damp and the steady drizzle which clung to their half-folded umbrellas. Trains ran from here as far as Hastings, Canterbury and Guildford. The third type was the fascinated, gawping bystander, who had been drawn to the station for one purpose: to see the Prince and Princess of Wales. A holiday had been arranged for Prince Edward, who regarded his round of official duties as an inconvenient interruption to his extensive and seemingly never-ending social life. He would always rather shake hands with a bottle of champagne than a stuffy official or dignitary. He would always rather charm a chorus girl than exchange tedious pap with an ambassador for the sake of fulfilling what he believed to be a pointless obligation. And he would rather attend dinner parties or go for a night at the theatre than plough through a heap of official documents and papers. Most of us would feel the same way. But – and it is a considerable one – the Prince had a tendency either to neglect or to deliberately avoid the boring in preference to the pleasurable even if his decision was detrimental to his own reputation and to royal interests. Queen Victoria allowed 'her Bertie' no serious role in running the country. He was an unreliable waster, never to be let loose on the most important state papers, and too frivolously indiscreet to even have access to the gold key which opened her red government boxes. The less trusting the Queen became, the more frivolous, gluttonous and promiscuous the Prince grew as a result of his deliberate exclusion. It would be over-simplistic to say that his gambling, reckless romps and numerous affairs – with, among others, the actress Lillie Langtry and Jennie Churchill – were displacement, occupying the space where preparation for kingship ought to have been. But the Queen's lack of faith left him with energy to burn; and so he burnt it. His engagement book was never empty, and he almost never slept. Whether it was wonderfully good shooting, an afternoon at the races or attending Evans's Music Hall in Covent Garden, where he ogled the female singers and dancers from a 'screened box, Bertie was wholly committed to the pursuit of a good, grand time. This, after all, was a man who'd been carried around a party all night in a sedan chair before the supports broke and he dropped like a stone to the floor and rolled across it; and someone who appalled Archduke Rudolf, Crown Prince of Austria, by dancing a 2 a.m. cancan with the Duchess of Manchester in 1887 at the Corinthian Club in St James's Square after ordering the band to play the quadrille from *La belle Hélène*. Rudolf (who shot himself eighteen months later) would have been more appalled if – as many others did – he'd caught Bertie and a prostitue luxuriating in his favourite swan-necked bath in the Paris brothel Le Chabanais, also frequented by Toulouse-Lautrec and Guy de Maupassant. The bath was filled with champagne.

On this trip filial responsibility forced him to avoid the brothel. Bertie was bound for Genoa, where the royal yacht awaited him and his family. There would be only the briefest of stops – for dinner – in Paris. With him were his wife, the long-suffering but still lovingly tolerant Princess Alexandra, and his daughters Victoria, 24, and Maud, 23. A specially commissioned train, taking them in supreme comfort on the first leg of this long journey, was stoked and ready to depart from Charing Cross as soon as he and Alexandra arrived from Marlborough House. Police and well-scrubbed porters roped off the platform to give the Prince and Princess a clear path from carriage to compartment. The Prince arrived with his entourage wearing a dark three-piece suit, a watch chain draped across his slightly portly stomach, and a bowler hat. In one hand he carried a black, silver-topped cane. With the other he waved at the crowd. Even those who had no idea the Prince would be walking through the station, or had little interest in his activities, turned or stood on tiptoe to glimpse his entrance. There was only one figure in the station who took no notice of him whatsoever.

Harry the Valet was looking elsewhere.

A society crook needed to devour the society pages. The Valet insisted he was an 'assiduous reader of the Court Circular and other papers', which he said 'recorded the progress of people who moved in the best circles'. The *New York Times* said that he knew 'everybody of wealth and consequence in Europe'.

The newspapers and magazines he bought from bookstalls – sometimes on his way back from stealing jewels – included *The Times*, the *Illustrated London News* and the *Daily Telegraph*. He was ferreting out news and gossip, often those tucked-away items which few others would bother to scan because they were too dreary, too obsequiously compiled or too divorced from everyday middle-class life to be of much value to them. What some might consider irrelevant, the Valet viewed as being as precious as mined gold. It was like ransacking private address and appointment books or combing through the bedside cabinets of a titled gentleman and his wife.

He recorded the habits of the gentry in a hardbound book. In it he kept details of births, deaths and marriages, and of friendships too – the lineage of double-barrelled toffs and the nicely well-heeled, who were close enough to spend weekends together in the country or to summer with one another in the South of France. There were lists of who used which box in London's theatres; who went regularly to Christie's showrooms for auctions; and who was partial to an afternoon's horse racing. All this and more he could glean from ostensibly trivial snippets.

The aristocracy used *The Times* as a means of communication as well as for pernickety point-scoring and disclosed an enormous amount of invaluable intelligence to the Valet as a result. They talked to one another in its pages. Since it really *was* better in London society to be spoken about – rather than not spoken about at all – this newspaper coverage stroked the vanity of people who regarded themselves as superior enough to feature, as if by right, in these deferential titbits. Lives were not so much chronicled as superbly flaunted, albeit in dust-dry language which often led to outrageously snobbish acts of one-upmanship relating to who was moving up the social ladder or sliding down it. The upper classes were able to follow one another, like a private detective pounding a daily tail. Who went where, as well as who was seen with whom, could not be kept secret – and most of the aristocracy didn't want it to be hidden anyway. High or low status was thus apportioned.

For a few scrappy pennies, the Valet found inside each edition of his favourite newspapers and magazines more information than he could conceivably handle. He came to know, as though it had been whispered discreetly in his ear; who was marrying whom, where the marriage would take place and the identity of most of the guests; which philanthropic duke or duchess was holding a fund-raising ball and the location and the hour of it; which date a member of the nobility would be heading off to the Riviera. From his knowledge of the railways, the Valet worked out the time and platform of departure. In particular he studied group photographs – the so-called 'shooting galleries' of men in dinner jackets and ladies in long dresses – so he could plainly recognise from whom he was stealing, and register any new faces likely to turn him a profit. It helped to make him an utterly believable gentleman cum prosperous businessman. Clad in his fine suits, he could abandon his true self. He would pose and mingle, catching the elite unawares in his stealthy, silk-smooth way because he'd been privy to the same innocuous tittle-tattle as them. He could therefore trade it as though, at worst, he was on the periphery of their esteemed circle. The Valet was frank about it. 'These journals,' he said, 'often gave me a useful tip which resulted in a rattling good afternoon's fun at a garden fete, a fashionable bazaar or the laying of a foundation stone.' He went to these jollies in search of what he described as 'a few prizes', which he defined as a 'diamond necklace or anything sparkling which might be within reach of my nimble fingers'. Believing the Valet was someone of means, the men and women with money and position told him what he wanted to know. He asked the right questions. He got the right answers. And he noted them down. The Valet made it appear that these conversations wound coincidentally down the avenues which all along he wished them to take. In punctuating each one with both banal and juicy society gossip he created a provenance for himself.

Immersed in the social scene, he turned himself into an encyclopaedia of who was who. He knew the Prince of Wales was not only leaving Charing Cross for the continent, but also that his presence on the platform would be a distraction. For when everyone's gaze but his own became fixed on the Royal party, the Valet would make his move. At most he'd only have a second or two. But it was enough for someone who was the master of concision, capable of stealing a jewel case in less time than it took to inhale and exhale a breath. The Valet's target was the former Duchess of Manchester – the Prince's one-time cancan partner.

In her early carefree days, still in the first bloom of her beauty, Louisa Frederica Auguste Grafin von Alten was a gorgeously attractive woman. She was born in Hanover in 1832. Her hair, the colour of anthracite, was parted down the centre and fell in a wave over slim shoulders which were as pale as Michelangelo marble and beautifully shaped. The skin of her face was pale and finely sculptured too – firm cheekbones, a narrow line to the nose and slender eyes, above which the brows were plucked and tapered. Her hands were fluted at the wrist. She was delicate without being brittle, graceful without being over-dainty. She had only to look at a man to win him. Among them was Spencer Compton Cavendish, who became first the Marquess of Hartington and then – in 1891 – the 8th Duke of Devonshire. He was foremost a politician, who led the Liberal Party, then the Liberal Unionist Party and finally the Unionists from the House of Lords. Asked to form a government after Benjamin Disraeli lost the 1880 election, Hartington shook his head, declining with regret because he felt his claim was, at best, tenuous and his position consequently untenable. Six years later he refused to become Prime Minister again, partly because he felt his own party lacked sufficient strength for the task and partly because he feared losing his seat at the next ballot. Instead he supported the Conservative leader Lord Salisbury. And in 1887 Hartington rejected a generous overture from Salisbury, who was willing to step aside and allow him into

Downing Street in his place. For a third time Hartington said no, which suggests one – or perhaps a combination – of the following: lack of confidence or ambitious lust for power; that an unselfish gene was rampant in his make-up; or that he took a rigorously practical view of the political circumstances and on each occasion calculated that short-term glory would lead to long-term misery.

With his full beard and high forehead, Hartington looks formidably stern and stately in Sir Hubert von Herkomer's portrait of him, which was painted in 1892. But he was a spirited, kindly figure who waited three decades to marry the true, lasting love of his eventful life. Without the slightest exaggeration – and meaning it wholly as a compliment – *The Times* claimed he was Louisa's

The so-called 'double' Duchess of Devonshire, who was described as the grande dame of the Victorian era.

'devoted and constant admirer'. The two of them began an almost thirty-year affair in 1863, and his infatuation with her was an open secret. Hartington was unable to comprehend the idea of marriage to anyone else. However, Louisa was already married to Viscount Mandeville, the 7th Duke of Manchester. But when the Duke of Manchester died in 1890, *The Times* put it bluntly: Louisa had 'recovered her freedom through widowhood'.

She married the bachelor Hartington – by then a duke – in mid-August 1892. She was 60; he was 59. Some called her 'the double Duchess'. To others she was 'The most typical grande dame of the Victorian era . . . the 'kind and attentive hostess', who 'greatly enjoyed' herself and never lost her 'slight' German accent. The newspapers generously emphasised the romantic nature of the clandestine Mayfair wedding. 'The strictest precautions were taken to keep the marriage a secret,' said one report. 'Even the vicar did not know until the last moment the hour of the ceremony . . . even while [it] was in progress the pew-opener of the church had been stationed at the outer door to warn off any individual who might by chance present himself for admission.' Indeed, only Queen Victoria, the Prince of Wales and the outgoing Prime Minister Lord Salisbury (he'd left Downing Street the previous day) knew of the wedding.

When the Valet decided to steal from them, the Duke and Duchess were still in honeymoon mode, as if Cupid had only just released his arrow. They couldn't stand to be apart from one another, the Duke reluctant to let the Duchess out of his adoring sight because marriage had made the world such a rosier place for him. It was agreed nonetheless that she would head off alone for a break in Monte Carlo. He would follow a week later after finishing off pressing political business. He was pining for her before the train left Charing Cross.

The Devonshires owned seven homes and land totalling 186,000 acres, including Chatsworth House in Derbyshire, Bolton

Abbey in Yorkshire and Holker Hall in Westmorland. The Valet was more interested in what were regarded as three 'glittering items' the Duke had given his Duchess as a sign of his commitment to her: a diamond tiara, a five-row pearl necklace and a diamond necklace. The Valet was convinced that the Duchess would never travel without these tokens of her husband's love – especially as she would miss him at the start of the holiday. The Valet had no difficulty in recognising either the Duke or Duchess. As soon as the wedding was officially announced, photographs of the couple in respectful oval crops appeared side by side in the newspapers, as if husband and wife were caught in separate halves of a gold locket. The Valet was already familiar with the Duke. Like the Valet, he was an avid man of the turf, a follower of form and odds, who enjoyed the green furlongs of Epsom more than the green benches of the Commons or the red of the Lords. The Valet was already familiar with the Duchess too. She liked to play the tables at Monte Carlo.

Preparation and execution of the Valet's plan was flawless. In retrospect, it would be seen as a dry run – a near-perfect rehearsal – for the theft of the Duchess of Sutherland's valuables from Paris. The Valet arrived at Charing Cross, went through the painted, arched sign that read 'To the Continental Train' and hid among the crowds. He moved out of the way of the porters' wheeled trolleys, which threatened his shins and ankles, and wove in between travellers and well-wishers, alighting close enough to the first-class carriages to linger as he spied on the Duke and Duchess's arrival and made them the focus of his attentions. The Duchess's train was due to depart at 11 a.m. The Prince and Princess of Wales would leave from an adjoining platform at 11.05 a.m. The Valet waited for the hubbub and kerfuffle, which he knew their appearance would stir. Rather than use his trusty Gladstone bag – too cumbersome to grip on such a packed platform and too likely to be knocked or bumped out of his hand

– he brought with him a smart beige canvas sack with long tied strings, which he folded inside his jacket pocket. On the front of the sack was an embroidered S. He borrowed the initial for no other reason than he thought it looked more distinguished than the other letters of the alphabet – even royal in appearance, as though it belonged on the Prince's coat of arms. 'The bag always commanded respect and averted suspicion,' he explained. After taking the Duchess's jewel case, he would drop it into his sack and then saunter through the ticket barrier without glancing at the guard. The Valet believed one thing: if he looked as though he knew where he was going – and acted as if he had a legitimate reason to be there – he would never be challenged.

The Duchess arrived punctually, and the Duke fussed over her on the platform, ensuring her carriage was comfortable and airy and that the windows opened without sticking. A maid and a footman took care of what the *Pall Mall Gazette* would later describe as 'a good deal of baggage' and 'a number of small packages'. Among them was a green leather case, locked and strapped. 'It would not take an expert thief to identify [this] as a jewel case,' added the *Gazette*. As ever, the maid took charge of the jewels. But the Valet saw the footman take the case from her and put it under the maid's seat in the Duchess's first-class carriage. The Duchess and the Duke remained on the platform; the over-anxious Duke asking time and again whether his wife was satisfied with the arrangements; she calmly reassuring her husband that he needn't fret. And then – as if a theatrical curtain had parted and set the footlights ablaze – the Prince and Princess came into view.

Just as the Valet predicted, the sight of the Prince provoked an instinctive reaction. Heads turned. Low bows were made. Eyes followed the Royal couple, as if each was a rare specimen of wildlife. Most importantly for the Valet, no one took the slightest notice of the Duke, the Duchess, the quick steps he was now taking towards the carriage and the jewel case, which was soon in his right hand. The Prince and Princess disappeared inside the Royal carriage. The Valet disappeared down the platform. Only a minute before the Duchess's train pulled away, her maid called out in a high-pitched shriek: 'The jewel case has gone!' So, of course, had the Valet – and without anyone knowing he'd been there in the first place. He'd been an amorphous and transparent presence at Charing Cross, as though starring in the glass and light trick of *Pepper's Ghost*, the popular stage illusion which fooled and fascinated the Victorian public in equal measure.

The Valet was exultant. He'd smoothly pulled off what he regarded as one of his greatest criminal exploits. The train was delayed, and a hasty search took place. The Duke seemed more distressed than his wife – because she knew something he didn't. Within ten minutes the Valet found out why the Duchess had reacted so impassively, as if she'd simply misplaced a handkerchief. When he forced the lock of the case, expecting the glittering majesty of the jewels to tumble out and blind him, the Valet discovered he'd been outwitted. The case contained a spirit lamp, three scent bottles with silver tops and a trinket or two of fake jewellery. The real jewellery had been packed elsewhere, and he had fallen for its decoy. As the *Pall Mall Gazette* wrote with a barely suppressed sense of *Schadenfreude*: 'There is somewhere in London today a gang of high-class thieves with a grievance as big as Charing Cross Station. The world to them is the dreariest of deserts.' The rest of the account encompassed the 'huge bustle' at the station, the simultaneous departure of the Prince and Princess of Wales and the fact that 'no one saw any suspicious persons about'. The *Gazette*'s anonymous writer came to the conclusion that 'Without doubt a gang of high-class thieves had brought off a grand coup for which they had been plotting and scheming and watching perhaps for months.' No one believed that a criminal acting alone could possibly be responsible for it. The same thing would be said – and virtually the same phrases used to say it – after the Dowager Duchess of Sutherland theft five years later. The *Gazette* calculated that the content of the Duchess of Devonshire's jewel case was worth £10. By his own high standards the Valet's efforts were worthless. He'd barely made enough to buy a decent dinner. And how could a thief of his reputation try to palm off a few scent bottles on London's most discerning fences? The Valet was inconsolable and crimson-faced. 'The jewels were paste,' he spat in disgust, as if the Duchess had both wronged him personally and been spectacularly unsporting in hiding them in an ordinary piece of her luggage. She had wrecked a moment of perfection. Remembering it as an affront to his dignity, he winced whenever he thought about the incident, which he marked down as 'the biggest mistake I ever made.' Word of the deception, and the way in which he had succumbed to it like a knave, greatly amused the criminal fraternity. The Valet out-thought and left empty-handed by a duchess? Surely, it couldn't be so.

The Valet wasn't familiar with failure or the sourness of defeat. Since those terrible four months in Pentonville had hardened his attitudes to crime, he'd been in jail only once more. In 1891, after an uncharacteristic lapse, he was found guilty of stealing a diamond merchant's wallet from the splendour of the Holborn Restaurant. Momentarily losing concentration, afraid he was being watched from another table, he'd pushed for the wallet too soon and too forcefully. The merchant felt the hand inside his pocket, and gripped his wrist. The Valet could not shake him free. In court he claimed he was Thomas Johnson, a fact which the under-resourced police took at face value without bothering to check. As there was nothing to link his pseudonym to any previous offence, the Bow Street magistrate imposed only a three-month sentence. After his release, the Valet went back to his business as if nothing untoward had happened to him. Brimming with self-belief, he dismissed the incident as a painful inconvenience; just one of those mishaps from which he would soon recover. He put on his disguises again, bought his copy of *The Times* as usual and adopted the unruffled philosophy that Raffles would eventually espouse in the pages of E. W. Hornung's books. 'Why should I work when I could steal?' It was pointless to tell him that crime was amoral. Again, he would shoot back a line similar to one of Raffles': 'We can't all be moralists.'

He was morally indignant now, however. The Duchess of Devonshire piqued him because he wasn't used to losing. She had trounced him, and it felt like coming second on the Derby favourite. 'It was a mean trick,' he said, never forgetting it.

He took out his revenge on others. In the middle of the summer the Valet decided to work his way along the south coast, typically taking no interest in the beaches or the bathing, or even the promenade variety shows of the sort which so attracted him in London. He sent no postcards, bought no gifts to take home. Ignoring the start of the grouse-shooting season, he decided to go sailing instead. Or – to be more specific – he went fishing; for jewels, of course. The Cowes Regatta on the Isle of Wight was a festival of competition, in which gentleman amateurs raced against one another in cutters and raters. The Valet wasn't interested in wet sails or the sight of another yacht's sharp white prow spearing through the Solent. For all he could fathom it, the specialised vocabulary of the sport – even the basic terms fore, aft and starboard – might as well have come from the pages of a foreign phrasebook. He was a landlubber, a word he did understand perfectly well.

Off the water – or in the harbours, where the long, most expensive yachts and big ships had been turned into floating bars – the Regatta became a non-stop round of cocktails. The peacocks of the wealthy fluffed out and paraded their plumage beside the choppy water. This was London society on holiday. But, for once, the Valet wasn't interested in sharing vermouth or gin and tonic with them. Stealing jewels on the Isle of Wight was too dangerous for him. It meant somehow smuggling his catch from shore to shore without being apprehended. The Valet knew the police would descend on, and block off, the harbours as soon as any theft was reported. It would be like trying to break his way through a chain-mail fence. Nor did the Valet have a boat of his own to take an alternative route to the mainland. It was far safer to lift jewels 'on the dry' in Portsmouth and leave the port by rail, usually heading west before tacking back to a bolt-hole in Brighton.

Glorious Goodwood race week preceded Cowes. Racegoers would travel by train from there to the Isle of Wight in a boisterous party. The Duke of Richmond commissioned his own carriages to take him and his friends to Portsmouth Harbour railway station. The prize passenger was Prince Edward of Saxe-Weimar-Eisenach, former commander-in-chief of Ireland, and his wife Augusta. Among the Duke's other guests was Isabella Maria Katherine Anson, the 61-year-old Countess Howe, wife of Richard Penn Curzon-Howe, the 3rd Earl. A steam packet, which the Duke intended to use to cross to the Isle of Wight, had already moved off from the station pier so he decided to commandeer another boat and join the steamer at Clarence Esplanade at Southsea. Newspaper reports said afterwards that porters were 'busily engaged' in loading an iron cage, which would 'hold a large quantity of goods'. The cage swung on a hoist from the train and on to the boat. Countess Howe's maid and butler put her luggage inside – including a dressing case containing her jewels and a lawyer's brief bag bearing the letters IKC. 'It looked impossible to get it,' admitted the Valet, 'but not to your humble servant . . . a thing was never impossible to me as long as it was under my eyes.' He sidled up to the cage with his Gladstone bag, constantly glancing around him. Under the impression that the cage would reach the boat as soon as she did, the maid walked down two flights of steps to complete what she thought would be the straightforward task of retrieving her mistress's baggage. When the cage arrived, the dressing case and the brief bag were missing. The maid raised the alarm, unable to believe that the precious things she'd left on the platform – with the cage door about to snap shut on them – were now gone. It seemed as mysterious and miraculous as end-of-the-pier magic. All the trick lacked was a drum roll, a puff of smoke and a forked flash of lightning. But there was no gadgetry or gimmickry involved. The Valet had patiently waited until the maid was looking elsewhere. 'I slipped the box into my bag and walked quietly into the street,' he said. The Countess of Howe's case and bag contained jewels which included a green Indian enamelled necklace set with pearls and diamonds, two ruby rings, a blue pin in the figure of dove, another in the shape of a serpent, two gold watches and a Persian gold coin pendant. These were worth more than £1,000. There was £90 in banknotes and gold too; the newspapers speculated that 'three suspicious-looking persons, evidently racing men' were responsible. Not for the first time – or the last – the Valet was mistaken for an entire circus troupe of criminals.

The crime inspired a letter one month later in the Morning Post, it called on the government to recruit more and better-tutored detectives. 'What's the use of the police as at presently constituted trying to discover the authors of robberies like that . . . of Countess Howe's?' it demanded. 'The men who do these robberies are moneyed . . . and, worst of all, are most highly educated and of good personal appearance. The ordinary CID inspector is quite out-classed in such cases.'

Outclassed? Never a truer word was written in relation to the police versus Harry the Valet.

Chapter 5

The most powerful crook in London

He was in the peak of condition and in the prime of his criminal life; though, of course, he did not realise it then. Since he kept no account books, and filed no tax returns, it is impossible to know Harry the Valet's annual income precisely. But, given his high success rate, and extrapolating a figure from the number of jewel cases he readily confessed to taking, the probable – but highly conservative – estimate is £5,000 to £10,000 per year: well over £1 million today. 'In the course of my career,' he claimed, 'I made enough money to have bought myself a house in Park Lane and an estate in the country.' At his zenith – when fortune favoured his particular brand of bravery – the Valet said: 'I simply could not make a mistake and did practically what I liked.'

It was as if he'd been blessed – born under the luckiest of stars. Although life was fraught with exhilarating danger, the threat of being unmasked and caught made him bolder. He saw the chance of profiting from his crimes more clearly and brightly than before. And he got out of the most awkward entanglements with a contemptuous shrug. He wriggled away with aplomb – and without embarrassment – even after being found with the jewels in his hands.

At Euston station, during the typical, early morning rush to board the weekend train, the Valet glanced through the window of a first-class berth and saw the 5th Lord Cadogan reading his broadsheet newspaper. He saw, too, that Cadogan's wife was standing on the platform beside the open carriage door. She was talking to a friend without a thought about, or a backward glance towards, the jewel case she'd left behind. It lay, unguarded, on the empty seat next to her husband. The train was only a few minutes from departure. The Valet waited until the Lord was concentrating so hard on a story in one of the inside pages of his paper that he wouldn't notice the entrance of a stranger into the compartment. It was an arrogant assumption. As the Valet stepped off the platform and blithely lifted the jewels, Cadogan abruptly pulled the newspaper away from his face. 'What on earth are you doing with that case?' he said. He flung the paper aside, stood up and barked: 'Put it down.' The Valet faced him directly, the jewel case dangling from his fingers.

At his moment of crisis, expecting Cadogan to shout for the guard, his confident gusto didn't let him down. As though he'd been caught taking nothing more incriminating than a biscuit from the pantry jar, he looked directly at Cadogan. 'I beg your pardon, My Lord,' he said. 'I thought you were so deeply engrossed in your newspaper that you would not notice my little attempt to purloin your jewels. May I wish you good morning and myself better luck next time.' The Valet's supreme display of steely nerve astonished Cadogan so much that he convulsed with laughter, as if the thief had told him a joke with a killer punchline. The Lord was a philanthropist and committed donor to good causes (his money notably funded the rebuilding of Holy Trinity Church in Sloane Street). Now he extended this charitable disposition to the Valet's bungled feat. Cadogan took the jewels back and then, the Valet said, 'he replaced the case on the seat and watched me making tracks along the platform without endeavouring by sign or word to queer my pitch'. For this vein of passivity the Valet called him 'A rattling good sport' – the exact opposite of the Duchess of Devonshire.

Another incident confirmed his talent for escapology. An Italian proverb says that 'In life you meet everyone twice.' The Valet had stolen from so many of London's well-to-do residents that he was bound to discover the wisdom of that expression eventually. At a theatrical garden party, which took place in Slough, he went to buy an admission ticket and heard the woman selling them ask: 'Haven't I seen you somewhere before?' She thought his face 'very familiar'.

The Valet looked at her. She looked at him more intently still, taking in the detail of his features and waiting for an answer to her question. In the few seconds it took for the Valet to study her, he

Lord Cadogan, who had a charitable disposition and a sense of humour – even when his wife's jewels were taken from him.

recreated in his mind the place where their paths had crossed. It was very recently too – in the first-class carriage of a train carrying both of them from Cherbourg to Dijon. 'I had nearly, but not quite,' he said, 'taken her jewel case.' Some would have made a run for it – turning tail, as if hopelessly cornered, and retreating to the sound of the woman's scream as she alerted the police. A less coolly confident thief would certainly have given himself away, stammering out an excuse immediately. One of two scenarios would then have been played out – and both of them would have dragged the Valet into deeper, murkier waters.

He could have anxiously listed probable mutual acquaintances – entirely false, of course – in the hope that one of them registered with her. If the woman assumed there was an innocent explanation behind the stab of recognition she'd experienced, then her curiosity would be satisfied. But this strategy was akin to calling your opponent at the poker table after you'd been dealt a hand of shoddy cards. For every name the Valet got wrong would heighten her interest in him. There was also the chance – however infinitesimal – that whoever he mentioned might also be at the party and that she would summon them to verify his claim. The Valet could even have tried to underscore his innocence with short, jabbed protests. No, she couldn't have come across him in the past. He didn't recognise her; so how could she possibly recognise him? However, the stresses in his voice and the worried crease of his expression could have been traceable, making his guilt apparent. She'd have put two and two together as neatly as a dovetail joint.

But he had planned for moments such as this. Like an actor in character, the Valet couldn't be shaken out of the role he was playing. He neither betrayed fear nor appeared flustered. Rather than speed up his reactions out of panic and in a rush to brush off his inquisitor, he purposefully slowed them down before framing the flourish of his reply. He smiled at her. 'It's most unlikely,' he said, taking his ticket in an unruffled way. He then delivered the most disarming of lines, which he'd rehearsed to wriggle free of further questioning. 'I've just returned from Burma. I was there on military service for ten years.'

Still striving to fasten down her vague memory of him to a definite time and place, the woman didn't challenge his story. The Valet completed a circuit of the party so that his departure would not appear suspiciously hasty, then slipped away into the hot afternoon.

He was more fortunate elsewhere. If he thought it wise to take a break from the railway stations, or if he found the *Times* columns bare of suitable social functions to attend, the Valet would pad along the corridors and patrol the lobbies of Northumberland Avenue's finest hotels. The gossip columns acted like a liveried barker, always announcing in an over-loud voice dignitaries arriving in London from the country or visiting from abroad. The Metropole and the Victoria hotels were among the likely destinations for the duration of any stay. Businessmen with bulging pockets to be picked would be invited to lunch there too. These hotels were fertile ground for someone who fitted the identikit description of the typical hotel thief laid down by the crime writer John C. Goodwin. The hotel pilferer was 'a generally handsome scoundrel, well tailored, sociable, suave . . . who usually confines his attention to jewellery or cash.' The Valet was just such a man.

The plan was first to find out in which room a specific guest was staying. The Valet could always take a short cut, charming – with words or bribery – hotel employees, such as barmen, waiters, maids or cooks. Or he could win over the servants of the guests; especially, he claimed, the women who were wooed by his looks and his soft, flattering patter. If this failed, he would fall back on the hackneyed but reliable ploy of handing a distinctively coloured letter – carrying his chosen guest's name – to the clerk behind the reception desk. He would sit in the foyer of the hotel and wait until his quarry returned and collected his mail. The coloured letter acted like a raised flag, which the Valet simply followed. Alternatively, he would wait until the clerk was overrun with work and lay the letter on the counter. He would then watch as the clerk placed it in the appropriate pigeonhole.

There were crooks who used 'twirlers' or skeleton keys, made wax impressions to create duplicates or drilled small holes in the wood before using looped steel wire to negotiate the locks and bolts. Others would take the room directly above and affix a rope to a balcony, which could be climbed down to gain access and then back up again to make it appear that no one had ever broken in. The Valet didn't like to burden himself with clattering tools or the paraphernalia of the cat burglar. Why risk rope burns or serious physical injury? Why risk, too, being apprehended with a bag of implements in his possession? If it happened, what plausible explanation could he give to the police?

The Valet preferred to talk his way into a room instead of descending through it like the swinging clapper of a bell. After discovering the correct number and staking it out, he would return early the following day and wait until the sheets were being changed and the bed re-made. He'd then concoct a tale which obliged the busy maid to leave, enabling him to ransack the room. Or he would arrive having previously persuaded her to look the other way. It was a more straightforward and much cleaner operation. There were occasions when the Valet even claimed to be a real-life valet, insisting that he needed to search the room for something his employer had left behind. The employer, alas, hadn't given him the key. Would the maid be good enough to open the room for him? It was a discreet and very private item. Would she also be good enough to remain outside the door while he hunted for it? He could find what he wanted and be gone in less than sixty seconds. And, as he knew every side and back exit, it wasn't difficult to enter and leave the hotel without being seen. In this way he once got away with £1,000 after a maid voluntarily unlocked the door and let him waltz through it. 'I much prefer a gentleman's room to a gentleman's company,' he used to say.

The jewels would remain in the Valet's possession only as long as it took him to hail a hansom cab and for its horses to travel to Stoke Newington, where he had struck up a business arrangement with the most notorious of fences. His name was Joseph Grizzard, but he was known as Kammy. Born in 1867, Grizzard had the face of a stockbroker – a shaggy moustache, dark, short, slightly curly hair and a prominent forehead. The eyes were sad-looking and round and full, like black marbles. The heart was blacker still. An atmosphere of menace surrounded Grizzard, who became known as a cross between Moriarty and Fagin for the intricate, scheming way he plotted his own crimes and controlled a stable of thuggishly brutal criminals who dared not answer back or run away from him. Grizzard would simply hunt them down and inflict his revenge. The punishment meted out after capture would be gruesome enough to lead to the miscreant's maiming or swift or slow death, entirely depending on Grizzard's mood and the degree of his displeasure. It was a convincing deterrent to anyone else contemplating a similar moonlit flit.

Anxious never to stain his own hands with marks of the crimes he perpetrated, Grizzard detached himself from the robberies themselves. Those on his payroll were manipulated through threats, blackmail and extortion. If one of them was caught and sent to jail, he would be rewarded for his silence. For not grassing up, or implicating Grizzard, he'd generously be allowed to continue breathing and would serve his sentence without harassment by other prisoners. Grizzard would also protect the man's family or loved ones financially and physically, which made the debt owed to the gang boss all the greater on his release. The Valet called Grizzard 'The most powerful crook in London, surrounded by bullies who would not have stopped at murdering me'. The Public Prosecutor Sir Richard Muir once tried to reckon up the maths of Grizzard's crimes. 'How many hundreds of thousands of pounds went through Grizzard's hands is impossible to say – it may, indeed, have exceeded a million,' he estimated. As if half admiring the uncommon skill of his opponent who, like the Scarlet Pimpernel, had a knack of disappearing after the fact, Muir also said that Grizzard 'possesses rather a fine face with nothing in it to tell the world of the evil, intriguing brain'.

Grizzard was awesomely successful not only because he adopted the motto of Caligula – 'Let them hate so long as they fear' – but also because early on he fashioned a convincing front for himself, which Scotland Yard found almost impossible to penetrate. In a move both simple and ingenious, he camouflaged his violent and venal streak – and his real intentions – by setting up as a legitimate jewellery dealer. Describing himself as a merchant in Hatton Garden, Grizzard was able to deal legally in gems – or at least pretend to do so – whenever the police moved in to collar him. The seedy underbelly of his trade was hidden in plain sight, which is always the best disguise. If he was asked to turn out his pockets, or open his bag, Grizzard could always offer an innocent explanation for the jewels in his possession. He even flaunted some of the diamonds he received by embedding them in rings he wore on his own fingers, as though challenging the police to prove that the stones were stolen. Grizzard was so astute he responded to one raid – held as he was eating dinner – by dropping a pearl necklace into a bowl of pea soup. This was the one place officers never thought of searching. A police report on Grizzard in 1913 outlined the difficulty of finding sufficient proof of his villainy: 'He is a diamond cutter by trade, but has no established business premises. He does undoubtedly do a little business, but the greater portion of his time is taken up by organising crimes and buying and disposing of stolen property.' The report lamented the heinous

*Kammy Grizzard, regarded as a cross between Moriarty and Fagin because of
the scheming way he plotted his crime and the retribution he meted out to anyone
who opposed him.*

grip he exercised on small-fry crooks and other fences. 'We have
been unable to prosecute him for lack of corroborative evidence,'
it concluded.

The relationship between the Valet and Grizzard was based on
mutual need and dependency. The Valet was prolific enough in
the amount of business he generated for clients at home and
abroad to interest Grizzard. Grizzard paid handsomely in return,
which persuaded the Valet to take jewels to him rather than peddle
them at a lower rate elsewhere – even though trading with one of
Grizzard's competitors was a less fraught exchange and unlikely
to end in fisticuffs, a blow on the head or a broken bone or two.
With a wide web of contacts overseas, and a chain of associates
capable of moving jewels rapidly across London in a criminal game
of pass the parcel, Grizzard was crucially prepared to dispose of
the most distinctive brooches, necklaces and rings which other

fences were reluctant to touch. The Valet's penchant for stealing from the aristocracy meant many of the pieces he took were either heirlooms or had been specially made, which meant most were instantly recognisable and easy to trace. Grizzard willingly took a gamble on these jewels because he was so well insulated from the original theft and distanced from the subsequent handling of them. The Valet and Grizzard became so intertwined that each man found it impossible to separate himself entirely from the other. And the police found it equally impossible to lay a firm finger on either of them.

London's most feared and experienced plain-clothes officers chased the Valet, who made it his business to know his enemy and 'keep him close'. Whenever a new detective was appointed, he considered it imperative to be able to recognise him. In this respect

Walter Dinnie, who possessed a clever and analytical mind. He always used brainpower rather than brawn to catch crooks.

the hunted became the hunter. The Valet sought out the man and filed away a mental picture of his face; so he was always aware of which 'copper' was trying to blend into the background in Hatton Garden or at a railway station. The Valet was up to date on each prominent policeman's career path, and also knew which major crimes he had investigated. This provided him with the inside track on the most prominent figures in Scotland Yard. From it he deduced not only their strengths, probable weaknesses and specialisms but also their thinking and procedural technique. Generally the dectectives at the Yard were unoriginal, hidebound and repetitive in their methods. But there were exceptions. Principal on the Valet's roster of foes was the triumvirate of Walter Dinnie, Frank Froest and Walter Dew. The author George Dilnot said of them: 'No three men in the world could have been drawn together who had greater knowledge of crime and criminals.' The facts support his claim.

Dinnie, Froest and Dew were a disparate bunch – a mix of audacity, tenacity, cerebral strength and gut instinct. 'Dinnie the Demon' was a Scot, born in 1850. He worked as an Aberdeen bank clerk before moving to the West Riding Constabulary as a clerical officer in 1873. After joining the Metropolitan Police in 1876, he spent six years behind a desk – processing the paperwork that resulted from crime rather than solving it on the streets – before volunteering to become a detective. By 1889 his consider-able brainpower had enabled him to rise to inspector. Dinnie was a thinker, able to work out complicated problems. Diminutive and slender, with thinning hair, he looked like an accountant. Without doubt figures were his métier. He specialised in fraud, and his investigations led to the arrest in 1893 of a 'bold and successful swindler' called Charles Wells – otherwise known as the Man who Broke the Bank at Monte Carlo. When Dinnie hauled Wells off his yacht, the *Paris Royal*, moored in Le Havre harbour, the prisoner had twenty-four warrants against him for obtaining money under false pretences. He took it from investors who expected inventions to be filed on their behalf at the Patent Office in Chancery Lane. Wells usually did half the job, obtaining provisional protection. In 192 instances – lodged between 1885 and 1892 – just one patent was fully completed: for a musical skipping rope. With the money he made – said to be £4,000 – Wells went to Monte Carlo in 1891 and broke the bank a dozen times, winning on 23 out of 30 successive spins of the roulette wheel during an eleven-hour spree. He left with a million francs. He went on to defraud his clients of £40,000, claiming he was perfecting a propulsion device that would revolutionise marine traffic. In 1892 he was sentenced to eight years. The composer Fred Gilbert's music hall song made Wells famous rather than infamous. Especially catchy was the chorus:

> As I walk along the Bois Boolong
> With an independent air
> You can hear the girls declare,
> 'He must be a millionaire.'
> You can hear them sigh, and wish to die,
> You can see them wink the other eye
> At the man who broke the bank at Monte Carlo.

The capture and prosecution of Wells turned Dinnie into the Man who Caught the Man who Broke the Bank at Monte Carlo. His career took off because of it.

Froest was a much more robust and physical character. Tagged the 'policeman with the iron hands', he was the sort of character who would take a hammer to mend a watch. Froest had pebble eyes, a round, full face and a narrow, slightly hooked nose. Beneath it was a bushy but well-groomed moustache. In uniform he resembled a Prussian field marshal. He was described as 'one of the most famous' of Scotland Yard detectives, and

Frank Froest, one of the toughest policemen of the nineteenth century and whose interest in police procedure led him into a crime-writing career after retirement.

someone who possessed a 'natural capacity for adapting himself to any circumstance'. He was genial and good natured, said Dilnot, 'blue of eye, light of step'. He had thick fingers and large, wide palms. One of his party tricks was to tear a pack of cards across with his hands; another was to snap a sixpence 'like a biscuit'. The Valet came to know him as a 'cool, intrepid and brainy man'.

With a resourcefulness and strength of purpose, which was said to carry him ruthlessly through obstacles if he could not go around them, Froest fought off a mob near Hatton Garden and survived being stabbed in four parts of his body. Often the American police, admiring his cool proficiency and his criminal clear-up rate, recruited him for 'special cases'. Crooks who dodged or shook off other policemen were undone by Froest's persistence and unflinching courage. Among them was the US confidence trickster Winford Moore, the perpetrator of a fruitful 'next of kin' scam across every state. Moore's spiel was a tearful tale about his pennilessness and the tragic passing of a relative, who he claimed had died with millions stashed in the Bank of England. The hapless victim was asked to provide funds so Moore could mount a legal challenge and access the blocked account: he would naturally return the loan many times over after reclaiming his rightful inheritance. The most gullible believed him. Froest dragged Moore into court. He also chased down a train robber throughout the US and England, despite the fact that the criminal carried a gun and promised to shoot him dead. Tracking him to a table at Gatti's Restaurant in the Strand, Froest yanked the weapon away in a struggle. The revolver he took eventually hung over his mantelpiece as a souvenir. Froest's throttling grip next disarmed a murderous cowboy called Harold Kuhne who shot and mutilated half a dozen men. With each killing, Kuhne added a notch to the butt of his gun. His pet eccentricity was to dress in his 'murder suit' of jet black. In these clothes – and these clothes only – he would kill, explained Dilnot.

Froest's reputation for refusing to be intimidated dissuaded crooks from trying to bully or beat him. At the beginning of his career, which began at the age of 21 in 1879, he was responsible for inflicting a long sentence on an especially violent criminal, who threatened his life from the dock. Years later, after his release, the two of them met unexpectedly in the Strand. Froest was then Superintendent of the Criminal Investigation Department.

'I suppose you're a sergeant now?' the ex-prisoner said to him.

'Better than that,' said Froest.

'An inspector?'

'Better than that,' said Froest again.

'A chief inspector?'

'Better than that.'

'Ah, well,' said the crook. 'I think I better be going.'

Of these three detectives, however, Dew turned up most often in the Valet's line of vision. He had wanted to be a railway guard rather than an officer. He admitted: 'For some reason or other, I had an instinctive dread of the London policeman, which lasted more or less until I became one.' He only did so because a friend suggested that his methodical approach and rational mind equipped him for the Force. Aged 19 in 1882, he found himself posted to X Division in Paddington. Promotion to CID's H Division in Whitechapel came five years later. Within another twelve months, Dew was enveloped in the red terror of the Jack the Ripper murders. He claimed to know by sight one of the Ripper's victims, Mary Jane Kelly, and said he was among the first on the scene after her murder – though both claims were challenged. He called it nonetheless 'the most gruesome memory of the whole of my police career'. The victim's abdomen and thighs had been removed, along with internal organs, which were placed beside her. The face was hacked and scarred beyond 'all recognition'. She lay in a bath of her own blood, and the walls of her room were blood-splattered. Dew slipped and fell 'on the awfulness' of the floor, smearing his suit. He called the Ripper 'a frenzied, raving madman' guilty of 'bestial brutality'. His closeness to the case gave Dew a taste for fame. He criticised the Ripper investigation for its cold and untrusting attitude to the newspapers, which he saw as a 'great potential ally'. He became a convert to the art of public relations and self-promotion. Seeing its benefit in furthering his own claims, Dew made a point of always backing into the limelight. The swell of his ambition was diminished only by the size of his ego. He began to shape an image of himself as thoughtful and modestly erudite – a plain man's Sherlock Holmes without the stained-glass mind.

The futile search for the Ripper was ideal preparation for what turned out to be the capstone on the monument of his career. In 1910, after a transatlantic boat crossing and the first use of Marconi wireless telegraph to trap a criminal, Dew caught Dr

Hawley Harvey Crippen, the wife murderer who tried to flee to Canada with his mistress Ethel Le Neve. The poisoned remains of Cora Crippen, more popularly known by her stage name, Belle Elmore, were supposedly dug up from the cellar of the family home in Hilldrop Crescent, Holloway. A twenty-first-century DNA test, however, has shown that the body parts belonged to a man. Another theory is that the police – Dew led the investigation – planted the crucial evidence of a striped pyjama jacket belonging to Crippen in the shallow grave to conclusively ensure a conviction.

The photograph of Dew, in his black bowler and soft grey overcoat, leading the handcuffed doctor down the gangplank of the SS *Montrose* and on to Liverpool's dockside appeared wherever in the world newspapers – however obscure – were published. It became the seminal image of the case, and Crippen made Dew more than a name. He became a super-policeman, and wallowed contentedly in his international recognition.

But Dew never forgot the Valet, because in one sense the two of them had something in common. Just as the Valet did not appear like the archetypical criminal, so Dew did not resemble a plodding policeman. The man who didn't look like a lag was chased by the man who did not look like a copper. A *Saturday Post* profile of Dew put it into perspective. 'If a swell "nobleman" had to be shadowed the usual order was "Send for Dew". He doesn't seem like a policeman,' it said. The article went on: 'No one could suspect the faultlessly dressed, military-looking man of being an emissary from Scotland Yard.' With his nondescript oval face, anonymous bland features and oracular tone, Dew could move around 'fashionable houses, restaurants and theatres' and 'mix in society without the slightest difficulty'. He recognised the same traits in the Valet, labelling him a 'clever, audacious criminal'. To Dew there was 'something very disarming about Harry . . . handsome, debonair and plausible . . . no one would ever have taken him for what he was'. He viewed him as one chess grandmaster views another, aware of his abilities to dominate the board. The elusive Valet was nearly always one thought and two moves ahead of the game. It chafed Dew that a thief who plundered jewels so prolifically could fade away after the skilful deed was done, as if he wore Gyges' ring of invisibility. As Dew pointed out, with apparent terseness, he was 'well known to us'. That knowledge of him seldom resulted in capture because the Valet was too slippery. But the Force, it must be said, did not help itself.

A crook of the Valet's cultured stripe had the distinct advantage of being pitted against a disorganised, occasionally shambolic ragtag Scotland Yard. Before 1907, there was no extensive training for policemen beyond the tedium of foot drill. Some were illiterate and innumerate, ignorant of basic legal proceedings and unable to carry out elementary detection. Candidates simply had to be physically fit and of decent character – though even these rudimentary parameters were bent and broken; and in instances of a minor criminal past were never seriously investigated. Educational tests for policemen did not begin until the end of the 1850s. A White Book of instruction was given to each constable; no one, however, checked that it had been read and understood.

Other mistakes were not only made, but perpetrated. In the Valet's rampaging heyday an officer needed special dispensation to operate outside his own division. If a crime took place in one part of London, but the thieves hid in another, the task of following them across 'the border' could be hampered by resentment – chiefly the accusation of poaching – and the isolationism of small-minded detective inspectors, who protected their own patches as if everything and everyone in it belonged to them alone. Information was withheld rather than made freely available, which would have enabled one division to join the dots and connect a criminal to a crime, or vice versa. Given his habit of stealing and moving on, the Valet was easily able to hop safely from one district of London to another without risking arrest.

At first, the police didn't know that he'd passed himself off as Thomas Johnson during his imprisonment in 1891 and then as Thomas James after another brief stint inside in 1894 for taking a 'ladies dressing case' from a carriage at Charing Cross. The truth was only revealed in 1895, after he was caught with his hands on a diamond merchant's wallet. It was taken from the inside pocket of a coat hanging from a hook in the Holborn Restaurant. The jury ignored the fact that both the victim and a waiter categorically identified him as the culprit, who had been loitering near the cloakroom. Calling himself Henry Williams, the Valet fell on the pathetically lame excuse that he'd mistaken the man's coat for his own. It was, he maintained, a completely innocent error. No one was expected to believe such obvious nonsense. But the jury were hardly an intelligent species. They were taken in by the Valet's cultivated manners and found him not guilty. The judge – Sir Peter Edlin – was apoplectic. Edlin's *Vanity Fair* portrait reveals a plump, sombre and grumpy-looking fellow with a wide, smoky-grey goatee-like beard cut square at the base. He has a choleric complexion and drooping, baggy rings beneath each eye. Edlin was a severe judge, unafraid to mete out the hardest of sentences. In this instance, however, he turned his ire on the jury, which he first resoundingly mocked as moronic and then dismissed as not fit for purpose. In a rare act, he sacked them, angrily telling the usher to remove them from the court and to swear in another twelve men instead. The Valet had scarcely left the dock when he committed another crime. He came to the conclusion that neither the police nor the courts were able to restrain him. Only a mistake of his own making, the Valet decided, could ever lead to his conviction.

His disparaging opinion of police methods was valid. Scotland Yard inadvertently conspired to make life easier, rather than harder, for the Valet and his ilk. The police were ponderous in trusting, let alone adopting, new methods or embracing much-needed change. The CID wasn't created until 1878. Widespread photographing of criminals had not begun until 1871. A rogues' gallery was preserved and updated in stoutly bound, brown-covered albums kept in a square room with high shelves and a huge reading desk. Eight criminals appeared on each page, photographed face and side on. Smaller volumes detailed the marks or physical peculiarities, as well as the records of ex-criminals. But it was a long and often frustrating process. By 1893 – as the Valet was cursing the Duchess of Devonshire's ingenuity – it was said that only seven crooks were identified from twenty-seven searches in a single day. From the mid-1870s the Black Museum – the gathering together of the gruesome tools and instances of crime – could be used educationally. The various implements of the criminal, which covered everything from robbery to forgery, as well as its most famous cases, could be explained and discussed. But the Criminal Record Office, which pulled together and co-ordinated the distribution of information, didn't come into existence to properly synchronise the Force's efforts until the dawn of the First World War. The result was confusion caused by constant breaks in the line of communication; or little communication at all.

In combating jewel-takers such as the Valet, the young policeman was told, 'Get to know thieves, my boy,' which meant going undercover. The total abstainer would have to drink conspicuously in a pub where supping a glass of lemonade would expose him. Someone else would pose as a waiter or barman in a club to collect material. One officer spent a week delivering milk to gain intelligence on a particular gang. These detectives mostly relied on 'reckoning them up' – guesswork allied to expertise in which the best and the brightest could supposedly deduce from the suspect's eyes or manner whether he was innocent or guilty. It was as if the trademark of crime was found on the face as obviously as a scar or a tattoo. Charles Dickens compared the most accomplished of these policemen to a sherry-taster. Just as he could recognise, said Dickens, 'the precise vintage of a sherry by the merest sip, so the detective at once pounces upon the authors of the work of art under consideration by the style of the performance; if not upon the precise executant [then] upon the "school" to which he belongs'. Dickens added that 'The experience of a detective guides him into tracks quite invisible to other eyes.'

Frank Froest proved it. He once found an unknown man - head down in a water-butt – outside a country house. The gash on his head made it look like murder. Froest dismissed the idea. 'That man was a tramp,' he said. 'He hurt his head in climbing through the fence – he was probably going to break into the house. He went to bathe it in the water-butt. As he put his head down he slipped, over balanced and fell in.' His hypothesis was treated with disdain. Froest, after all, had made up his mind instantly. 'That couldn't be so,' he was adamantly told. The sceptic who said this went to the water-butt and lowered his head to prove his point. What came next was a 'smothered scream, a mighty splash and a pair of feet waved wildly in the air' as he also fell in.

There were other laudable examples. A sergeant made an arrest in a fashionable hotel purely on the basis of an ordinary shirt-button he found on the carpet. A theft had been committed from one of the rooms but the button did not fit any of the clothes belonging to the guest. The policeman spent the rest of the day loitering around the hotel until he found someone with a button missing. The match was indisputable. The Valet always made sure his buttons were tightly sewn. And he never wore a ring in case it got caught on the loose threads of a jacket or snagged someone else's button, or became entangled in the lace or fine stitching of a lady's dress. But he also knew he could flit around London without worrying overmuch about being caught through stray traces of evidence. Sweat and saliva stains, a particle of hair or a sliver of fingernail left behind were not going to incriminate him. Providing he didn't discard a monogrammed cigarette or a handkerchief, which could be read as easily as a printed calling card, there was nothing to tie him to the geography of a crime, let alone the crime itself. If there was trace evidence, the police often overlooked it. If it wasn't overlooked, it would more often than not be so inefficiently compiled, bagged and stored as to make the effort useless. And if none of those amateurish mistakes were made, it was unlikely to be interpreted correctly or be cross-referenced and distributed widely enough to be of value. The Valet seldom had a bad night's sleep over it.

He was fortunate in Scotland Yard's lack of enterprise and slack approach to the new science of fingerprints. It was as if forensics was a disease from a faraway country. In *The Tragedy of Pudd'nhead Wilson*, which appeared in 1894, Mark Twain made clear: 'Every human being carries with him from his cradle to his grave certain physical marks which do not change their character, and by which he can always be identified. These marks are his signature, his physiological autograph, so to speak . . . [it] consists of delicate lines of corrugations with which Nature marks the insides of his hands . . . ' But *The Principles of Forensic Medicine* by William A. Guy, published at the start of Queen Victoria's reign – a final edition coming out shortly before she died – was more concerned of other things, such as existence and removal of 'scars and tattoo markings', the shape and position of the nose, ears and eyes in identifying a criminal from his photograph, the 'alteration in the colour of hair' and the 'detection of blood stains'. The uniqueness of fingermarks is absent; such were the curious ways of late Victorian 'CSI'.

It was left to Francis Galton to make the most irrefutable

contemporary argument for the benefit of fingerprints. His 1892 book, *Finger Prints*, included diagrams, charts and tables too. Most Victorians had never taken much notice of, or seen any relevance in, the whorls and swirls and the loops and arches of their own hands. The more enlightened learnt of their importance – and the potential for using them to catch criminals – through Galton, a half-cousin of Charles Darwin. He highlighted the 'cheiromatic creases' and the 'centesimal scale of relationship' and said: 'Let no one dismiss the ridges on account of their smallness, for they are in some respects the most important of all anthropological data.' He went further, calling them 'little worlds within themselves'. Galton expanded the ideas of early fingerprint pioneers, among them the Italian Marcello Malpighi in the seventeenth century; William Herschel, who began collecting them as specimens from 1859 onwards; and Dr Henry Faulds, responsible for urging Scotland Yard to adopt prints in 1886.

The Frenchman Alphonse Bertillon developed something different: an anthropometric identification system based on the fact that the proportions of specific body parts (such as the size of the head, the length of the fingers, the shape of the ears) are never the same. By 1894 Scotland Yard had opted for a haphazard hybrid of Bertillon's anthropometry and the use of fingerprints to nail criminals such as the Valet. It still jailed the entirely innocent Adolf Beck, a 55-year-old Norwegian who once owned a copper mine and was considered 'something of a rolling stone' because of his various ventures and wandering past. Beck's tragedy is pertinent in illustrating the buffoonery and comic blunders committed by Scotland Yard. It also explains how the Valet was able to roam unchecked for so long.

On a winter's afternoon at the end of 1895 Beck was mistaken for the swindler Augustus Wilhelm Meyer – alias John Smith. The female victims of Smith's chicanery (he always cheated women out of money or jewels) queued up to condemn Beck – despite the fact that his eyes were blue compared to the brown of Smith; despite the fact that he bore none of Smith's distinguishing marks on his flesh (Smith was Jewish and circumcised, and had a scar on the right of his neck); despite the fact that he was a gentleman of impeccable record who didn't speak with a minor American twang like Smith; and despite the fact that he had been in Peru when one of Smith's previous offences had taken place in 1877. Hard though it is to believe, two retired police constables swore Beck *was* Smith. A handwriting 'expert' swore, too, that the inky samples of penmanship from Beck and Smith were identical. Even Beck's slightly protruding ears were markedly different from Smith's – betraying the weaknesses of the Bertillon system, which relied on accurate measurements being taken at the outset. The trial lasted just three days. Beck was found guilty, sentenced to seven years as a repeat offender and dispatched to Portland Prison to break rocks. The investigating officer in the case was Frank Froest.

Beck, who felt cursed, experienced further ignominy and injustice. He was accused of being Smith again in 1904 and escaped jail only because Smith – this time calling himself William Thomas – was arrested a week later. Eventually even the dim-witted police had to concede that Beck was not Smith or Thomas or Meyer. But if Scotland Yard couldn't tell the difference between Beck and Smith when the discrepancies were so flagrant – Beck was nine years older and photographs of them reveal only vague similarities – how did it ever expect to identify correctly and then capture someone of the guile and mobility of Harry the Valet?

Never still for long, the Valet was always making fresh starts. One of them took place every summer – a yearly jaunt to Monte Carlo. He was drawn to the place predominantly because of its status as a gambling haven. It was a gold-trimmed play-pit for the rich who were prepared to squander chips at the card and roulette tables.

To lose a few hundred pounds on the rapid spin of the wheel or the wristy turn of a spade or heart was all part of the fun of the holiday for them.

Monte Carlo began to flourish after the French outlawed gambling in 1857, which enabled the tax-free principality to become the only gaming centre in Europe apart from Aix-les-Bains. The creation of a railway line meant that it was attracting one million visitors annually by the closing decade of the nineteenth century, and turned over £1 million per year, too. Queen Victoria called the French Riviera a 'paradise of nature'. She regarded Monte Carlo, however, as evil and squalid and full of 'very nasty disreputable people'. The Queen thought the Charles-Garnier-designed casino, with its cream stone and marble steps, was the epitome of sin. 'The harm it does . . . can't be over-emphasised,' she said, avoiding the place as though betting was as contagious as the plague. The views of sea and sky, as well as the sunshine, pulled the aristocracy to its rocky promontory and into more than twenty-five hotels, each of which arranged for horse-drawn cabs to collect guests from the station – even if the distance covered from platform to lobby was less than a hundred yards. 'People come from near and far to throw good money after bad and make a pauper of themselves in the bitter and inevitable end,' wrote the *Chicago Daily Tribune* in 1898. It described the clientele as an eclectic mix of 'Princes, Dukes, Countesses, tradespeople, professionals, gamblers, rakes, cocottes and tourists'.

With its wide terrace, carved stone balustrades, fountains, tropical shrubbery and beds of flowers, the casino was imposingly exotic and the luxurious surroundings inside encouraged excess. Five palace-like gaming rooms were fitted with polished inlaid floors, chandeliers and comfortable seating, huge panel frescos and tall palms and potted plants. Uniformed attendants whirled down and through a curved white entrance – a triple doorway beneath a gilded balcony – to fetch and carry for the patrons. The attendants responded to instructions conveyed with nothing more than a finger-click or a snap of the head, which sent them obediently scurrying like a trained butler for drinks or the house currency. There were coquettish cigarette and cigar girls who always smiled – especially at the gamblers who lost, urging them to try their luck again. And the slick managers and croupiers of each establishment recognised at first sight who to smarm and flatter and make special. The visitor was made to feel that entering the casino counted as a privilege; and that it was also a privilege to lose in it. The police made daily examinations of the hotel registers. To qualify for a gambling ticket, which allowed admission to the casino, each visitor had to stipulate name, residence, occupation, 'last halting place' and duration of stay. Aliases were frequently used. In fact, when Lord Salisbury gave his real name the casino initially refused to believe he was the British Prime Minister.

Wherever the Valet turned he came across someone fantastically wealthy. He only had to follow the scent of money to make the excursion worthwhile. Here he was known as Mr Harry Villiers or Mr de Villiers – an upstanding London-based businessman who liked a bit of sport. He found it terribly easy to pick a pocket, take a jewel case, sneak into a room and scoop up whatever he liked. He knew and trusted French fences who would accept the jewels – and give him a decent price without too much dispute – less than half an hour after he appropriated them. He could post others on to his receivers in London. No one around the tables ever regarded him as anything other than a gambler with enough in the bank to absorb whatever losses he stacked up. And no one ever suspected him when a wallet went missing or a diamond necklace was stolen. Again, clothes were important. He would take large trunks of bespoke tailoring with him. As Dew stressed, the Valet was conscious of the fact that he couldn't be seen wearing the previous summer's fashions. It would suggest he'd fallen on comparatively hard times and hadn't been able to pay his tailor. The very rich noticed these minor flaws. 'Every new fancy of the Paris dressmakers is aired here, and the richest of hats and gowns is worn,' said the *Chicago Daily Tribune* of Monte Carlo's obsession with style. So, from the society magazines, the Valet made sure that the sharp cut of his jacket and the toes and heels of his shoes were not out of kilter with the sartorial etiquette of the new season.

He was especially careful about attracting the attention of what he described as the 'foreign police', who he thought were 'more troublesome' than Scotland Yard. 'I always took off my hat, metaphorically speaking, to them,' he said. 'In France or Belgium, the gentleman thief cuts no ice. You have to look slippy if you want to get away with anything crooked.' The Valet would arrive at Calais or Boulogne and spot a detective disguised as a workman sitting on top of one of the pillars, 'watching me the way a cat would watch a mouse'. He rated the French detectives more highly than Dew, Dinnie or Froest or – at least at the time – two other men who often tailed him: Edward 'Tricky' Drew and Edward 'Gentleman' Gough. The Valet said Drew was so good he could 'tell a jewel thief by his shadow on the wall around the corner'. He rated Gough as 'the best-dressed detective at the yard, a man who could go anywhere and be at home in any company, from a doss house to a West End club'. But the continental copper, he added, was 'more thorough' and did 'things that the average British detective dare not do for fear of red tape'. He admitted: 'Once one of these fellows gets his eye on you he never leaves you until he has run you in.'

Still, the Valet was crassly presumptuous enough to think that he could outmanoeuvre them and Scotland Yard simultaneously. Providing he was careful and resourceful, he saw nothing in his future except prosperity. He later confessed to being a 'conceited young ass'.

The Valet miscalculated in one important respect: he forgot the human factor – the beat that his lovelorn heart was about to skip. It occurred in April 1898. He'd never be the same man – or the same thief – again. As one newspaper eloquently put it, 'Like Samson, he fell to a woman's charms.'

Chapter 6

The blind lovers

All through his criminal life Harry the Valet was susceptible to the following – though not necessarily in this order:

Luxury and fine clothes
Champagne and whisky
Jewels and women

Like a rare astronomical arrangement, in which more than two planets simultaneously align, the things which most attracted him came together in astonishing conjunction in the gold-leaf splendour of the West End's Alhambra Theatre in 1898. The Valet was sitting in the stalls when he glanced up at a woman occupying a crimson-curtained private box near the stage. Around her neck hung a string of diamonds. It proved to be one of the few occasions when the Valet was attracted to the face long before he noticed the jewels. She had a curvaceous, full figure and striking features: a small, kissable mouth, wide almond-shaped light brown eyes, a petite slender nose and smooth pale cheekbones. Her shoulder-length hair was wavy and fair. He studied her more closely than the performance he'd paid to see. To the Valet, she was clad in the beauty of a thousand stars. Something about her was irresistible to him. Within 'twenty minutes' of the curtain closing, he'd uncovered the basic details about her. She was an actress and singer, and a former Gaiety Girl too. The Valet floated along the Strand, already convinced he'd found his perfect match.

Even the romantic poets, striving to explain it, never quite distil into verse a definitive answer to the question: What is love? It always slips away and escapes them. Just as beauty depends on the uniqueness of the beholder, so love depends on the capricious heart. So, 'Love is heaven, and heaven is love' . . . or 'Love is a sickness full of woes' . . . or 'Love is more cruel than lust'. Or, of course, it is none of these things. Or it is an amalgamation of them. Or it is a million others instead. The Valet could not describe it to his satisfaction either. But he recognised love when it came to him unexpectedly, and he knew how he felt. He was like John Clare, who wrote in his poem 'First Love':

> I ne'er was struck before that hour
> With love so sudden and so sweet

At a discreet distance, the Valet followed the woman to Romano's, one of theatre-land's most fashionable restaurants. Despite being warned off by her friends, who told him 'half of London is head over ears in love with her', the Valet was undeterred. He was also blatant in his tactics. What he'd seen he must now possess. With disdain, he described rival suitors as 'London cavaliers'. Striding uninvited to her table, he ordered a bottle of champagne and sat down.

From the start, the thief and the actress were less than truthful with one another.

She told him her name was Maude Richardson. She was actually Louisa Lancey, who had taken Maude as a stage name. She said she came from Dorset, and added that her father was a farmer. But she came from Devon – near Ilfracombe – and her father, William was a cordwainer or shoemaker. She said she was born in 1869. The real date was 1863. Her mother, Ann, gave birth to her at the age of 36 after raising five other children – three daughters and two sons. The Lanceys barely scraped a living, moving first to Swansea and then back to Devon, returning no better off than before. When she was 16, Louisa willingly left the coast and countryside – or what she called 'the old homestead'. The small-town existence was stupefyingly claustrophobic to her, like being imprisoned. She didn't need a clairvoyant's powers to forecast what lay ahead if she remained there; she only had to look at the plight of the mature women around her. As Louisa Lancey she would melt into a decent but dull marriage. She would cook, clean and care for her husband and the nursery full of children that would surely follow. Rural poverty would restrain and confine her. She would never move far from the sea or the soft folds of the fields enveloping the town. The world would shrink to the size of a bedroom and a parlour and the walk to church twice on Sunday. She would age prematurely into a wrinkled crone, always thinking about how different life might have been.

As Maude Richardson she could enjoy the racket and upheaval of London. At last she could see for herself places others had only ever read about in the *Illustrated London News* or spoken of second hand; places, moreover, presented in drawings and etchings that were incapable of capturing the scale of the architecture – the Gothic spread of the Palace of Westminster and the high finials of the Abbey, the slow drag of the Thames and the imposing white-walled town houses of Belgravia where she aspired to live. She could walk down Regent Street, admiring the fancy dresses of the richer shoppers, and pick her way past the billboards and theatrical posters of the Strand, where she wanted her own name to appear. One of her sisters had already married and moved to Camden. She encouraged Louisa to follow; for anything might happen in London. She could become somebody. Louisa had three discernible talents – a decent singing voice; a long, wonderfully shaped pair of legs; a face cute enough to hold the attention in a room. She was made for the music hall.

She became engaged to a solicitor, who worked in Lincoln's Inn Fields. But her ambition lay in acting and in particular the Gaiety Theatre. Her interest in these appalled her husband-to-be and the engagement was broken off. At that moment Louisa Lancey became Maude Richardson. Competition to join the chorus of the Gaiety – and become a Gaiety Girl – was formidable. Only the beautiful need apply and only a minuscule number were successful. Auditions were conducted by its impresario, George Edwardes, who looked and sounded like Phineas T. Barnum, the American circus owner and showman. Edwardes was known as 'the Guv'nor' because his booming word was absolute and final. As a benign dictator, he dominated every aspect of the Gaiety. To be part of his show brought rewards and status. The Gaiety Girls of the late nineteenth century were the equivalent of today's It girls. They were written about in the society columns. They received letters and gifts from admirers and attracted the kind of worship that Hollywood's silent movie stars would enjoy when the 'picture houses' began to dominate public entertainment and sweep aside the variety theatres and music halls. They always dined in Romano's, where it was important to be seen and spoken about. The restaurant owner deliberately reserved window seats for them to attract other customers and generate publicity for his business. In return, he gave them a half-price lunch and dinner. Passers-by, half or totally in love with the girls, would drool over them, as if staring into a shopfront at an attractive but unobtainable jewel. Framed pictures of actresses such as Maude were displayed in the window of Barraud, a photograher's studio on Oxford Street.

The theatrical historian W. MacQueen-Pope summed up the Gaiety Girl as 'a thing complete in herself'. Stressing her importance still further, he added that 'She was worshipped and adored.

George Edwardes, known as 'the Guv'nor' because of his benign dictatorship of the Gaiety Theatre and the long-legged girls he hired.

She stood as a criterion for all that was enchanting.' The chosen few were expected to be the embodiment of ideal womanhood too – wholesome and winsomely well behaved, like the girl next door, but also sparkily suggestive and alluring. They had to give an extravagant wink to the front rows without losing a modicum of their dignity. Maude mixed sassy vitality with Devonshire country sweetness.

The Gaiety Theatre was described as a sexual hothouse and those within it, like Maude, as 'often willing victims of sexual intrigue'. The girls brushed off or coyly accepted the overtures of what the profession disparagingly called 'stage-door Johnnies' or 'mashers'. These were genuflecting chancers in top hat and tails, who occupied the boxes; or men about town clustered in the stalls wearing tight trousers, carrying crutch sticks and using toothpicks.

They snidely became known as the 'Crutch-and-Toothpick Brigade'. No other theatre attracted so many of these swooning young bloods clutching long-stemmed roses and wrapped gifts or bribing the doorman to personally deliver letters and notes to a favourite girl. Dinner and drinks were always on offer. It was said that the Gaiety carried on 'more or less openly' the tradition of the *coulisses* of the famous continental opera houses where noblemen and plutocrats picked mistresses from among the members of the *corps de ballet* who dressed the edges of the stage. As the Gaiety girl flounced across the stage, she could be assured that there was someone in the audience who wanted to win her with his wealth – everything from jewels and a monthly allowance to a furnished flat or a house. When this infatuation waned or was extinguished, it was taken for granted that the girl would be materially compensated for her broken heart. The interest rate for borrowing it in the first place was high. Were she living in splendour at her beau's discretion, she was entitled to expect him to maintain her in the style to which she'd become accustomed. Otherwise, the gentleman would have violated an unwritten code and find himself barred from the Gaiety.

The theatre came to resemble a matrimonial agency. Along with the stage-door Johnnies came the highest of high society. One actress named Connie Gilchrist, who post-dated Maude at the Gaiety, later married the Earl of Orkney. Another, Rosie Boot, wed the Marquess of Headfort. A third, singer Irene Richards, went down the aisle with Lord Drumlanrig. Baron de Rothschild and his brother, Sir Alfred, rented the Royal Box by the year merely to watch the chorus. And the Sultan of Zanzibar became infatuated with the singer Madge Saunders, whom he followed wherever she went. Worried about an exodus from stage to altar, Edwardes eventually inserted a nuptial clause into every contract to dissuade his chorus from accepting proposals.

By the time Maude joined the Gaiety, it was regarded as a

bohemian circle, able to straddle society establishment and the stage, and its productions specialised in what became known as 'elaborate burlesque'. Edwardes said he wanted 'tall fair mannequins'. Qualifications other than appearing stunningly gorgeous in costume were unnecessary. Edwardes personally schooled girls such as Maude, arranging a schedule for each of them and then charting their progress in singing, dancing, elocution and – for purposes of grace and balance on points – the art of fencing. Maude fitted the bill. She was soon able to accumulate wealth and possessions from men who wanted a Gaiety Girl to impress their friends, as if acquiring a valuable work of art. The money and jewels she collected to supplement her wages were akin to an investment account, which could be cashed in after her beauty faded and she was forced off the stage by younger, fresher rivals.

Maude was in her element. In 1887 she found herself cast in *Miss Esmeralda*, a burlesque of *The Hunchback of Notre-Dame*. A year later she was given the role of a prison warder in *Frankenstein*. The columnist of the *Penny Illustrated Paper and Illustrated Times* was more than won over in 1888. Styled 'The Man about Town', he wrote about her fulsomely in his column, called 'Chat of the London Gossips', and claimed to 'flatter himself that he discovered her at The Gaiety'.

Edwardes thought the purpose of his life was to 'entertain the public' and he did so beyond London by sending the company into the provinces. Maude travelled the country, from the Grand Theatre in Leeds to the Lyceum in Glasgow, from the Shakespeare in Liverpool to the St James's in Manchester. Reviews said she 'filled the parts with great credit'. She also appeared in *Robinson Crusoe* in Drury Lane in 1893 with the rubber-faced pantomime dame Dan Leno, and Marie Lloyd, who seldom uttered a sentence without a sniggering double entendre somewhere within it. She specialised in the lewd and the bawdy, her hidden mucky meanings attracting the disapproval of the censors. The production costs of *Robinson Crusoe* – and the salaries of the two leading performers – were so high that it lost £30,000. One newspaper article about Maude said: 'In the provinces she became very popular . . . money flowed in and the entrancing Gaiety actress took palatial chambers in Regent Street.' She was able to employ a cook cum maid and a footman. The article went on to detail the end of her London career: 'She left Gaiety (in 1893) after a glorious time on the stage and began to see the country. First she went to York, where the 10th Hussars were then quartered. She dined with the officers and was introduced to some very smart and distinguished persons, who afterwards became great friends.' The phrase 'great friends' was loaded with the sort of nudge-nudge, wink-wink innuendo that Marie Lloyd would have understood perfectly.

The Valet didn't care. He was hooked on Maude. The question was: How could he persuade her to become hooked on him? Champagne glass in hand, he began with a formal introduction. He didn't use the name Jackson or Wilson or James. He didn't reveal himself as Henry Thomas either. Maude came to know her new, infatuated admirer as Harry Williams.

He followed the same template in pursuit of her as he did when chasing a pearl necklace or a jewel merchant's purse. He discovered as much about her as he could – where she shopped, which perfume she liked to wear, what she liked to drink and eat. This gathered intelligence cannily enabled him to fit his table talk specifically around her interests. His words were always tenderly woven. Within a few days he was taking Maude to Ascot, where he impressed her with his knowledge of horses. At the beginning she coquettishly toyed with the Valet, drawing him into her circle and then pushing him away from it again. 'Being a cautious girl,' he said, as if defending her as well as explaining his willingness to endure any sleight, 'she was allowing me to visit her frequently, yet holding me at arm's length until she could find out a little more about me.'

A fortnight after Ascot, he followed her to Brighton, where she stayed at the Cyprus Hotel. He arrived unannounced, clutching another bottle of champagne and claiming to be passing through, as if pure coincidence had dragged them together. The season was under way. The long, wide strip of pebble beach was covered in bathing machines and visitors. Children shrieked and dug with spades; coloured sailboats and clipper schooner-yachts rode shallow waves in the middle distance, charging one shilling a trip. Maude and the Valet strolled along the seafront past the Grand Hotel with its nine tiers of rooms and partway along a three-mile line of tall, whitewashed houses with bow-fronted windows and balconies. A noonday cannon was fired from the West Pier, which stretched like a thick finger into the Channel. The Palace Pier was rising from the sea, already more than a skeleton of metal and wood. It was said that if you lived in Brighton for three years you would meet 'everybody you had ever known'. For everyone went there – including the aristocracy. The air was filled with the tangy, pungent taste of salt and the sound of competing brass and minstrel bands. Hawkers and street-sellers tried to bawl above the pitch of the music. In its relatively small acreage Brighton had a disproportionate number of pubs and beer shops – more than 600 by the late nineteenth century. The Valet took Maude drinking in its more salubrious establishments and to the theatres where she had previously performed, such as the Empire, with its decorated scrollwork and historic emblems, and the red-brick Theatre Royal.

Maude's wealth stoked the Valet's enthusiasm for her. His prime motivation nonetheless was to satisfy his beating heart. The fact that he was able to woo her in the first place emphasises how plausible his performance as a cultured, rich businessman had become. He was always kindly and well-mannered, as though it would pain him to cause the slightest offence. He opened doors and stood aside for others to pass. He helped ladies on with their coats. He treated waiters with courtesy and as equals. He tipped everyone – from cab drivers to shoeshine and telegram boys – and allowed shop owners to keep his loose change. He posed as a multimillionaire. 'The only way I could press my suit was by telling her that I was a man of great wealth, who could give her all the beautiful things which a woman craves,' he said. The Valet admitted he began to 'spin her yarns'. About houses he owned overseas. About investments. About grandiose plans for the future. About jewels and lavish nights out during which she could wear and flaunt what he would buy for her. She could have whatever she wanted, he said. He told her he owned valuable American mining rights. To prove it he would give her £20,000 as soon as these were turned into stock and sold. In reality he had just enough in his wallet to make Maude think that genuine riches were locked up in bonds and securities and overseas banks; money, he said, which would be released as soon as some trifling technicality was resolved about its transfer into his main accounts.

At most, the Valet intended to remain in Brighton for a week before returning to London. He stayed for almost two months, until the end of June, moving with Maude from the Cyprus Hotel to rooms at the Coach and Horses. 'I began to make an impression upon her,' he said, pleased with his own showmanship.

Neither suspected that the other – for markedly different reasons – was brittle and vulnerable. That life was hard, and might be about to implode for both of them, was masked behind one long and high-spirited act of fakery and self-invention.

In the Valet's case, age was catching up with him. At 45, he was no longer a live wire – or as lithe and acrobatically nimble as he used to be when it came to entering carriages and weaving along station platforms. His reflexes had slowed appreciably and his fingers seemed slightly stiffer, less able to perform the once rudimentary act of gripping the handle of a jewel case in a clean swoop. He was more ponderous and heavy-legged than before too, as if trying to run underwater. Most crucially, he was prone to dithering and hesitation where none had previously existed. Once the Valet used to weigh up his prospects instantaneously – plunging without pause into a first-class compartment. Now he began to vacillate and suffer nervous bouts of hand-wringing before making up his mind about whether to strike. Once he saw only positive signs in front of him; now he saw only the negative. And once he had an unshakeable belief in himself, as though no one could hold him in check. Now he began to doubt his talent for the first time, as though it had mysteriously left him and would never return. The idea spooked him. In a business where a split second could determine success or failure, the Valet became over-cautious. He missed chances through delaying his move, or otherwise lunged too soon, which botched the operation completely and forced him to bail out of it. Like a surgeon with a twitchy scalpel, he had lost his touch – and with it his confidence. What used to be done unthinkingly was now a labour. The Monte Carlo police were to blame for this abrupt lack of form.

The Valet's nagging concerns about the ruthlessness of the 'foreign copper', who was more dogged and organised than his London counterpart, had proved valid in late summer 1896. As usual, he'd taken his fine wardrobe to Monte Carlo, where he planned to pick pockets and infiltrate the rooms of the gentleman gamblers who had more money than sense. But he was caught stealing banknotes. He served fifteen months of a year and a half sentence before returning to London in early 1898, where he managed to survive on the meagre leftovers of previous thefts and supplement them with the odd new one. As well as being physically diminished – thinner after the diet of prison food – he also experienced a strange sense of dislocation, as if he needed to renew his acquaintance with London before becoming its master again. When the Valet fell in love with Maude at the Alhambra Theatre, he was only just beginning to regain his poise. But his poor streak continued. He was like a once-prolific batsman now unable to score a run anywhere around the wicket – and unable to work out why.

Maude was in a worse state at the time they met. She was an emotional wreck, but determined not to betray it. The cause of her distress was another broken relationship, and the money she had lavished on it.

Harry Andrew was a lieutenant in the 42nd Regiment of the Gordon Highlanders – the Black Watch. He belonged to a family of 'credit and renown' near Liss in Hampshire. Although openly regarding him as a 'weak-minded fool' – an assessment less of an insult and more an example of impeccable judgement – his father paid him a monthly allowance.

Andrew met Maude during a holiday she took in Cape Town in 1894, where he was serving with his regiment. Maude was 31 and still a spinster despite the attentions of the Gaiety Theatre's stage-door Johnnies and the occasional profitable dalliance with society gentlemen. She lied barefacedly, telling Andrew she was 24 years old. He was 27. 'She was loved by all,' said a report of the couple's time together, 'but could return only his affections.' Maude and Andrew lived together in Monte Carlo – as Mr and Mrs Anderson – and then in London and Bombay. At the beginning of the relationship Andrew paid Maude's expenses from his parental stipend. But, by late 1895, he was beginning to borrow considerable sums without repaying her. Andrew convinced Maude that his father would eventually take financial care of the two of them. There'd be a house in London and another in the country; she would want for nothing – especially his love.

As Andrew represented her best chance of settling down – and being kept in relative comfort – she agreed to marry him in August

1896 at St Mary's Church in Aden, a settlement then called a 'simmering cauldron of abominations'. Maude financed the wedding with a 'gift' of £100. As if ashamed to be betrothed to a Gaiety Girl, and afraid to tell his father in person, Andrew insisted that secrecy was imperative. On no account should his father or his regiment be told of the marriage. He would break the news in a tender letter on embossed paper. Written in his looped hand it would, he promised, extol Maude's virtues as the ideal wife and explain the breadth and depth of his unqualified love for her. The wedding took place on an infernally hot afternoon, and the bride and bridegroom both adopted pseudonyms in case word of it leaked out. Maude became May White. Andrew called himself Robert Bertram Crichton. The honeymoon lasted less than 24 hours.

With much pleading, Andrew had already persuaded his new wife to allow him to trek to a mostly unknown corner of East Africa on an expedition organised and paid for by the gadabout explorer Henry Sheppard Hart Cavendish. Less than a day after the marriage ceremony, Andrew set off to join him. He did so to satisfy his wanderlust, create a new career for himself after the army – which allowed him paid leave – and also to convince his doubting father that he could achieve something significant in his life. He put his adventurous spirit and personal ambition well ahead of his marital obligations and his wife's heartfelt needs. He would receive no payment from Cavendish, but was able to keep any 'big game' he shot; it hardly seemed an equitable deal. Maude graciously wrote him yet another cheque and also said in a letter: 'How glad I am that you are going to try to make a position for yourself.' The new bride was told to sail alone to Australia, where he would meet her the following year. As a parting gift, Andrew gave Maude the brief letter, intended for his father, which she was instructed not to post. 'It is in case of my death,' he loftily explained. The night after her wedding Maude dined and slept alone. Andrew was already chasing celebrity and clinging to Cavendish's expensive and highly connected coat-tails.

A distant relative of the Duke of Devonshire, Cavendish eventually became the 6th Baron Waterpark and the 7th Baron Cavendish of Doveridge. He married five times before his fiftieth birthday. At the time of his and Andrew's African sojourn, he was only 21. With more than £100,000 of his own money – and another £50,000 privately raised among aristocratic friends – he hired Andrew, eighty-four porters, a headman and enough horse-drawn caravans to cart all of them along narrow tracks and through expanses of deep uncharted vegetation. He planned to fill in blanks on the map. For protection against the natives he took six Maxim guns and a large Parrott gun slung between two mules. Cavendish and Andrew, who in effect became his second in command, travelled from Somaliland to Lake Rudolf and then moved along its eastern edge to the mouth of the Omo River. The next stage of the plan went disastrously awry. Abyssinian soldiers had looted the village of the tribe living there. Cavendish and Andrew found themselves running out of food and water. There was no possibility of finding fresh supplies nearby. The two men were forced to split up: Cavendish took one caravan section to Murle, on the western bank of the river and then headed for the western shore of Lake Rudolf; Andrew backtracked, taking the greater load down the eastern shore of Lake Rudolf. The explorers met at Lake Baringo in July 1897. Andrew's bravery went unrewarded. When Cavendish gave a lecture about the expedition to the Royal Geographical Society, illustrating it with lantern slides, Andrew was barely mentioned, as though he was no more than an irrelevant servant rather than a practical and reliable partner.

Oblivious to it all, Maude arrived in Australia, docking at Melbourne before moving on to Sydney. She disliked the country. She hated the sticky heat and the dry, rising dust. She felt homesick and lonely and pined for London. Every day she waited for a letter from Andrew, who thought writing to her was a waste of good paper and black ink. In the back of beyond, the African postal service was almost non-existent. The letter would simply go astray and so there was no point in attempting to write to her. Maude became distraught, and then despairing. Depression's black dog soon consumed her. She was confined to bed behind drawn curtains, her room a dark tomb. Life itself seemed worthless. Why, Maude asked herself time and again, had she married such an uncaring man? Would he ever come back to her? If so, how long would he stay? If she wanted to live, Maude decided, she had to sail back to England. There was nothing for her in Australia; least of all her husband.

After the Cavendish expedition ended – and failed to bring Andrew either the fame or social status he sought – Maude remained ignored and abandoned, as though she'd become an inconvenience to him. The wedding anniversary came and went without a word from him. So, in late October 1897, she wrote to Andrew at his parents' home in Hampshire. The letter she sent is as painful to read as a suicide note. It conveys in crisp but tortured sentences the misery of a desperate, lonesome wife who could not understand the level of cruelty meted out to her.

'I have been very ill and am still so,' she said. 'This last 15 months has nearly killed me. I feel broken hearted . . . I do not know what will be my end. Death would be better after all I have endured for your sake.' She signed the letter 'Your Maude'.

Even the glacial Andrew could not ignore it. The couple met in a Soho restaurant – a brief, edgy coming together of two people who were now manifestly strangers and wholly resentful of one another: Maude because she'd been pushed to the precipice of madness; Andrew because she no longer interested him and he wanted rid of her. There was no trust, let alone any love, between them. They were different people now, each trying to forget the other's name. The squabbling and rowing gathered pace. Accusations of desertion and callousness were levelled and denied. Andrew claimed Maude could have joined him in Paris, where he'd relaxed after his exertions on the Cavendish expedition. Maude counter-claimed that he'd made life intolerable for her. They parted unsatisfactorily and without determining anything except their hostility towards one another. Four months later they met again. By this bleak stage the coupling of grief and rejection had worked destructively, like poured acid, on Maude's self-esteem, almost nothing of which remained. Stricken with the irrational thought that she might never find another husband, Maude pleaded with Andrew to return to her and make a home for them both in London. He refused.

The Valet was ignorant of Maude's wretched state when he began courting her four weeks later. Given the malicious treatment Andrew inflicted on her, it might have been reasonable to expect Maude to withdraw from the Valet's overt advances. But, for the time being, she saw him as a palliative cure. He offered an arm to steady her, a shoulder on which to sob. The Valet knew Maude was already married. She spoke openly about the circumstances – though not the depth of the wound it had created. He knew, too, that her husband was unlikely to return. Nor did she seem to want him back; Maude referred to Andrew in the most disparaging terms, which the Valet interpreted as proof that she was now pre-pared to live with him instead and eventually marry. It was as though her loathing of Andrew contained within it a subliminal statement about her affection for the Valet. She made him feel furiously alive, and he was experiencing the strange, ballooning lightness of love. 'I thought everything was going splendidly,' he said.

The Valet had begun to view his relationship with Maude as a triptych. In the first frame he courted her with candlelit meals and seductive promises about his wealth. In the second she fell in love and became inseparable from him. In the third he married her. There would be a town house or apartment with domestic servants as well as a cab and driver. There would be a country retreat in which to relax. And there would be regular departures to the casinos of Monte Carlo and the couture designers of Paris. He would introduce her to grouse-shooting in Scotland. She would introduce him to London's stage glitterati. In this perfect, unblemished fantasy, the Valet would 'go straight', forsaking his forays into railway stations and hotel bedrooms, turning away from crime because it would not be necessary to commit it. Maude would fund his extravagances. He imagined no one else for him. More to the point, he imagined no one else for her. They seemed to share common interests, after all – a gluttonous desire for good clothes and finery, expensive wines, a devotion to the theatre, a penchant for a flutter on the horses or a hand of cards, and late nights and early mornings spent drinking in clubs and bars. What inspired both of them – or at least it appeared so to the Valet – was the longing for a sybaritic life, which ought to be a romp and should never be taken too seriously. Nothing else mattered very much, and few things actually mattered at all, beyond the pursuit of frivolity and pleasure. Here, he thought, were well-matched epicureans, relieved to have found one another.

His sweet dreams of togetherness soon broke apart.

The Valet had arranged to call on Maude and take her to supper. His rap on the door was answered by her maid, a 25-year-old called Georgiana Summers, who had previously worked at the Cyprus Hotel in Brighton where the Valet found Maude. As she was there at the birth of their courtship, and became aware of its intimacy, Maude subsequently hired her. But she preferred the Valet's company to her employer's often wayward ways. 'The mistress,' she now told him gently, 'has left London and gone to Ostend for a holiday.' The Valet thought he'd misheard her. His cheeks flushed; there was nothing convincing he could mumble to cover his embarrassment after being stood up so deliberately. He was immobile on the doorstep, caught awkwardly between the need to bundle aside the maid and check for himself inside the house, and to make a tattered retreat.

The firmest tenet of his faith had always been that every decision to steal must be based on reason and not emotion. But everything he did in relation to Maude was governed by the gut. 'Being impetuous and madly in love with my inamoratas [sic],' he said, 'I resolved to lose no time in following her and insisting on making her my wife.' There was just one difficulty. As he admitted: 'My money was nearly at an end.'

The Valet knew just one way of funding the cost of his ticket. But it was already too late in the evening to tackle the railway stations. No society hostess of any significance was likely to be leaving London with her valuables at such an hour. He hailed a hansom and went to Northumberland Avenue. He said: 'Going up to one of the hotel bedrooms when the coast was clear, I found a jewel case'. The Valet fenced the contents for £500. The next morning he took the boat train from Waterloo and then caught the eleven o'clock steamer to Ostend. The maid had told him that Maude was staying at the Hotel Splendid. The Valet arrived there and smoothed down his clothes, wrinkled by travel. 'I asked the head porter if he had seen her,' he said. The answer he got – 'she has gone for a walk with a gentleman friend' – sent his heart on another downward lurch. 'This looked as if all my rosy dreams of making her my wife were to be upset,' he said.

Silver-topped cane in hand, the Valet strode out of the lobby and began searching the streets. 'I had not gone far before whom should I see but the woman I loved so madly.' She was arm-in-arm with the gentleman. As the Valet had come so far – and had nothing to lose – he was recklessly bold. 'Without waiting to think what I was doing I marched straight up to them,' he remembered.

Staring directly at Maude, and refusing to glance at his rival, the Valet raised his bowler hat and said: 'You see, you can't get far away from me after all.'

He was not clasped in a fond embrace. 'It was plainly evident at once to me that my presence was unwelcome to both of them,' he said.

'What has brought you to Ostend?' Maude asked tensely.

The Valet shot back his lover's reply. 'To be with you,' he said with tenderness. 'What else do you think would bring me? Haven't I got a right to come and see you?'

The gentleman, whom the Valet recognised by sight but not name, intervened, as if protecting his own hold on Maude's affections rather than her honour.

'Look here, sir,' he said, which the Valet knew was the polite preface to the rebuff that would follow. 'I don't know who you are, but it is plain to me that my friend here does not wish your presence nor your attentions. Will you have the goodness to allow us to pass?'

The Valet took the question – and the superior, arrogant tone in which it was asked – as blatant provocation. It was as though he was being flicked aside. He responded with a 'snarl of rage'. He said: 'I raised my cane to strike him – at the same time demanding: "And who the devil may I ask are you?"' Afraid of a brawl, in which she would be caught in the middle, Maude implored the Valet not to bring the cane down on the man's skull. 'He is my friend,' she shouted. 'And that ought to be sufficient for you. Please do not make a scene on the street.' The becalmed Valet saw sense, let the stick drop by his side and retreated half a pace. Maude understood that only by mollifying the Valet, rather than barking out a military-style order, could she persuade him to step aside. The Valet said she gave him a 'sweet smile' before promising: 'When you are able to control yourself better you can come and visit me at my hotel.'

The Valet watched them walk away. Maude did not wave or turn her head back towards him. He felt stranded and snubbed. The sight of them together – and the knowledge of how foolish he must appear to both – inflamed him all over again. He admitted: 'Far from being able to control my feelings, I flew into such a rage at the thought of the insult I had received from her cavalier that I walked straight from the front to the Town Square.' The Valet was looking for a gun. 'I went into the gunsmith's shop and bought a revolver and some cartridges.' Around his jealous mind ran one thought: 'If that fellow insults me again, or tries to come between me and that girl, I'll shoot him like a dog.' It was no 'empty brag', he added. The Valet bought the gun, loaded it and tucked the weapon into his coat pocket. In the afternoon he went back to the Hotel Splendid and learnt 'to my utter dismay' from the head porter that Maude had left Ostend. The Valet refused to believe it. 'Being suspicious I inquired at various other hotels.' As a skilled investigator and inquisitor, locating her was straightforward. 'Ostend,' he said, 'is a very small town.' He discovered that Maude and her gentleman had moved a few hundred yards to the Palace Hotel. In his pique and foaming envy – and fuelled by drink he'd consumed in various bars to anaesthetise his sorrow – it never occurred to the Valet that he was behaving appallingly. Or that Maude was now scared of him. Or even that he had no claim whatsoever on her. He was just 'mad with rage and the liquor', he said.

He found them sitting in the lounge; 'a sight that dispelled all my dreams,' he added. The Valet withdrew the gun and pointed it at Maude's companion. In an act of remarkable bravery, she threw herself across him. As she did so, she began to scream. The hotel waiters rushed to disarm the Valet, and the manager ran into the street and returned with two police officers. 'They promptly arrested me on the charge of threatening to commit murder,' he said. The Valet was handcuffed and taken to the railway station, where armed gendarmes pushed him roughly into a carriage. 'Where they were taking me or what was to happen to me I neither knew nor cared,' he said.

The Valet, still drunk, found himself in a cell in Bruges. After sobering up, he realised one thing. 'But for the finger of fate . . . I might have been hanged for murder.'

He never expected to see or speak to Maude again. She was gone, he decided, and her departure was entirely his own fault. Buried in their files, the police in London and Monte Carlo would discover that he'd only recently emerged from jail. His next sentence would be harsher and longer because of it. There'd be no more theatres or late night revelry; no more well-made suits; and no more hand-in-hand seaside walks with Maude in Brighton. There was no hope for him now. The Valet described the night he spent in prison as 'terrible'. The following morning he was awoken by the jailer who shouted through the solid door, 'You've got a visitor.' He heard the loud, scraping turn of the key in the lock. The cell door swung open, letting a narrow oblong of light into the tiny cell, where the Valet sat bent over on the bed. He was 'half dazed' from sleep and alcohol, and dazzled by the brightness of the corridor lamp. He became more dazzled still by the sight in front of him. Maude stood in the doorway, as if making one of her stage entrances. 'I could scarcely believe my eyes,' said the Valet, struggling for breath. 'At first I thought it was a vision.'

Maude was contrite. She told the Valet that she'd come to 'beg forgiveness for being the innocent cause' of his arrest. She added, almost as an afterthought, that he'd given her friend 'the scare of his life'. She said: 'He thinks he is too young to die and he has gone back to London.' If the Valet promised to behave himself, Maude said, she would 'endeavour to affect [*sic*]' his release. Even in his relief, and with the peculiar sense of pyrrhic victory he felt, the Valet was determined to extract as much drama as possible from her unexpected arrival and apology. 'It is very good of you,' he said. 'But, all the same, I would rather stay here if I have lost all claim on your affections.'

'Don't be a fool,' she replied. 'We shall have some good times together – you and I.'

It never occurred to the Valet that Maude had only recanted because her previous suitor had fled at the sound of gunfire. He was too much in love to notice; and too elated to have her back to bother about the reasons behind it.

Maude, whom he called 'this remarkable young woman', arranged his bail, handing over £150. By mid-afternoon she and the Valet had left Bruges. At the railway station he saw two familiar faces on the platform – Scotland Yard's 'Tricky' Drew and Edward Gough. The shock of recognition almost solidified his blood. He assumed the men had been sent to arrest him. 'When I saw them looking at me I crossed my hands – figuratively speaking – for the handcuffs.' To his astonishment Drew and Gough behaved as if the Valet didn't exist. 'I discovered afterwards that they were in Belgium on their annual holidays and were not in the least concerned about my doings,' he said.

It was safer in Blankenburg than Bruges. He and Maude went there and booked into the Hotel Terminus. As a result of her benevolence – and the proceeds of his jewel theft in London – the romance flowered again as though nothing had ever disturbed or sullied it. They 'moved among fashionable society', as the Valet put it, and shared the same bed again. The black spot on this rising sun was the Valet's imminent court case in Bruges. Which is why the two of them decided that he should 'skip bail'. They would take a room in Aix-la-Chapelle's Hotel Majestic – comfortably beyond the jurisdiction of the Belgian police. The Valet and Maude acted as if on a Grand Tour, each stop of which was marked with champagne and rich food and evenings at the theatre. To celebrate their escape the Valet took Maude to the opera house to see *Faust*. In the matter of love, he was almost totally blind.

The days passed serenely and expensively. The Valet, almost broke, was unable to deny Maude anything; and, of course, she wanted *everything*. He was locked in self-denial – too much in love to think constructively about how he'd continue to meet the costs of entertaining her. He wouldn't let Maude go, but he couldn't afford to keep her either. And if she caught him out as a fraud, he knew the relationship would never survive. With his wallet almost empty, his tipping point approached. It arrived when Maude announced that she was tired of Aix-la-Chapelle and wanted to go to Paris. The Valet could no longer hide his parlous financial state, which would soon become all too apparent. There would be another hotel and one evening after another in Parisian clubs to pay for. All of it would run well beyond his budget. The Valet could think of no way out of his predicament except the obvious one. 'If I was to hold her I would have to do something to convince her I was all I had pretended to be,' he said.

The Valet could stall Maude in Aix-la-Chapelle, where it was possible to insist with conviction that the complicated wiring of his financial affairs could not be untangled unless he could walk into a major bank or contact a firm of brokers directly. That argument would collapse in Paris. He tried to persuade Maude not to go there. Surely, the Valet ventured, it would make sense to return directly to London, where he knew he could gather cash more easily. Maude was stonily silent, ignoring whatever alternative to Paris he proposed. She had set her heart on it, and he must take her there.

With reluctance, the Valet arranged for tickets and hoped, like Mr Micawber, that 'something would turn up'.

Something did. It was the Dowager Duchess of Sutherland.

Chapter 7

A prison cell as big as the Ritz

It seemed to Harry the Valet as if the bright things Paris offered had been arranged specifically for him, and catered to all his natural inclinations: the nightclubs and gambling dens, the lit-up revues and flashy shows, where he drank good champagne and watched long-legged dancers who applied make-up thickly, like a red and white mask. He browsed the bars with vermilion awnings, which trapped the smoke from pungent cigarettes and strong cigars and congealed it into an intoxicating blue fug. In the mornings – recovering from the revelries of the night before – he could wander through its quarters, awake to the warm smell of the bakers' shops with their misted-up windows and the fragrance of roasting coffee before finding a discreet pavement café in which to hide. Most of all, he liked the style of the city – the fact there was an insouciant, party-like feel to it; that every fad or fancy was given a carefree embrace; and that sartorial elegance – the minor details of appearance and the cut of the tailor's scissors – were noticed and truly mattered. He fitted into Paris as though he'd been born in the fourth arrondissement, beside the filigree glory of Notre Dame, rather than beneath the plain tower and low roof of St Luke's Church.

He felt safe in Paris too. He could navigate through it without the shaking fear that Scotland Yard's detectives were stalking him, loitering in shadowed corners or hiding in niches. As no one knew him, there was no need to be perpetually on guard. He could relax a little and allow himself to enjoy the sights and the pleasures, as if he was on holiday. There was no danger of finding Walter Dinnie or Walter Dew at the bar of the Moulin Rouge or the Casino de Paris. Or Frank Froest eyeing the frilly, high-kicking cancan dancers at the Folies-Bergère. Or Edward Gough and 'Tricky' Drew scanning the seats of the opera house with a pair of borrowed theatre glasses. The width of the Channel protected him from such bothersome intrusion. On his way back from Monte Carlo, the Valet always headed for Paris because most of the businessmen and aristocracy, who had sat around the roulette and card tables with him, would spend a day or two indulging themselves and their wives in its shops, bars or clubs before finally returning home. There was the possibility of pulling off another job or two before catching the boat back to London quite separately from his former fellow travellers. In the early spring, he would catch a continental train for a long weekend, returning refreshed and usually several thousand francs richer.

Whenever he went to Paris he scarcely ever wanted to leave. Now, for the first time in his life, he didn't want to be there at all. Under any other circumstances – with the love of his life beside him – the Valet would have strutted in the manner of a king on a state visit. He'd have paraded Maude, like a prize he was proud and boastful to have won. He'd have dressed her; bought her jewellery; made sure of securing a prime pavement seat at a café to show her off. But on this occasion he experienced only dread: the dread of being unmasked as an impostor; the dread of losing Maude for ever because of it; and the dread of what to do next – plus the realisation that, whatever he decided, there was a need to do it urgently. The Valet rarely panicked or let his rhetoric run ahead of his judgement; but he did so now. As a sign of his desperation, he tried to borrow money from Maude in the belief that 'I might tide myself over for a day or two till I could bring off a job'. He asked for £50.

With his intriguing promises of bonds and investments, and the property deals and mining stocks which he claimed had made his fortune, the Valet succeeded in convincing Maude that he was no mere millionaire. He was super-rich, a man capable of buying at whim whatever he needed to amuse himself. To hear him ask for money – and such a piffling amount too – made Maude catch her breath. It was rather like discovering that what you thought was gold is actually tin underneath. The Valet's request for a loan was expressed in a polite but pained manner. The badly thought out ruse didn't work. Rather than eliciting sympathy and under-standing, it sparked Maude's temper and aroused her doubts. The well-dressed gentleman in front of her had suddenly lost his immaculate sheen. She realised she'd been duped. The request was met with disgust, as though he'd dropped a dead bird at her feet. Maude looked at him sceptically.

'But I don't understand it,' she said. 'I thought you were a very wealthy man.'

The Valet tried to offer some comforting charm, as though his lack of money was an accounting error that would soon be sorted out. 'So I am, my dear,' he replied with as much ease as he could muster. 'But I cannot cash any of my securities.'

Maude looked more doubtful than ever. 'But you can wire to your banks?' she suggested.

The Valet had his reply ready: 'I am afraid I can't. The fact is I have overrun my monthly allowance and the only way is to sell some shares. This will take a week at least.'

The Valet was running out of what he confessed were 'lame excuses'. Maude was running out of patience. 'She seemed to be very taken aback,' he said. 'It seemed she had suddenly become suspicious of me altogether, as she refused point-blank to give me a penny.'

The more he tried to reassure Maude, the more she scowled – seeing through his lies as if each was clear glass. She began to gather up her things. She was now insisting on separate rooms. She wanted nothing more to do with his claims of temporary poverty. If he was so wealthy, there was surely someone he knew in Paris able to guarantee him credit. She went off 'in the sulks', said the Valet.

What can a desperate serial thief do except plan another theft? The Valet, alone and fretful, reverted to type. He roamed the streets, eventually finding himself on the Rue de Rivoli. 'I had a good look in a jeweller's shop, and wondered if I could rob it that night,' he said. An hour later he returned disconsolately 'to see how the land lay' and prepared to smooth over his disagreements with Maude. He rehearsed what he might say to repair the rift between them, sure he could win her back with the same emollient phrases that had seduced her in the first place. He knew there'd be something to steal eventually; precious stones that he could convert to cash. He planned to convince Maude that everything would be resolved within a few days; that what had occurred was purely an oversight on his part which would never happen again. He would reiterate his unconditional love for her. But the Valet didn't get the chance to launch into his prepared speech. 'To my utter astonishment,' he said, 'I found her room vacant.' He dashed to the desk to see whether Maude had left a note for him. 'I was told she had gone from the place and left no address.'

The Valet was abject in his distress. 'There was only one thing in my mind,' he said: to find her. He supposed that Maude had already packed for London or intended to set off soon. 'For days,' he remembered, 'I spent my time running between the Saint-Lazare and the Nord stations watching the London trains. When I wasn't doing that, I was going around all the hotels in Paris studying the books for her name and making inquiries about her.'

At the Hotel Bristol, in the Place Vendôme, he found instead the Dowager Duchess of Sutherland – someone to whom Fate seemed especially attached.

The Dowager Duchess was not an easy woman to ignore or forget. Journalists of the day euphemistically described her as 'colourful', which was a gross understatement. Scandalous would have been more appropriate. Her biographical chart is painted black. From the newspaper coverage she attracted, she emerges as a cross between the Duchess of Malfi and Lady Macbeth – intolerant, ruthless, self-possessed, greedy and rapacious.

Mary Caroline Michell was born in 1848. She was one of seven children – five boys and two girls. Her father, the Reverend Richard Michell, was a Fellow at Lincoln College and then Vice-Principal, and eventually Principal, of Magdalen Hall, Oxford. After Magdalen was refounded as Hertford College, he became its first Principal too. Most memorably, he was Public Orator at Oxford, a convincing, tub-thumping presence on the podium and at the lectern – though his speeches were often too intellectually highbrow for his audience to absorb with complete understanding. Mary Caroline's eldest brother, Edward, became the King of Siam's legal advisor. The second, Richard, rose to be Professor of Law at Madras's Presidency College and a High Court judge there. Another, Roland, became Companion of the Order of St Michael and St George and Commissioner at Limassol in Cyprus. The Michells' other two sons, Herbert and Walter, made decent, if largely ordinary, lives for themselves. Herbert graduated from Hertford College; Walter rowed and played rugby, and became assistant headmaster of Rugby School. Mary Caroline's more attractive sister Elizabeth married an

Oxford student and lived contentedly with her four children.

Mary Caroline was short on raging beauty – with black, curled hair pulled away from her face to reveal a strong, slightly too prominent jaw and a mouth with wafer-slender lips – but unlimit in her ambition. She unquestionably became the most successful and talked about of the Michell siblings; though rarely for the right reasons. Gossip columnists were particularly attracted to her.

In January 1872, then 24, she married her cousin, the 37-year-old Arthur Kindersley Blair – a former officer of the 71st Highland Light Infantry – at the medieval St Peter-in-the-East Church in Oxford. Blair had bought his ensignship in 1855 for £450. Five months later he became a lieutenant without paying for the promotion, which underscored his suitability for the rigours of military life and suggested he would climb higher still within its ranks. He never fulfilled his potential. As a sturdily reliable, but undistinguished, soldier he was embroiled in the siege and fall of Sebastopol in 1854–55, during the Crimean War. He left the regiment in 1861. He and Mary Caroline had two children: a son, Arthur Guy Fraser, who died less than a year after his birth in 1873, and a daughter, Irene Mary, in 1876. By the time of the marriage Blair was working quietly as a general land and business agent for George Sutherland Leveston Gower, the 3rd Duke of Sutherland. He negotiated on his behalf and handled whatever paperwork the Duke – too occupied with outdoor pursuits to bother with nit-picking detail – pushed his way. He met prospective investors or dealt with anyone who wanted the Duke to invest in a new scheme or development. But he was soon cuckolded. According to the diarist and socialite Walburga, Lady Paget, the Duke 'Spent half his life doing his accounts and the other half mooning by the sea with a lady who . . . had established supremacy over him'. She was icily referring to Mrs Blair. Lady Paget, it must be stressed, was scarcely favourable towards the Duke, because of his unfeeling disregard for the original Duchess

– her close friend, Anne Hay Mackenzie, Countess of Cromartie. But she accurately portrayed the truth of the matter. The Duke had fallen out of love with his wife, and fallen in love with Mary Caroline.

The Duke was an odd fish, indeed. *The Illustrated London News* memorably described him as possessing 'a touch of the modern knight-errant' who was always 'in the midst of more than one thrilling adventure'. Pro social reform yet endearingly eccentric, he smoked cigarettes by the crate-load. He piloted his yacht, *Sans Peur*, across to Norway to chase salmon or through the Mediterranean to chase the sun. He also used it to carry men and goods in support of Giuseppe Garibaldi and the Red Shirts of the Risorgimento. He searched for oil, dug for gold and mined for coal. He supported the Suez Canal scheme. The *Illustrated London News* said of his restless exploration: 'Few ports of call in the

The Duke of Sutherland, who relished the outdoor life and steam trains.
He liked to attend fires in London in his private fire engine.

civilised or uncivilised world . . . were not familiar to him and his yacht.' He revealed a childlike wonder for anything mechanical, such as the chug of steam trains and the clang of fire engines. He became Director of the Highland Railway – partly subsidising lines to Wick and Thurso and Ardgay, across the Kyle of Sutherland to Golspie, and fully subsidising another from there to Helmsdale. The total cost was in excess of £500,000. As though it was a miniature track with model trains laid out in the gallery, down the main staircase and through the dining room of his home, Dunrobin Castle, the route became known as the Duke of Sutherland's Railway. He was cheerfully christened 'The Steam Duke' and 'The Iron Duke'. His penchant for fire engines bordered on the infantile. He bought his own engine and frequently attended blazes in London dressed in a fireman's uniform. It was said that after the Alhambra Theatre caught alight, the Duke and his friend, who just happened to be Prince of Wales, clambered on to the roof for a better view of it.

The Duke dressed to his own unique taste. Everyone knew him as the Duke and so there was no need to show off with expensive clothes. During the day he liked to wear red flannel shirts, worsted stockings and a Norfolk jacket. The Sutherland tartan was held in place with a leather ring. A knitted glengarry sat on the top of his head, which was a mass of shaggy hair. The outfit was completed with a pair of 'the heaviest' hobnailed boots. For the evening he 'swayed between blue serge and black velveteen' suits made by local tailors. Lady Paget regarded him as 'a little unwashed and rough, but kind and bon enfant'. With a silvery, Father Christmas beard, the Duke looked rather like a caricature of Scottish nobility. Twenty years older than Mary Caroline, he had a portly gut, baggy eyes and round shoulders. Her attraction to him was primarily based on his ownership of 1.3 million acres of land, three palatial homes and his established place among the Prince of Wales' 'Marlborough House set'.

The properties alone were mesmerising. Dunrobin resembles a fairy-tale fort, replete with turrets and towers and grounds that overlook the north coast of the Moray Firth. The principal designer was Sir Charles Barry, architect of the Palace of Westminster, who intermingled Scots Baronial and French Renaissance in his design. The castle, part of which dates back to the 1300s, contained almost 200 rooms. The Duke also owned Lilleshall in Shropshire and Trentham in Staffordshire. With its arches and white walls, as well as a clock tower, Benjamin Disraeli thought Trentham's impressive house and gardens ideally suited his imaginative purposes so he used them in his novel *Lothair*. He stole its look and layout and rechristened it Brentham, describing the owners of the stately mansion as 'a family with charm'. If this wasn't sufficient – for how many homes does one man need in which to live? – Stafford House in St James belonged to the Duke too. This glorious place was best and most accurately summed up by Queen Victoria, who once told the Duke and Duchess: 'I have come from my house to your palace.' Made of Bath stone, and spread over three floors, it housed a fraction of the Duke's art collection, which included the work of Raphael and Rubens, Tintoretto and Van Dyck, Hogarth and Reynolds.

Mary Caroline saw herself as mistress of all she surveyed – both the Duke and in particular his fiefdoms. So, too, did the Duke, who shared the vision of the two of them locked harmoniously together for ever. He shut out his wife to dote on his willing, supine lover. Because of his devotion to Mary Caroline, the final years of Anne's life, which ended abruptly, were miserable and remorseful. Because of Mary Caroline's devotion to him, the last act of Arthur Kindersley Blair's life was grislier still.

Arthur Blair died in 1883. That bland line is made vivid by the whispers and innuendo entwined with it. The likelihood is that the Duke either shot him dead or had a hand in shooting him.

If he didn't, the assassin was Mary Caroline. And, if neither physically yanked the trigger, Blair was pushed into suicide. A shameful cover-up followed.

Blair was staying temporarily with Mary Caroline and his daughter, Irene, in the grey-stone Bohespic Lodge, about a mile from Tummel Bridge near Pitlochry. The official version of what happened to him ran like this. On an October afternoon – a murky hour when patches of fog, like wispy low cloud, hung over the moors – he went grouse shooting alone. Between 5 p.m. and 6 p.m., returning home, he slipped on the banks of a burn called Allt Dalriach, less than half a mile from Bohespic Lodge and less than 100 yards from a farm at Dalriach itself. His gun went off and the bullets lodged in his heart and his left lung. The gunfire alerted Mary Caroline, who left the Lodge and found him dead, the gun beside his body. His tearful wife was too distraught to talk about the catastrophe. A local doctor travelled five miles in his pony and trap to pronounce him dead. There were no witnesses and the newspapers took almost no interest in Blair's death. The 'incident' was passed off in a paragraph near the middle or at the bottom of a page as nothing more than an 'accident of a melancholy nature'. But another doctor, who carried out the post-mortem because of the sudden and suspicious circumstances, scratched two words at the foot of his report: 'Supposed accident'. Six days later Blair's death notice, which Mary Caroline published in *The Times* and other newspapers, could not have been briefer. It contained fourteen words, which ended with the letters RIP – a terse and inadequate farewell.

On 4th October Arthur Kindernley Blair, the Highland Light Infantry, died aged 48. RIP

The notice is fascinating for what it does not reveal. It does not say where Blair died. It does not hint at the unfortunate events that must have preceded his 'accident'. It does not say he has a wife and children. It does not mention his funeral or ask for flowers. In a final insult, Blair's name was wrongly spelt; he was described as Kindernley rather than Kindersley, a mistake that at least *The Times* corrected in its next edition.

The doltish plods of the police carried out superficial questioning and a cursory search of the scene before accepting the theory that Blair's death was nothing more than a classic example of rotten luck. The case, however, pricked the interest of a reporter from a local newspaper. He embarked on some rudimentary investigations and footslogged his way to the inn at Tummel Bridge in an attempt to discover what lay beneath the understated account of the 'accident'. In his book on the family's history, *A Prospect of Sutherland*, Gilbert T. Bell relates what happened next. The reporter spoke to the inn's hostess, who described Blair as 'such a nice frank gentleman'. She added that 'everybody liked him'. Asked how the shooting had occurred, she replied: 'According to the doctor, who is a very careful man, and weighs things on every side, it was an accident; and I suppose that's the most charitable view to take of the matter.' Charitable, indeed.

Tongues wagged at piston speed. One embroidered rumour followed another. The locals said that Blair had been a nuisance to both his wife and the Duke. He had refused to remain silent about the affair or be bought off to ignore it. The Duke, it was suggested, concocted the account of Blair's lone grouse hunt to protect Mary Caroline, who had actually killed her husband out of anger and frustration after asking for a divorce and being turned down. How, for example, did she appear beside her dead husband so swiftly? How did she know the precise location of her husband's corpse purely from the echoing sound of the gunshots? Why were tenants of the nearby farm not on the scene first? More tittle-tattle claimed that Blair had committed suicide, spiritually broken by his wife's infidelity and his impotence to do anything about it because of his role as one of the Duke's paid servants. One school of thought said the Duke was benevolent in covering it up to prevent the disgrace that would have descended on his family, including Mary Caroline, if the truth became known; especially because Blair had been one of those hard-bitten soldiers on whom depression could not possibly have settled.

However it was achieved – and the Duke was a formidable figure to a county policeman or doctor – the suppression of the facts was so successful that no fatal accident inquiry was ever held. No one was called to answer difficult questions or cross-examined. None of the evidence was ever tested. Victorian scientists knew that the rotation of a bullet meant several factors needed to be considered when examining wounds – whether contused or lacerated – to determine what *The Principles of Forensic Medicine* categorised as 'accident, suicide or homicide'. These included the distance from which the gun was fired, the diameter of entry and exit allied to angle and direction, the position of the body in relation to the weapon and the question of whether the skin or clothing was burnt. An inspection of the barrel would also indicate when the gun was last fired. None of this – thankfully for the Duke and his lover – was ever carried out. 'As a general rule,' added the manual crucially, 'the suicide fires only one shot.'

Sherlock Holmes was right to announce in *The Sign of Four*: 'When you have eliminated the impossible, whatever remains, *however improbable*, must be the truth.' It is especially true in this case. Did Blair commit suicide? Probably not. Why shoot himself on a cold moor – especially when his daughter was so close by? Was his death accidental? Again, probably not. Blair was a soldier who had extensive training and combat experience with firearms. He was hardly likely to have marched across the moors with a fully loaded double-barrelled gun primed to fire. Even if he had been – stretching incredulity – the gun was hardly likely to discharge on being dropped; and, if it had done, the bullets were hardly likely (unless he was damned unfortunate) to pierce him so accurately in what was tantamount to a bull's eye hit.

In his 1965 book *Land of the Mountain and the Flood*, the writer, photographer, poet and chronicler of Scottish folklore Alasdair Alpin MacGregor said: 'The Duke was whispered to have been responsible.' Much earlier still the *Glasgow Herald* had reported categorically in 1889 that Blair was 'accidentally shot by the Duke'. The *Evening Times* repeated the claim in 1893 beside an unflattering, matronly drawing of Mary Caroline. 'Mr Blair was killed by the Duke accidentally while they were out hunting,' it concluded. In both instances, no one came forward to dispute the assertion or suggest it was a slur or smear. A profile of the Duchess circulated to overseas newspapers in 1898 was unsparing in its criticism. It talked about her as a 'woman of unconventional habits' and added that her life was 'stranger than that penned by any fiction writer . . . none but the trashiest of tale spinners would dare to spin her life in a plot'. The piece went on: 'One day the Duke lifted his rifle and he downed not the game, but the gamekeeper.' In a review of the 'accident', the *Northern Times* – admittedly from the safe distance of 1935 – was most scathing of all. Underneath the headline THE BLAIR DEATH MYSTERY it said of Mary Caroline: 'Who fired the fatal shot was not legally proved, although suspicion pointed to a certain individual who would, for the good of the country, have been none the worse of a hanging.'

At the time of the 'accident' the Duke was already estranged from his wife Anne, who in 1878 had bought a two-storey, white-fronted villa in Torquay. She changed its name from Bella Vista to Sutherland Lodge, and then to Sutherland Tower – though no tower existed. She began to use it more frequently or retreated instead to two rooms in Stafford House, where according to Lady Paget she 'spent much time lying on a sofa under a red silk eiderdown'. She surrounded herself with mynah birds and parrots, which perched everywhere. She ate alone every day. Lady Paget called the Duchess's circumstances 'wretched', as though she were being shut out and then obliterated from the marriage. So Blair was the only impediment to the Duke and Mary Caroline's cavorting. With him out of the way – Blair was even buried almost 500 miles away, his grave firmly out of sight, in London's Paddington cemetery – the affair carried on as if he'd never existed and the shots which killed him had never been fired.

With her talons firmly dug into the Duke, Mary Caroline performed the very belligerent and public act of selling her home in Hyde Park Gate and moving a short walk from her lover in Park Place, St James. She could not have been more blatant about her intentions if she'd stuck posters proclaiming it in capital letters on every wall across London. The Duke and Duchess Anne grew further apart than ever. The Duke took Mary Caroline with him on *Sans Peur* and spoke only briefly – if at all – to his wife. Lady Paget said she 'refused to go to Dunrobin since the Duke invited Mrs B there'. (She could not bring herself to spell out Mary Caroline's name in full.)

A forlorn, forgotten Anne, increasingly an encumbrance to the Duke, arrived in London from Torquay to wave off her husband on another of his voyages in November 1888. She found Mary Caroline on the passenger list of his yacht, which was bound for America. Anne retreated to her bed and in less than a fortnight had died from what the *Northern Times* described as 'a sudden and mysterious illness'. The *Glasgow Times*, which was too tactful to say that the Duke had slipped anchor with his girlfriend in tow, added that 'The acute symptoms to which she finally succumbed had not been in existence until ten to twelve days ago.' Alasdair Alpin MacGregor insisted that: 'Broken hearted, she had taken poison.' It is impossible to prove – but not impossible to conceive as a stark reality. As Lady Paget said: 'Her misery had been very great.' When she fell ill, the Duke was in mid-Atlantic. Told of his wife's sickness, he refused to turn back. Told of her death, he said it was impossible to return in time for the funeral. Asked what should be done with the body, he is said to have barked: 'Bury it.' He never saw the coffin at the foot of the grand staircase at Stafford House, where it was covered with crosses and floral wreaths. He never saw her burial, which took place in Torquay rather than at Trentham's Sutherland Mausoleum. He didn't much care. The Duke was free to marry Mary Caroline, which was all that mattered to him.

The Duke owned 40 acres in Florida's Tarpon Springs. On it, north of Lake Butler, he built Sutherland Manor – a white weatherboard property with a shingle roof and a long veranda. He sailed *Sans Peur* along the bayous of the Anclote River and staged cocktail parties in his vast garden. There was no mourning, no funereal black for his dead wife. Instead there was the fizz of champagne, the pouring of fine wines, long meals and longer conversations with Mary Caroline. Their engagement was announced in February 1889. Neither he nor his bride considered it bad taste. The wedding took place on 4 March – the same day that Benjamin Harrison was inaugurated as America's twenty-third President. They were married in Dunedin by the Bishop of Florida, Edwin Gardner Weed, at the neo-Gothic Church of the Good Shepherd, which the Duke's bank account largely constructed. The bride carried white roses and wore a white silk dress trimmed with coffee-coloured Chantilly lace. From her white bonnet flowed ostrich plumes spiked by diamond pins, as though she was being crowned.

The Duke and Anne had five children: Cromartie (Marquess of Stafford and future 4th Duke of Sutherland), Francis Mackenzie, Alexandra, George Granville, who died in 1858, and Florence, who died in 1881. None of the three remaining offspring attended the ceremony. They were disgusted in equal measure by their father's insult and impropriety, which disgraced the Sutherland name. The former Mrs Blair was considered arrogant and repulsively avaricious. They hated her with venom. The Duke wrote to his children, explaining his decision to wed so soon, which had shattered the Victorian convention that widows and widowers ought not to remarry until at least twelve months after a spouse's death. The Duke and the Dowager Duchess had waited exactly 100 days. The letter was coldly received. The children were just as alarmed by scare speculation, which leaked across the Atlantic, that Stafford House might be sold to the American socialite and workaholic Cornelius Vanderbilt II, who was a dollar billionaire. He already owned opulent properties on Fifth Avenue in New York and The Breakers, a vacation home in Newport, Rhode Island. But no home in London was finer or more coveted than the Duke's residence; and for Vanderbilt to buy it – given his extraordinary wealth – would be no more than passing over a bagful of coppers. Rather than throw the couple a party to mark their honeymoon and homecoming, the Duke's daughter, Alexandra, went through Stafford House like a locust on a corn hunt. Paintings, ornaments and relics were removed from the private rooms and hidden in a warehouse in case Vanderbilt appeared at the door one morning gleefully flourishing the buyer's deeds.

The breach between the father and his resentful offspring was never mended. Constant pettiness made harmony between them impossible. There were interminable squabbles and tugs of war over houses and furniture, status and heirlooms. The children spoke to the Dowager Duchess only when it was absolutely unavoidable. She was now seen as far more than an interloper, a tart or a carpetbagger who had snared the father with her dark, feline wiles. She was regarded as a particularly virulent bacteria which had infiltrated the Sutherland bloodstream and turned it poisonous. They believed, quite justifiably, that she was working cleverly towards one aim: paring down the inheritance the Duke would bequeath them in his will. The Dowager Duchess believed, quite justifiably too, that they were stealthily manoeuvring to remove her from the family circle as soon as the Duke breathed his last. Whenever official duty or a function brought the children and the Dowager Duchess together, the atmosphere turned sulphurous. The Duke showed no inclination to mediate. He seemed not to understand the fuss over his remarriage. Eventually the exasperated, wearied Duke – unable to claim any moral high ground but still dominant – reduced the allowance of his eldest son, Lord Stafford, after two disparate disputes, which were intimate and emotional at one end of the spectrum and farcical and ludicrously trivial at the other. First, and revealing a remarkable insensitivity, Lord Stafford expected the Duke to settle the bills accumulated during the medical treatment of his sister, Alexandra, who died in 1891, aged just 26. As executor, Lord Stafford ought to have paid them himself. Next, the two men fought over the cutting down of trees at Trentham; the son thought the father was being deliberately provocative towards him, and turned to the courts to prevent the axe doing its work. He emerged well beaten.

The friction became so persistent, and so intensely pernickety and bitter, that in 1892 the Duke and his Duchess took the unprecedented step of producing a written record – privately printed – of these tit-for-tat spats. As an act of self-defence and justification, the title was laborious but plainly factual: 'Record of Events about Quarrel between Themselves and Lord Stafford'. It was like trying to douse a fire with kerosene. Gilbert T. Bell identifies the author of all this rage on the page. 'One senses the Duchess's hand behind the pen,' he says, calling it 'tactless'. He adds: 'Although it purports to be a joint exercise, unmistakably it is her work.' The Dowager Duchess was explicitly pitting the Duke against his children for her own profit. Were he to be fully or semi-reconciled with them, she could feasibly find her own largesse appreciably cut. The ramifications of this slim volume rippled well beyond the minuscule readership it attracted. It fulfilled its purpose in exacerbating tensions and provoking further bickering. In doing so it made the conflict between the Duchess and the Duke's children more personal than ever, like a split in fundamental faiths. The Dowager Duchess would soon be dragged into a prison cell partly through her own hubris, but also because the family hated her sufficiently to let her rot there.

This chain of events began because the Duke developed a liking for the written word. The pen and the inkwell attracted him again in August as he drafted and signed a new will. Less than six weeks later, he died, aged 64. The print was still fresh on the will and on the unfortunate book he and the Duchess had produced. The gouging wounds both created were fresher still.

The Duke died of a perforated ulcer. In apparent roaring health, he had gone to bed in Dunrobin, and then complained of stomach pains. Only twenty-two hours later, he was dead. *The Times* reported that his funeral at Trentham was blighted by a 'downpour' of 'unremitting severity' and a 'raw wind which blew from the east'. Draped in the Union Jack, the oak coffin was surrounded by wreaths. One was in the shape of an anchor from Lord Stafford. Another took the letter S as its centrepiece, spelt out in Neapolitan violets. Attached to it was a card from the Dowager Duchess with the handwritten valediction: 'With a wife's undying love'. A pipe band played him to his maker. The melody had barely faded away on the cold autumnal air when the legal tussle began between the Dowager Duchess and the new Duke.

The old Duke left everything to his widow. The new Duke's solicitors regarded the document as akin to treachery. In their view it was 'difficult to imagine a will less in keeping with the spirit of the times, or more calculated to inflame feelings of distaste and mistrust'. The benefits given to the Dowager Duchess, they said, 'were so extensive that it looked as though those documents might almost have been written at her dictation'. That final qualification was unnecessary.

The Duke's personal fortune amounted to £1.4 million – the equivalent of almost £600 million today. As estate duty or capital transfer tax were penalties that future governments would create, the Dowager Duchess collected almost all of it. The hard cash went with a lifetime interest in substantial coal and iron shares, a lump sum of £100,000, virtually every non-heirloom in Stafford House and Lilleshall and assorted other chattels, including 'any six carriages of mine and any eight carriage horses'. The Duchess's daughter was even left a legacy of £12,000. For the Duke's immediate family . . . well, there wasn't a bean. The 4th Duke was dependent on the benevolence of his stepmother and beholden to her. Worse still, on the day he fell ill the old Duke had signed a codicil to the will, which increased his wife's cash legacy to £150,000.

As much out of financial survival as damaged ego and anger, the 4th Duke immediately challenged the will. In March 1893, the court had ordered that documents in 'locked tables and boxes' at Stafford House should be examined to make certain the Duke's intentions were not being misinterpreted. The Dowager Duchess bridled at the prospect. She said these items were of a 'personal and highly confidential nature'. The Duke, she added, had ordered her to destroy them. The court took no notice of her complaint and instructed the removal of the papers to the neutral ground of a solicitors' office in Whitehall, where the Dowager Duchess and the 4th Duke could inspect them under beady legal eyes. At the meeting, the Duchess was explicitly told that no document could be destroyed. The 4th Duke's counsel, Richard Taylor III, stressed the point.

The two sets of solicitors in the *Sutherland* v. *Sutherland* case sat like duelling armies on either side of a long oak table. Several documents were produced and scrutinised. The Duchess became tetchy and agitated. She began accusing the 4th Duke of tampering with them. 'These papers,' she said, 'were not as I first saw them.' She surreptitiously swept a private letter off the table, climbed from her chair and walked calmly over to the Adams fireplace. She pushed the letter carefully through the bars of the grate, as though it was a piece of garbage. The first lick of flame consumed it. Taylor was incandescent, protesting at the 'most improper proceeding'. The Dowager Duchess treated him like a footman who had dared question whether she really wanted two sugars in her tea. She said dismissively, and as though she was above the law: 'That document was a letter from me to my husband before I was married. I shall do as I like.' Taylor was said to be 'not the sort of person to allow himself to be spoken to like that by a Duchess, or by anyone else'. He didn't hesitate to prod the court into prosecuting and imprisoning the Dowager Duchess for contempt.

Six days later the case was heard in front of Sir Francis Jeune, President of the Probate, Divorce and Admiralty Division of the High Court. Sir Francis had been a Fellow at Oxford in the college where the Dowager Duchess's father had once held sway; he liked the Reverend Michell too. The Dowager Duchess apologised, though hardly fulsomely, and now claimed the letter had been written to her by the Duke 'in the course of a yachting excursion in the winter of 1886 . . . it related to an unpleasant experience between the steward and a maid'. Sir Francis was unimpressed with either her mock sorrow or her highly dubious explanation of what the letter contained. He could not have been more forceful. 'The lady,' he said, 'has committed an act, which, as far as I know, is without parallel . . . The scheme of obtaining a document must have been deliberately planned beforehand by the Duchess. Her intention – carried out by an act of deceit and violence – was a gross contempt of Court.' In simple terms, he was calling her a liar and a criminal. She was fined £250 and sentenced to six weeks in prison.

The Glasgow *Evening Times* described the Dowager Duchess's appearance in court. It said she was: 'A splendid-looking woman with a masterful will, rare power of self-control, and a voice and variety of facial expressions which are seldom found off the stage'. The public face was far different from the private one. Instead of being taken from the dock to Holloway Prison, she climbed into her cab and ordered the driver to take her to a home she'd built for herself in 1889: The Willows in Windsor. Her guilt – and the consequences of it – penetrated her like a spear. With the doors locked and the curtains drawn, she collapsed into an exhausted, lachrymose heap. Her doctor insisted she was suffering from 'severe nervous depression and the shock resulting from the mental strain which she had endured the previous day'. The Dowager Duchess sent medical certificates to confirm her unfitness for prison at precisely the same moment as moves began to be made to arrest her for absconding. But to emphasise the latitude given to a member of the aristocracy, as opposed to mere ordinary, grubbing citizens, the court allowed her to remain at The Willows until she felt healthy enough to travel to Holloway for her appointment with justice. If she expected wholesale sympathy, she did not receive it. The *Daily Mail* said she had done a 'contemptuous as well as a contemptible thing'; the *Daily Chronicle* vigorously supported the court, too, implying that the 'horsewhip' ought to deter those who make insincere apologies. Only *The Times* continued to be slavishly lenient, as though the Dowager Duchess were an innocent victim of a harmless mistake. It spoke of her 'weak heart and other troubles', as if writing to the lament of a dozen violins, and stressed her anxiousness to serve the sentence imposed, a claim she'd already disproved by running away from court. Even when she was unable to prevaricate any longer, she revealed contempt for the legal system. Due to reach the prison by 6 p.m., she arrived two hours and forty minutes late. She was still given her own 'welcome party': two doctors to care for her health and the chief warder, who greeted her like a visiting dignitary. Her incarceration was hardly pokey or grim either.

Other cells contained a metal washbasin, a rough table and chair and a small iron bedstead. She was taken to F Wing on the prison's east side and into a room 25 feet long and 15 feet wide. The 'cell' was arranged in a very comfortable style by the furniture dealers Maples. There were blue velvet chairs, tapestries on the walls to disguise the austerity of the brick and stone, a brass bedstead and adjacent toilet suite, a fireplace with brightly polished irons and a fender. *The Times* talked about the 'cheerful appearance of the room' as if it were an apartment at the Ritz. 'Additional comforts,' it pointed out, 'were presumably contained in a number of trunks conveyed in a small wagonette which was kept outside long after Her Grace had been received into prison.' She ate only the best food, off her own plates, and drank her own wine, wore her own clothes, and newspapers, books and magazines were delivered to her daily. She received 'hundreds' of letters and elaborate arrangements of flowers. Bread, water and a circuit of the yard it most certainly wasn't. She was exempted from all menial work. A servant was also available to make her bed and clean out her 'cell'. It was said that the hardest part of her incarceration was rising at 6 a.m., taking breakfast at 7.30 a.m. and attending chapel at 9 a.m.

A fortnight had barely passed before the Dowager Duchess's doctors were lobbying for her release on health grounds. An unedifying procession of feeble arguments was trotted out. Implicit in each was the fact she was a duchess and so her treatment ought not to be beastly, harsh or prolonged. It was a tender wail of 'she has suffered enough'. Her weight was cited as a sign of prison's destructive powers: it had fallen from 12 stone 2 pounds to 11 stone. One of the prison physicians, Dr Philip Francis Gilbert, said: 'I believe that further imprisonment may be permanently injurious to her health and might produce serious consequences.' The doctors spoke as though she were an ailing, tottering and decrepit 95-year-old grandmother, rather than a woman of 45 who was being given the choicest cuts of beef. The Home Secretary, the future Prime Minister Herbert Asquith, dismissed the appeal. When the Dowager Duchess at last left Holloway, she received a solid silver casket containing £250 to cover the cost of her fine. The lid of the gift was inscribed by 'sympathising English and Scottish friends' with their 'expression of indignant protest against the severe order made by a Judge for having unflinchingly carried out a dying request of her husband'. The Dowager Duchess took it as confirmation that her sentence stemmed from the whim of a merciless and despotic judge.

If only the Dowager Duchess had been conciliatory – both before and after her husband's death – to her stepson. If only she hadn't been so mercenary. And if only she hadn't been so obviously Machiavellian in her dealings with, and barely concealed loathing for, the Sutherland family. The meeting in the solicitors' office would then have been unnecessary. Even if it had not been, and she'd burnt the letter nonetheless, no doubt the 4th Duke would have demurred before submitting her to a court case and a jail term. But the Dowager Duchess was her own worst enemy, which made other enemies superfluous. However short and comfortable, her stay in Holloway severely injured her pride and prestige, and devalued her self-esteem. Afterwards she felt soiled and abused by it. In hindsight, however, she knew she had no one to blame but herself. Her own nastiness, marble-hearted approach to money and swollen self-importance – the crass need to beat down the 4th Duke and his brother – had led her to prison and kept her there. She had shown no compassion; so the 4th Duke would show no compassion either. No one could blame him for it.

Aware that litigation could make *Sutherland* v. *Sutherland* into a real-life *Jarndyce* v. *Jarndyce*, the Dowager Duchess and the 4th

Duke nonetheless arranged a settlement over the will, but without striking a peace accord. It was announced in June 1894, and took eight QCs and five junior counsel to ensure no loophole or embarrassing clause snaked through unseen in the small print. The 4th Duke retained the estates and homes that he'd previously feared losing. The Dowager Duchess retained her financial treasure trove – believed to be anywhere between £500,000 and £850,000 and at least £5,000 annually. The Dowager Duchess – typically aggressive in business and neurotic about plots against her – insisted on cash: not cheques, not banker's drafts and certainly not the transfer of columns of digits from one account into another. For she always sensed betrayal. It was as if she expected the 4th Duke to swindle her spectacularly. The Bank of England issued special £1,000 banknotes on her behalf, which were taken out of circulation after she had deposited them. The 4th Duke's solicitor, wearing top hat and frock coat, collected the case, heavy as a flagstone, in a hansom cab and took it to the Dowager Duchess's solicitor, who counted the notes as if dealing out a hand of Patience. His client obtained both the flesh and the blood of an extraordinary transaction.

There was a lot of gossip about which scandalous skeletons the 4th Duke and the Dowager Duchess wanted to remain in the cupboard thus making it necessary to find a workable agreement. A fist fight in court would have led to a plague descending on both their houses. One mystery was never solved. Why did the Dowager Duchess burn the document? Asking that question leads directly to another. Why did she originally insist that she had written it, and later claim 'the letter' belonged to the Duke? Whatever the paper contained, it was sufficiently significant for her to make sure no one saw it. In her contempt hearing, Sir Francis Jeune highlighted the clandestine but awfully clumsy effort she made to do so. His words were damning: 'It seemed clear from those documents that the Dowager Duchess had picked out one that she had concealed from the administrator until a later period of the inspection,' he said. Jeune added that she had 'placed it between the bars before anyone could stop her', which proved malice aforethought. The power of the court – and the possibility of a prison term – was not enough to deter her. She evidently saw the document as the equivalent of nitroglycerine: so destructive that it had been got rid of. What she destroyed might have been evidence of her infidelity with the Duke before it became commonly known. It might have implicated either her or the Duke in the death of her husband. Or it might have immeasurably strengthened the 4th Duke's claim that his father's will must be declared null and void. The manner in which she burnt this single, incriminating sheet of paper stressed one thing. The Dowager Duchess was unmerciful – vicious, self-obsessed, vengeful and never able to let a grudge die.

Much later she would prove it again by building her own 340-room Xanadu in the Kyle of Sutherland. She deliberately constructed it to overlook the Sutherland estate, from which she was excluded. The family were unable to ignore her stately creation, which loomed over them. The tower of her castle purposely has clocks on only three sides. The side facing Sutherland is blank to signify that the Dowager Duchess refused to give 'the time of day' to the new Duke. The Duke, commuting to and from Dunrobin, drew the blinds of his carriage whenever he passed it.

The official title she gave her home was Castle Carbisdale; but it became popularly known as the Castle of Spite for reasons so obvious as to require no elaboration.

So this was the woman the Valet recognised from the pages of the newspapers he read – an adulteress, possibly complicit in murder and, above all, someone who thought she was above the law. It was stretching the point, but surely she was a thief too? She'd stolen from the Sutherland family and reduced to cinders the proof of her guilt.

When he saw the Dowager Duchess's name staring back at him from the register of the Hotel Bristol he had no reservations about stealing from a woman with so much wealth on behalf of a woman with so much beauty.

Chapter 8

The 11.50 train from the Gare du Nord

Paris was wrapped in a milky, autumnal light into which the pearl-grey formal façades of its grand buildings and the hard lines of its monuments faded to become from a distance almost indistinct, as if disappearing behind a veil along the wide boulevards. The prospect of rain hung in the air and the early seasonal winds had looted most of the leaves from the trees. Outside the Gare du Nord were the flower sellers with late blooms, which shone like shots of wet colour across a grey canvas, and the newspaper vendors, whose blackened hands gripped and held aloft the front pages of the papers for Monday, 17 October 1898. Harry the Valet took no notice of them. He walked through the station entrance with only one purpose in mind. What came next – and the consequences of it – briefly proved to be the Valet's best of times. He would be admired for his outrageous cheek and steady nerve, a piece of skill which seemed impossible to those who studied it afterwards.

Among the criminal underworld, there would be low bows and envious approval. Among the police, there would be grudging respect for the pluck and planning of an operation that irritated and frustrated them. And among the public, an appetite to discover everything about the Valet and a life led in imaginative, bold leaps, which carried him for three decades from one high-profile crime to another.

For six heady, helter-skelter weeks he possessed more ready money than he could ever spend. So much money, in fact, that his wallet was thick with notes. His drive to use them for personal pleasure proved insatiable. He seldom slept and was almost never without a glass in his hand. He lived on champagne and fine wine, and swept with imperious fanfare into London's theatres, night spots and clubs. Through a fatal combination of human weakness and self-delusion, which made the Valet feel invulnerable, he became a luminous presence, the toast and talk of the town. But he discovered as a result that joy and woe are truly woven finely together.

All this happened to him because he stole the Dowager Duchess of Sutherland's jewels and in an instant became a criminal celebrity.

In explaining the theft, and the madly impetuous and hysterical way in which he behaved after it, the Valet would always justify himself with an unblushing defence of the heart: 'The most romantic thing about the robbery was that I did it for the sake of a very beautiful woman,' he said. 'Bear in mind that I was madly in love . . . and imagine what I felt like.' To emphasise it, he called himself 'love-stricken' and 'heedless of the danger I was running'.

The Valet had reached breaking point. He could not conceive of living without Maude Richardson. He saw nothing when he closed his eyes but her face. He could think of nothing – apart from winning her back. He acted as if nothing mattered except marriage to her. She was everything to him. He cared more about her presence than he did his own. The Valet was driven by something else too. He was manically jealous that she might already have forgotten him and found someone else to take his place; another stage-door Johnnie or London cavalier, like the gent he'd scared off with a pistol shot in Ostend. Every waking moment away from Maude was torture. After she left him, the Valet said he had only one idea in his mind: to find her again.

It happened when he least expected it, a coincidence so unlikely that it could only otherwise be found in the pages of a romantic novelette. The Valet was strolling along the Champs-Elysées and glancing abstractedly at passing carriages. Seated in one of them was Maude, her profile unmistakable. With a hasty wave, he summoned a cab himself and discreetly followed her to the Hôtel du Nord, which was almost directly opposite the Gare du Nord station. He didn't rush to make an apology, buttressed by a lengthy proclamation of his love and a proposal of marriage. Standing outside the hotel, as she disappeared inside, he had the sense to understand that approaching her would achieve nothing. Where could he have taken her? And what present could he have offered her? There was no point in calling on her with empty pockets. The Valet needed to convince Maude of his wealth – not provide her with further evidence of his continued impoverishment.

The Valet was also aware that a trifling or minor theft would bring only temporary respite, a few days' grace before his money ran out again. There was a need to do something spectacular on her behalf; a job that would keep Maude permanently in the cushy style which she regarded as her entitlement; a job, moreover, which would make the need to pull off another unnecessary.

Enter, the Dowager Duchess of Sutherland.

The Dowager Duchess had spent five days in a suite at the Hotel Bristol, on the Place Vendôme, which had been laid out to salute the armies of Louis XIV. From her top-floor windows, she could view the column honouring Napoleon I and its cannon-bronze plates. She was accompanied by her third husband, the Francophile Sir Albert Rollit, an affluent, plump figure with swept-back hair and a bristly light-coloured beard. He was a one-time steamship company owner, a solicitor, former President of the Law Society, two-term Mayor of Hull, where he'd been born, and Conservative Member of Parliament for Islington South since 1886. Aged 54, he grew close, and then closer still, to the Dowager Duchess after his own wife died following a brief illness in 1895. The Duchess was in the mood to be courted. She'd been alone long enough. Given her wealth, there was no shortage of aristocratic admirers offering flowers and spurious concern, a restaurant table or a weekend tucked snugly in the country. Pitted against the blue-blood competition of dukes, earls and baronets, the odds of Rollit – not the most physically appealing of men – becoming her third husband seemed long indeed. In comparison with them, Rollit, knighted in 1885, seemed staid and humdrum, a businessman cum politician manifestly unlike the Duke of Sutherland in manner and enthusiasms. He didn't sail, shoot or socialise lavishly. Rather than the wide outdoors, his natural habitat was the cosy club chat of smoke-filled rooms and the benches and bars of the Palace of Westminster. But, for precisely this reason, the Dowager Duchess found him attractive. Not being cut from the same tartan as the Duke worked entirely in his favour. He was respectable, reliable and uncontroversial. In the eyes of his bride-to-be these were winning traits because her frictions with the Sutherland siblings – and especially her incarceration in Holloway Prison – proved so profoundly bruising that she longed for the emotional stability that Rollit's ordinary ways equipped him to provide.

Newspaper coverage of the Dowager Duchess's tribulations had not been flattering; indeed, some journalists took an almost sadistic pleasure in plunging the knife into her and twisting it with relish. She thought it prudent to remove herself as a possible target of the press blades. What she sought was an unobtrusive, but rich existence in which she could consort with her narrow circle of friends and travel abroad without drawing attention to herself – and without

The Dowager Duchess of Sutherland, who went to prison through greed and a thirst for revenge and became her own worst enemy, which made other enemies superfluous.

the recent past being raked up like cold ash and old coals. Rollit had fatherly qualities. He offered decent conversation, maintained and managed her financial arrangements and also protected her interests. More than anything else, he was dependable.

The widow and the widower were married in November 1896 in St George's Church, Hanover Square, at the altar where Percy Shelley re-married Harriet Westbrook in 1814. The church was decked in palms and white chrysanthemums. There was no white dress to match them. The Dowager Duchess, never again able to pass herself off as a paragon of purity, wore a petunia velvet gown with a trim of chinchilla fur studded with jewels. Hardly under-dressed, she added the ornament of a large diamond comb at the back of her hair. Just six days later – in retrospect the new Lady Rollit ought to have taken it as a portent – the tower of St George's

*Sir Albert Rollit, who won the Dowager Duchess of Sutherland's
heart simply because he was so unlike the Duke of Sutherland.*

was ablaze. Fire destroyed the church's original bell and its organ,
which had to be rebuilt nut and bolt. For the Rollits, however, life
went serenely on. It moved in a decadent procession from London
to the shires or to the South of France. The couple were regularly
in Paris. For the Duchess, the city was one enormous clothes and
jewellery store. For Rollit, it was a gentleman's parlour where
business could be successfully and pleasurably negotiated. As
President of the Anglo-French Chamber of Commerce, he
chaired or hosted meetings designed to stimulate trade. The
Duchess, who took no interest in her husband's work, occupied
herself with shopping, adding to her commodious wardrobe, and
searching out new jewels to buy.

Enter the Valet.

He went through the familiar routine, as if laying down markers and plotting co-ordinates across the platform of the Gare du Nord. A good plan was the authorial signature of his work. This became more important after his embarrassing error over the Duchess of Devonshire's jewels in 1893. He had presumed far too much of her, a mistake he would never repeat. To make certain of it, he gathered more reliable inside information than ever before. He was like a spy infiltrating an enemy camp. The best way to glean titbits came 'through the servants', he reckoned. A personal maid always knew what her mistress had brought with her and where it was kept. The hotel maid knew the same things too; she dusted the dressing table, moved bags and suitcases, opened wardrobe doors. The porters were constantly alive to the comings and goings of the guests and learnt to overhear and make mental notes of conversations without being obtrusive.

The Valet began canvassing the staff of the Hotel Bristol. He did so in a casual way, as if expressing a fascinated but completely innocent interest in the Dowager Duchess. He made it sound as though she was a former friend with whom he would like to be reacquainted. Well in advance of her departure from the hotel, the Valet knew that she planned to catch the 11.50 a.m. train to Calais. He knew that the maid would leave her first-floor room at approximately 10.30 a.m. with the jewel case, which was covered in green baize and carried by a leather strap. He also knew the maid would give the case to the porter and return around 11 a.m. to collect it. He knew the porter would place the case carefully back into the maid's hands; and that a railway omnibus would take her and at least one other servant on the two-mile route to the Gare du Nord. He even knew that 48 hours earlier the Dowager Duchess had lavished £5,000 on a pearl chain from a Paris jeweller. Finally, he knew that he was dealing with a woman obsessed with ostentatious jewels and her appearance in public.

In his will, the Duke of Sutherland had left his wife the Sutherland jewels for her 'use and enjoyment during her life'.

Some were subsequently classed as heirlooms during her early and feisty altercations with the Sutherland family. The Dowager Duchess had had no option but to return them – reluctantly, and with a residue of ill feeling and genuine grief that never left her. She did retain a plain string of pearls which the *Illustrated London News* rated as 'one of the great jewels of the world'. The string was long enough to pass three times around her neck and fall down in long curves over her chest. She also amassed a gem collection of her own. Jewels were irresistible to the Duchess, and showing them off gave her a distinctive sense of self. She was never without an array of jewellery; and she could never be persuaded – unlike the Duchess of Devonshire – to wear replicas as a precaution against thieves such as the Valet; only the real thing was ever allowed to adorn her regal personage. The Valet became the major beneficiary of her inflated pride. Her jewel case collection comprised twenty-six items. Even the briefest descriptions of less than half of these pieces make it glint in the imagination like Aladdin's Cave. To open it was to be in awe of the contents, which included:

A long gold chain set with fine pearls
A plain pearl chain
A long gold chain set with fine diamonds
A diamond and pearl necklace
A large cross of white enamel with diamonds
A heart of fine pearls
A horseshoe brooch, ornamented with diamonds and
    sapphires
A jewelled gold bracelet
A jewelled bracelet with small globes of diamonds
A gold bracelet bearing the name 'Mary' in diamonds
A large emerald and diamond ring
A fine pearl and diamond ring

A brooch, in butterfly form, set with precious stones
A gold purse, set with diamonds and other gems
A dragonfly brooch in diamonds

The Valet was particularly taken by the thought of the distinctive dragonfly brooch and the large cross of white enamel and diamonds. Any fence would accept them with alacrity.

The scene at the Gare du Nord resembled the one five years earlier at Charing Cross, where the Valet had stalked the Duchess of Devonshire. In fact, it was as if he was replaying that moment. There was the heave of passengers and porters sweeping across the booking hall and spread in wide but ragged lines towards the carriages. From the furnace fire of the trains came the smell of coal and hot ash. The air was full of dark mottled smoke and sugar-white steam. Smuts swirled among them like black ticker-tape. The noises were familiar too: the clunk of carriage doors being slammed shut, the din of lumbering trains in departure or arrival, the scuffle and shuffle of feet on the platform, the brisk tap-tap of brass-bottomed canes and the bump and scrape of luggage. There was an atmospheric crackle about the place – shouts and raised voices of every pitch and timbre, fulsome greetings and sobbing goodbyes. No one took much notice of the Valet. He headed towards the boat train as though anxious to claim a seat on it. The haste of the late traveller meant he didn't have to divert attention from himself. The genuine passenger was always looking elsewhere: at the clock, at the trains, at their ticket, at their case or at someone else who might barge into them. Everyone around him assumed the Valet had somewhere urgent to go. In this way, he slid into and out of stations such as the Gare du Nord with no more effort than it took to slide a letter under a hotel door. He had neither his trusty Gladstone nor his impressive canvas bag with its embroidered S. He'd forgotten both of them in his rush to pack and surprise Maude in Ostend, and he lacked the money to buy replacements. The Valet had no overcoat either. It had also been left behind in London. He would have to carry the Dowager Duchess's jewel case openly, and look as though it belonged to him.

The boat train was still gathering fuel for its journey, the coal being fed into it with wide shovels, as the Valet loitered unobserved and undisturbed beside it, counting the minutes until the Dowager Duchess and her entourage arrived. He was 'wildly excited at the prospect of a big capture'. As well as Sir Albert, she was travelling with her brother, Roland, and his wife. The Valet watched as the maid arrived clutching the Duchess's jewels. With her was one of the other servants, also loaded down with baggage. Rollit strode ahead of them with the gait of a military captain leading a platoon. In a mental rehearsal the Valet imagined each

Henri de Blowitz, the Paris correspondent of The Times
who shaped policy as well as reporting on it.

step of the theft to come. In between the to and fro of passengers passing in front of him, the Valet saw the servants put two boxes, plus the jewel case and a satchel, in to the Dowager Duchess's compartment and then spread a rug over them. 'I waited,' said the Valet, 'and at last a fourth person appeared and took her seat in the carriage. This was the Duchess herself.' He described her as 'a very stately-looking woman', and said she sat opposite her cases.

Momentarily the Valet was despondent. For the Dowager Duchess showed no inclination to move again before the train pulled out of the station. It was as though she was guarding her valuables, like a bull-mastiff protecting a gate. 'It was perfectly clear that unless she came out on to the platform I would be unsuccessful,' he said. The two paid retainers went to find an umbrella for the Duchess and third-class compartments for themselves. The Dowager Duchess was now alone. 'The time seemed interminable,' said the Valet, 'but still I waited patiently. After all, I had everything to gain and nothing to lose. A false move on the part of the Duchess at the last moment and the jewels were mine. It was worth it.'

Reward for his vigilance arrived serendipitously. It was the Valet's immense good fortune that a prominent journalist was already in the Gare du Nord. By chance he spotted the Dowager Duchess and decided to pay his respects and say farewell to her. Henri de Blowitz was the Paris-based correspondent of *The Times*, a well-fed, fastidious, flashily dressed and fussily mannered man, immediately recognisable by his long coat, shiny top hat and sprawling, immensely bushy grey sideburns, which were fashionably called Piccadilly Weepers. De Blowitz was described as omniscient and omnipotent, a writer so immersed in Anglo-French politics – and so influential in shaping it – that an article under his name could shift or even make policy. Anthony Trollope might have invented him. The scoop of de Blowitz's career came in 1878. He gained access to the Treaty of Berlin and enabled *The*

Times to publish the entire document on the morning it was signed in Germany. A Spy portrait of Blowitz turns him into several balls of fat – a swollen balloon of a fellow with a substantial paunch, stretching the buttons of his waistcoat, and a round head. Anyone of note who ever came to Paris found themselves both entertained and interrogated by Blowitz, who had a voluminous contacts book.

He went to the Dowager Duchess's carriage door. As he did so, the Duchess left her seat and came on to the platform to politely greet his full moon face. The Valet had already calculated the precise angle of his approach and exit, and also the fine margin of error in between. 'At last, to my satisfaction,' he said, 'I saw the Duchess rise from her place. The moment she stepped out, I stepped in.' He claimed the case and the satchel.

One of the most famous jewel thefts was completed in less than five seconds. With a nerveless few strides from platform to wood-panelled carriage, a hand outstretched on to the leather-studded seats, a side turn, like a dancer on points, and graceful exit, the Valet undertook what de Blowitz's own newspaper called the coup of lightning. Everything about it was as finely wrought as a watch mechanism. No one saw the Valet enter. No one saw him leave. No one – least of all the owner of the case and the satchel – was aware of what had happened. The Dowager Duchess was still talking to Blowitz, ignorant of the Valet's consummate performance. In a few hours she would find herself written about and interviewed, her past excavated like an archaeological dig, all over again; and just because she'd shaken hands with Blowitz out of courtesy.

With the satchel and the jewel case, the Valet was marching away from the Dowager Duchess as she resumed her seat in the carriage. She failed to notice the loss of the jewels.

The Valet was wary and nervy, however; another danger loomed directly in front of him. The metal and wooden barriers at the Gare du Nord were closely monitored to dissuade thieves. His task was to act nonchalantly, as if he'd just seen off a friend. A worried roll of the eyes, a flicker of apprehension in the set of the face or a twitch of his shoulders would be cataclysmic for him. Any sign that he was trying to conceal the satchel and the jewel case would alert the rail authorities to his guilt as surely as tripping a wire and setting off an alarm. Through body language – head up, spine straight – and a fixed, hard gaze, he tried to convince the porter that time was pressing; that a lunch appointment or a business meeting was next on his agenda; that he was too important to be interrupted by pointless questions about where he had been and what he was carrying.

But, in the end, it was simple.

There was an enormous crowd struggling to get on to the platform, and the attention of the porter and a detective beside him was divided. He vanished into the sea of that crowd and was gone, as if its waves had closed around him and swallowed him up. 'Everything seemed to be in my favour,' said the Valet. 'I simply walked through the barrier, got into a cab and told the driver to take me to the Rue de Rivoli.'

The Valet needed to buy a big piece of leather luggage in which to place the jewels. His cab reached the Grands Magasins du Louvre and he used the loose francs, which he found in the satchel, to purchase it. He was uncharacteristically giddy and exultant in his achievement – so much so that he became slapdash, acting like an amateur. 'I was so careless that I marched into the shop, leaving the jewel case in the cab,' he said. 'I deserved to lose it.' The irrational notion that he could have been followed dogged the Valet. The idea was nonsense. The police would have arrested him as soon as he reappeared from the shop in possession of his new purchase.

With the jewels inside the bag, he told the driver to head for the Gare de Lyon. 'I alighted and waited there for about ten minutes to see if I was being shadowed by detectives,' he said. From there the fidgety Valet hailed a second cab, which took him to the Hotel London and New York. Only in the dark privacy of his room did he break open the case and examine his haul. He didn't bother to lock the door. 'I poured all the treasures on to the table and gloated over them,' he said, without articulating what he saw. The best he could muster was the sentence: 'Words fail me to describe the beauties of the jewellery.' But, for the rest of his life, the Valet said that he was able to see them 'all before my eyes'.

The jewels emerged, each more gorgeous than the last. The large chain of diamonds and a necklet 'simply dazzled' him. The necklet had taken someone he described as a 'clever craftsman' five months to make. It contained five large pearls – one of which was 78 grains. The dragonfly brooch was stupendous. The large cross of white enamel and diamonds was 'another beautiful treasure' comprising four stones of blue and white diamonds worth £1,200 each. 'There were also brooches, earrings, bracelets and rings, which would have turned an Indian Rajah green with envy,' he said. The Valet believed the total value of the jewels was £16,000. His estimate was too conservative. The Dowager Duchess's valuables were worth £25,000 to £30,000.

The Valet composed himself. He sat down at the table in his room, took a sheet of the hotel's stationery from the leather tray in front of him and wrote a note to Maude. It read:

I have everything you require. See me at once.

He didn't elaborate, because it was impossible to do so. He couldn't explain in writing how the jewels had come into his possession. The Valet simply wanted Maude to believe that he had money; and that he was prepared to spend it solely on her. He gave the letter to a porter to be hand-delivered. When Maude received it, slitting open the envelope and reading his scribbled promise, she assumed it was a ruse to entice her back. She thought his claim was bravado, not to be taken seriously. That the Valet had the temerity to ask for a loan still rankled. She'd been taken as a fool once – and had acted like one herself too. She would not be won over by an unsubstantiated promise on paper. Maude's trust in the Valet had been so diminished that she wasn't prepared to go to his hotel and face disillusionment again. The two lines he had written didn't make sense to her anyway. If he actually possessed what she wanted, why should she have to travel to him to gain proof? Why wasn't he rapping on her bedroom door with the evidence of it in his own hands? No, she decided, it was another game; and she was fed up with playing. It would only lead to another row, another unpleasant scene in which one of them was sure to become angry and the other – no doubt her – would make an excuse and leave. The depressing, pointless cycle of it all would have to end. She could only rid herself of this man by ignoring him. Maude tore the letter into ragged squares.

The Valet hadn't prepared himself for rebuttal. He was expecting a summons to the lobby. He was brushing his hair, preparing his smile and framing his words of welcome. Instead he received nothing but silence. The afternoon hours passed slowly. The Valet realised that he had no option but to find Maude and present her with the jewels. He began stuffing them into his pockets, utterly convinced he could present them as evidence of his millionaire status. 'I went out into the streets with diamonds, sapphires and amethysts literally tumbling out of my pockets,' he said. 'If that was not asking to be captured, you might tell me what it was.'

The Valet needn't have worried about capture. The French police had no idea of his identity. In fact, they had no idea about anything at all.

The detectives and the newspapers were aghast at the audacity of the theft. It was the criminal equivalent of Dr Johnson's remark about discovering a dog walking on its hind legs – 'you are surprised to find it done at all'. Daring was the adjective most often used in reports to convey the enormity of it to the reading public. 'The robbery was cleverly and boldly effected,' said the *Daily Mail*'s Paris-based reporter. The jewels, it continued, were taken 'in an adroit and clever manner . . . so cleverly was it done that not the slightest suspicion was aroused . . . The whole thing must have happened in a few moments.' It concluded bleakly, and without attempting to be deliberately facetious: 'The authorities here have absolutely no clue.'

Strung together, the jumble of tantalising headlines is revealing. They lay out the theft succinctly, and convey the confusion of the police:

DARING THIEVES AT PARIS
HOW THE THIEVES MADE THEIR HAUL
STORY OF A SUSPICIOUS STRANGER
NO TRACE OF THE MISSING PROPERTY
THE ROBBERS STILL AT LARGE

No one knew how the jewels had been taken in such circumstances. No one knew how the criminals – and almost everyone assumed more than one man was responsible – could possibly have escaped. And no one knew on whom to pin the blame. Early reports – ironically, given the Valet's history – insisted the Duchess of Devonshire had been the victim rather than the Dowager Duchess of Sutherland. A retraction was demanded and published immediately.

The Calais-bound train was still travelling through the suburbs of Paris when the Dowager Duchess said she 'wished to obtain something from her little bag' and realised that the satchel and the jewel case were missing. The train continued to Amiens, where she and Sir Albert Rollit alerted the authorities and returned to the Gare du Nord. On hearing of the theft, the local police in Amiens immediately wired Paris, London, Calais, Brussels and Amsterdam in case 'the thieves' – perpetuating the idea that a co-ordinated team was behind the theft – could be rounded up by a border patrol. The Parisian police, attempting to disguise their own lack of gumption, tried to blame the Dowager Duchess for failing to respond with sufficient speed to the loss of her jewels. However delicately worded, one statement in particular didn't require decoding:

> Regret is felt by the police authorities that the Duchess, on becoming aware of the loss ten minutes after the train started, did not insist upon having all the passengers' luggage searched.

The coldly furious Dowager Duchess could not wait to leave Paris after her return there at 7 p.m. Within two hours, during which she and Rollit gave further statements, she was heading for Calais again. By then, she had issued a reward for the return of her jewels. The sum was £4,000.

The police made erroneous assumptions. Foremost among them was that some of 'the thieves' remained on the train after the theft. The theory was based entirely on the level of security on the Gard du Nord platforms, which the detectives regarded as impregnable, as though the ticket gate were double-bolted and fastened with a combination lock. The police also came to the conclusion that the Dowager Duchess must have been followed during her remaining days in Paris; and that the perpetrator had confederates who aided and abetted him.

Rollit and the Duchess hampered the inquiry with their own witness accounts. Each threw the police further off the Valet's trail. Rollit thought the couple had been shadowed during shopping expeditions. He said a figure appeared regularly in his peripheral vision whenever he and his wife left the Hotel Bristol. If so, it wasn't the Valet, who was careful never to give his 'marks' a sense of his presence. The Dowager Duchess was more specific. The *Mail* said she told police that 'a well-dressed man on the platform stared at her so persistently . . . she thought she must have met him somewhere'. She continued to watch him, endeavouring to recall his face, 'while he never took his eyes off her'. She made it sound as though he was more voyeur than observer and that his stare was like the glare of a lamp. Whatever the identity of the 'well dressed man', it wasn't the Valet either. He sought to blend into the swirl of the crowds rather than stand out from it so conspicuously. The police wasted more time after insisting – despite verbal evidence from the servants, the staff at the Hotel Bristol and the Dowager Duchess – that the jewels might have been left in her suite or with the porter, and not taken to the Gare du Nord at all. A search of the Duchess's rooms and a thorough scan of the offices unsurprisingly produced no fresh information about the whereabouts of the case.

And so the mistakes went on, as if the police were conspiring as allies of the Valet.

Scotland Yard fell into the trap of thinking the Dowager Duchess had been monitored by a gang – 'probably from the time she bought the jewels in the Paris shops or because she was known to carry costly jewellery around with her'. Within days, an unnamed senior officer at the Yard was prophesying: 'If I am right in my conclusion, the jewels are in the possession of the swell gang, who are experts in the matter of value. They will be in no hurry to get rid of them. Buyers in St Petersburg, Antwerp and other cities are always attracted to the French capital.' He added, as if to dismay the Duchess further:

Every day which elapses after an affair of this sort decreases the chance of the recovery. My opinion is that the metal has found its way into the crucible a long time ago, and the diamonds have been cut up and disposed of in various quarters. The chief hope lies in the possibility of the accomplices quarrelling over their booty. They generally do and then the maxim of 'honour amongst thieves' is thrown to the wind. Somebody informs, either in the hope of obtaining reward, or with the object of venting personal malice and then an arrest follows. Curiously enough, we get most of our best information in this way, either from the parties directly implicated or their lady friends – very often the latter.

His parting shot was depressing for the Dowager Duchess: 'It is doubtful that the jewels will be recovered.'

The French police made one raid on what was described as a 'low gambling den' in Paris after being convinced the thieves were hiding in it. They found, as a report put it, that 'the birds had flown'. Similarly lost, and lacking either map or compass to put them on the correct route, Scotland Yard began to speculate that a continental crook, rather than an English thief, was responsible. The following piece of conjecture appeared in several newspapers: 'It is by no means certain that English thieves robbed the Duchess. Though English thieves possess an unenviable reputation on the continent, there are plenty of accomplished foreign thieves on the railways.'

The likely mastermind was believed to be Sam Karmarzyn, an Austrian who had stolen diamond bracelets and necklets from a honeymooning couple in Charlottenburg at the beginning of October. 'Detectives at home and abroad have been closely inquiring into Karmarzyn's movements in the last few months,' said the *Police Gazette* after his arrest in Whitechapel. 'From what they have discovered, they believe he had something to do with the robbery of the Duchess of Sutherland's jewels.' The blameless Karmarzyn was questioned for hours about the theft, which

Scotland Yard became convinced he'd orchestrated well before his imprisonment.

The *Pall Mall Gazette* also scoffed at the French to the extent that it implied the Commissary of Police was guilty of bungling. 'The Paris detectives are rightly adjudged the most perfect of their kind in the old world. They admit their general incompetence and utter inability to deal with the diamond felon . . . They are utterly in the dark . . . and most reticent about the matter . . .'

But the Valet was no ordinary diamond felon. He was the archetypical clever and accomplished thief who appeared in reports which made regular, if fumbling, attempts to analyse the crime. One article was almost tantamant to an identikit portrait of him. It defined the jewel-takers as:

> . . . men of high intelligence with close powers of observation. There are not many of them, but they are, to use a phrase commonly and appropriately applied to the Royal Irish Constabulary, a highly organised body of men. You meet them without knowing them at the fashionable seaside resorts at home and abroad. They put up at the best hotels, where they scan very carefully the visitors and then they know from a catalogue of the 'family jewels' of Europe when a prize is within reach.

A mythology quickly built up around the theft and the perpetrator found the speculation amusing. 'Often, I have chuckled at some of these yarns,' said the Valet. 'Especially at the one where I had a confederate smoking a cigar at the door of the railway carriage, who by accident placed the burning end on the maid's hands, so that she dropped the jewel case, which I quickly replaced with one exactly like it.' The Valet was honoured to find himself anonymously credited with such brio and panache and mistaken for an entire performing troupe of criminals.

But, as far as he was concerned, the Dowager Duchess's jewels represented only half the prize. He needed Maude's love to make it complete.

In late afternoon, the jewels bulging in his pocket, the Valet failed to track Maude down. In the early evening he toured the cafés, and failed again. As darkness fell, he went into every nightspot, such as the Folies-Bergère and the Café des Américains. At last he found her – 'to my great joy,' he said – drinking champagne in the Casino de Paris. Exactly as he'd done in London and Ostend, he approached her directly and unsubtly. 'I asked what she meant by giving me the slip,' he explained. Maude responded with a dismissive, 'Oh, you have found me,' and then began to laugh, swilling another mouthful of champagne. 'Well, what are you going to do about it?' she added. Neither mentioned the note he'd sent her. The Valet took Maude to the Café des Américains. More champagne was ordered. 'Unfortunately,' said the Valet, 'she had been enjoying herself with some friends before I met her, and, the wine mounting to her head, she began to abuse me, and created such a scene that for the first time I began to be afraid, remembering I had the whole of the Sutherland jewels in my pocket.'

The Valet unsuccessfully tried to quieten her. 'She only got worse, and knocked my hat off,' he said. He called the waiter, asking him to summon a cab for them. As he and Maude drove to the Nord Hotel, the Dowager Duchess was leaving the nearby station for the second time that day. 'It was an audacious thing to do, no doubt, but I was always audacious,' said the Valet. After taking Maude to her room, his next move went beyond audacious and belonged in the category of the ridiculously rash.

He began to spill the jewels from his pockets, tipping them on to the bedside table. He was like a conjurer producing an endless rope of coloured handkerchiefs. Out came pearls, a bracelet, some rings and the necklace which had so enthralled him. 'Now, my dear,' he said to Maude, thinking she was going to be 'nice' to him, 'I have always told you that I was a very rich man, and I am going to prove it. I have just got some of my family jewels over from England and I am going to show you a few of them.' As the jewels appeared, the Valet asked her: 'Aren't they pretty, my dear? They have been in our possession for many years.' He saw Maude's 'beautiful eyes sparkle at the sight of the glittering jewels'. She began to gather them up, running each thread of stones through her fingers.

It had never crossed the Valet's mind – he was too swept up by the ecstasy of simply being with Maude again – that she might want to keep the jewels. He'd assumed the sight of them alone would be sufficient to lure back his love. Maude had another idea.

'You must give me this bracelet and this necklet,' she demanded.

Belatedly the Valet understood the awful position he now found himself in. She wanted to *wear* the jewels. 'They would be recognised by any Paris detective who saw them,' he said. The Valet described it as 'sheer madness'.

He tried to stumble out an excuse. 'But, my dear,' he said, 'I can't give them to you. They belong to the family.'

Maude snapped at him. 'You mean you don't want to.'

'No, my dear,' he replied with trepidation. 'I would like to, and you know it, but I simply can't.'

Maude picked up one of the jewels and threw it to the floor. 'I wouldn't have them if you begged me to take them!' she shouted. She began to shriek and then tossed the other jewels at him.

'I stood there too dumbfounded to do anything but watch her,' said the Valet. 'What a scene. I don't think I will ever forget it in my life.'

After pelting the Valet with diamonds and pearls, the unstable Maude then started to plead with him. Could she sleep in some of the jewellery for just one night? She promised to return everything in the morning. As a stalling tactic, he agreed. But with the dawn came an entirely predictable response. When the Valet awoke beside her, and asked for the jewels, Maude at first refused to take them off. She longed for them more than ever now. She pleaded with him again – a prolonged speech in which she claimed to be so attached to *all* the jewels that she could not possibly let them go. Clandestinely, the Valet began to push a stray necklace and a bracelet into his pockets, promising as he did so to provide replacements for her from his fortune. Gradually, and with great persuasion, he reclaimed every piece of jewellery.

The Valet thought it sensible to leave Maude alone, promising on his way through the door to be back within the hour. He left believing he had managed to pacify her. Again, he was wrong. In retrospect, he would say: 'What happened during my absence, I have never been able to understand.'

In truth, it hardly takes much understanding. The newspapers delivered to her room reported the theft and the Dowager Duchess's £4,000 reward. The thought that the jewels were stolen struck Maude in the way that the descending apple had once struck Isaac Newton. She was perfectly placed to receive the Duchess's cheque. When the Valet arrived back at her hotel, he was told by a clerk on the reception desk that 'a gentleman' wished to see him. The gentleman was from the Paris police.

Returning to her room, the Valet found Maude in a rage – pointing and gesticulating at him as the uniformed policeman stood, slightly bewildered, alongside her. She was linking his possession of the jewels to the Duchess of Sutherland. The policeman smiled accommodatingly. He treated her like a child who was indulging in a foot-stomping tantrum which would burn itself out. Maude reached such a decibel level that she had almost nowhere left to go on the vocal register. The policeman, who scarcely spoke English, didn't understand a word said to him. Maude, who scarcely spoke French, didn't appreciate that she wasn't making any sense: she took the policeman's silence and his expression of incomprehension as an example of the smooth, undemonstrative Gallic way of doing things. From her actions and wild behaviour, the policeman assumed he'd been called to defuse a lovers' tiff, rather than to arrest a jewel thief. He did not take her hysterics seriously. She came across as a hectoring battleaxe. The Valet seemed to the policeman to be one of those errant husbands who had come home late without offering a plausible explanation. Maude appeared to be an angry spouse at her wits' end; indeed, she looked as though she were about to spontaneously combust.

The Valet insisted he spoke French with a 'fluency that can always be acquired in the best French prisons'. He persuaded the officer that he would visit the Prefect of Police and sort out the confusion later on.

'You will allow me to change my clothes?' he asked.

'Of course,' came the reply.

The policeman, trapped in the middle of two warring factions, wanted to be rid of both of them. The Valet remembered, as if smiling as the words dropped from his lips, 'He bowed me out with all the Sutherland jewels in my possession, and I simply left the hotel . . . Ah my friends, they are a polite race, the French.'

The Valet threw himself into the first available cab, which took him to the Gare Saint-Lazare. From there he travelled back to London via Newhaven. The Dowager Duchess's jewels remained in his pockets. But Maude Richardson – despite her behaviour and despite her treachery – remained in his heart. The Valet, unable to think coherently, made excuses for her to reassure himself. Once the brooches and bracelets were sold, once he was able to hand her the proceeds of that sale and once the two of them were settled into a stable rhythm in familiar surroundings, he saw them unmistakably as a couple again. He told himself that Maude would be his alone. The profit from the jewels would dispel her doubts about him and put an end to the squabbling over money. The next time he saw Maude, she would greet him with a blizzard of tiny kisses.

He didn't realise that all the component parts of a tragedy were already in place.

Chapter 9

There's no one to love me now

Harry the Valet described his philosophy as the sanguine: 'What will be, will be.' He even went as far as citing it as 'the motto of my life'. And he was about to prove it true in ways which were impetuous, senselessly cavalier and utterly contrary to his natural criminal instincts.

On his return to London the Valet quickly lost his breezy optimism. He felt infinitely alone and lonesome. It seemed to him as though everything had been rendered worthless. If Maude was not with him to share the Dowager Duchess of Sutherland's jewels, what had been the point of taking them? Without her, he no longer cared whether the police handcuffed him for the theft, or whether the courts gave him a long sentence for the crime. As his hurt mind judged it, he was already in solitary confinement anyway. For to exist without the woman he loved was worse than the daily sadness of a small cell. He thought of no one else but Maude, and his imagination constantly wheeled with the images of the two of them together: the low bohemian or high society nightclubs, the dinners at Romano's, the theatrical boxes, the drama of Ostend and the flit to Paris, where the fragile scaffolding of his life collapsed around him. He became restless and depressed, as though mourning a death. The Valet didn't seethe with resentment or swear revenge after Maude's attempt to have him arrested. He pined for her more than before. His very existence seemed to be wholly dependent on hers; she was the fulcrum of everything. As a consequence, there was nothing rational about his actions or his attitude, which alternated between the euphoric – an unshakeable belief that the separation was temporary – and sunken dejection, a feeling that he could never be content again. During the downward mood swings, which induced a maudlin self-pity, the Valet behaved with a recklessness that suggested he wanted to be caught, as if jail alone could put him out of his misery.

In the past, when he sought to deflect suspicion after a major theft, he had always been ultra-cautious. As the Valet worked on his own, he didn't have to worry about the disloyalty of a talkative or inexperienced associate. There was no one to betray him – except himself. But he was steely in his self-discipline. He did nothing to draw attention to himself as a possible culprit. There were no flamboyant, stand-out purchases, which might attract gossip. He didn't indulge in all-night socialising in case it became apparent that he was inexplicably flush with money. He spoke to no one about the crime in case alcohol, or the bait of a high reward, loosened their tongue and incriminated him. He lay low and ticked off the days until he believed the police were resigned to defeat. He frequently moved addresses, switching from hotel to rented house or slipping into a friend's spare room at night, to make certain he wasn't being watched or followed. All this was a necessary ordeal, to ensure his safety and survival. But now – with the police in every European capital and coastal resort searching for the Dowager Duchess's gems – he ignored every one of his previous rules. 'Wealth and the glamour of night life lured me to the brightest spots in the Metropolis,' he said. The Valet strolled casually around London as if he'd joined the peerage and he spent his cash as though he had an inexhaustible supply of it. 'I had received something in the region of £10,000 from different fences,' he added calmly.

Some of the smaller and less distinctive pieces of the Dowager Duchess of Sutherland's jewellery were sold as he passed through France. These funded the Valet's ticket home. The more striking items – such as the dragonfly brooch and the gold bracelet with the name 'Mary' spelt out in diamonds – were immediately broken up to make them difficult to trace. The Valet made a crude job of it. In an effort to justify himself, he explained: 'I knew that Scotland Yard would be watching every receiver in London.' On the way out of Paris, lacking the tools to carefully prise out the stones, he took off his right shoe and spent an hour thumping the heel against the necklets, pendants and bracelets to dislodge the stones from them. He then turned to the reliable Kammy Grizzard, who was unfazed about handling whatever the Valet gave him. Grizzard became the main recipient of the Duchess's trinket box. As ever, he was able to distribute the jewels quickly through the extensive network of contacts that were always available to do his bidding – or face the dire consequences of refusal. The Valet hid or held back a few of the gems, which he considered presenting to Maude after she returned from Paris to either her rented house in Langham Street or to the hotel in Brighton where the two of them had consummated their love six months earlier.

As part of the deal Grizzard arranged temporary accommodation and shelter for the Valet until he located a safe house of his own. In late October, he found such a haven: 5 Cathcart Road in a residential byway in South Kensington. In a smartly respectable three-storey, doubled-fronted property, he took rooms on the first floor. There was a narrow, wrought-iron balcony and a view of a row of trees, which grew directly opposite the high rectangular windows of his bedroom. The wooden front door of the house opened directly on to the pavement. There was a bonus to living in this obscure corner of London. Her name was Edith Elman –

the Valet's attractive and widowed 30-year-old landlady. Instead of calling himself Harry Williams – or Henry Thomas – he politely introduced himself to her as William Johnson. Apart from changing his name, he made only one other concession to disguise himself: he shaved off his moustache before growing it back almost instantly. Elman immediately weighed up her newest resident and described him as a 'very wealthy gentleman of a sporting turn of mind'. Elman remembered him at his best as being 'so awfully jolly and so extremely liberal with his money'. Within a few minutes of meeting her, she added, the Valet had 'showed me a pile of money and a pile of handsome earrings, which he offered me'. She accepted a diamond half-hoop ring, valued at £150.

Accompanying the Valet was a 25-year-old called Moss Lipman. He was gangly and loping, almost 6 feet tall and with a dark complexion, which suggested he'd been born overseas. The Valet reassured Elman that Lipman, an apprentice tailor, was actually from the East End of London.

Already the Valet was flinging notes around in a parade of excess. He brought an expensive wardrobe of clothes with him to Cathcart Road. There were Savile Row suits – informal lighter shades of cloth replacing the darker ones – and silk shirts, a short top hat, a pair of lavender evening gloves, a pair of white spats, a satin-lined opera cloak and a silver-mounted malacca cane. It was hardly the outfit of a man who wanted to remain inconspicuous. He appeared on the streets like a London dandy. He flounced into clubs, dragging waiters to his table and ordering the most expensive drinks and food and buying a glass or three for whoever asked for it. Wherever he went, the Valet became the central figure around which any party turned. He was constantly toasted for his generosity, which made his face an easy one to remember.

The Valet's peculiarly eccentric antics, which in his situation bordered on the insane, attracted puzzling looks and comment.

At any moment he could easily have been apprehended. As some of the Dowager Duchess's jewels were hidden in a locked box on top of his wardrobe, the evidence against him was overwhelming and conclusive. He seemed not to care and confessed: 'I went around the West End with money to burn, advertising the fact that I was the man who had stolen the Duchess of Sutherland's jewels.' It is debatable whether he enjoyed himself – or looked back on his spree with much pleasure – after the glow of the moment was over. Drink, gambling, theatregoing and general entertaining were his displacement activities as he vainly hoped to forget Maude. However hard he tried, and however much champagne or malt whisky he consumed to anaesthetise the pain, it never worked. Or at least not for long.

The Valet slept during the morning and afternoon, and came alive in the evening. He would drink himself into a morose stupor until the early hours, take a cab back to Cathcart Road and drink some more with Elman. It was as if he was afraid of night terrors or the worst insomnia. He lived constantly on the edge.

The petite, dark-haired Elman became a token substitute for Maude and she and the Valet became lovers for no other reason than each was weak, needy and grateful to be able to depend on someone else. It was no foundation for anything but the most transitory affair; sex filled a void for both of them. Elman said he escorted her 'almost every night' to the theatre. He paid for a private box at the Shaftesbury to watch *The Belle of New York*, the plot of which was redolent of the Valet's own life – a virtuous girl strives to reform the spendthrift ways of a playboy called Harry only to discover he remains dizzily in love with an actress.

One incident especially underscored his lack of concern for his own future. He took Elman to a play called *The Great Ruby* at Drury Lane. As if wearing a sandwich board proclaiming himself a thief, he fastened what Elman described as a 'magnificent ruby' on to the lapel of his jacket. She was constantly astonished by his array of jewellery. He always produced something from his pockets that she had never seen before and asked her to wear it for him. 'I like to take you out, you know,' the Valet told Elman, 'because you look so nice decked out in diamonds.' She said the Valet 'inevitably wore lots of diamonds' himself. 'His entrance to the theatre glistening with gems always caused quite an attraction.'

In Oxford Street's Palm Club, his extravagance was more obvious than ever. 'He spent money almost as quickly as he could throw it away there,' said Elman. 'He thought nothing of spending £300 to £500 a night on champagne alone. Between 50 and 60 girls got around him and he would treat them all to two or three bottles of champagne each. Before he left the club he would order a dozen or two dozen bottles of wine for the musicians in the band and they would drink to his health.' Elman thought herself at the epicentre of a surreal event. 'He was always asking me to cash £100 notes for him,' she added. The more he spent, the more jewels he gradually offloaded. He used a variety of fences in case any one of them – including Grizzard – gave him away. Some of the Dowager Duchess's jewels were sold by one of the Valet's unwitting associates at a Sunday market in Houndsditch after a jeweller had re-set the stones. Others were traded for cash at the Brown Bear pub in Worship Street.

The ever-curious Elman knew nothing of his background. Apart from Lipman, he received no visitors and the postman never called with mail for him. Where had he come from? How had he made so much money? And why, Elman finally asked, did he spend it so freely and lead what she regarded as such a 'fast life', as though he was afraid to stand still. The answer she received revealed the level of the Valet's heartbreak over Maude. He told her the truth. 'He said he had loved and been jilted by a Gaiety Girl,' recalled Elman. 'He said he was very fond of the girl and would do anything for her.' Whenever Elman probed him about his unrequited love, she watched the Valet's expression become so sorrowful that he repeatedly broke 'into tears'. He was inconsolable. She said: 'He would often say 'there is no one in the world to love me now' . . . All his woes seemed to centre on the fact he had been rejected by this Gaiety Girl.'

Sometimes drink soured the Valet, and drew an aggressive response from him. He explained the circumstances to Elman, sketching out the way in which Maude had left London without telling him and how he'd dashed to Belgium before finding her arm-in-arm with a rival suitor in Ostend. 'Whenever I catch them together, I'll shoot them both,' he spat, omitting to add that he'd already tried and failed to do so. Through these conversations Elman came to understand the Valet's feelings for Maude. She saw him trying to erase, if only for a drunken hour or two, the memory of her.

He continued to make a spectacle of himself. It was as though he wanted to buy the love and affection he'd lost so abruptly. By his own admission, he walked into hotels with 'seven or eight hundred pounds in gold' in his pockets before pulling out 'a handful of sovereigns' and calling for 'drinks on the house'. As the Valet conceded, he was 'practically asking to be arrested'. The tittle-tattle about him intensified. 'All round the West End my conduct became the topic of the moment,' he said. ' "Have you heard about Harry the Valet?" people would whisper. "He's brought off another big coup. It must have been the Sutherland jewel affair" '. It was the obvious conclusion to reach. Scotland Yard alone seemed unable to make the critical connection.

As October 1898 was about to turn into cold November, the newspapers reported no progress in the search for the thief and the Dowager Duchess of Sutherland's gems. The original flurry of stories about the crime began to dry up. News of it came out – if at all – in a slow, depressing drip. The police, still naively unaware that the Valet was responsible, insisted that investigations were continuing: an orthodox but flaccid gesture which persuaded no one – least of all the ill-tempered Dowager Duchess or Sir Albert Rollit – that the jewels would ever be found. The police were dilatory and dawdling, and unable to make sense of the theft. Expecting never to see her jewels again, the Dowager Duchess pressed on with an insurance claim.

In charge of the case was Walter Dinnie. He called in Frank Froest and Walter Dew to assist him. The officers weren't even convinced that the jewels had been taken by a London-based thief. 'It did not follow from the mere fact that the person robbed was an Englishwoman, that the robbery had been the work of an English crook, or that we should find any link to it in London,' insisted Dew, offering a mediocre explanation as to why it took so long to pin the blame on the Valet. 'We concentrated on inter-national crooks and others who, from their records, might have pulled off such a coup,' added Dew. 'Our object was to find out if any such criminal had been out of the country at the time when the robbery took place.' He said Scotland Yard officers visited 'all the known haunts of such men – clubs, dives and dens of both east and west'.

The scenario which Dew carefully laid out – thinking, as ever, of burnishing his own image and ego in the process – suggested that the Valet was quickly established as a candidate for the crime. But almost a fortnight after the theft, the Yard were no nearer to identifying him – despite his high living and despite the tongue-wagging throughout the underworld about his free spending. Dew, only recently promoted to inspector, was typically anxious to push his contribution to the operation. He insisted: 'I played such a big part in it personally.' He wasn't as keen to spell out Scotland Yard's inability first to point the finger and then to apprehend someone who was already familiar to them. Dinnie, Froest and Dew lacked the guile to swiftly collar a thief who was making himself the easiest prey. While Scotland Yard's 'crack team' flicked through evidence files containing almost no clues, the Valet was taking long, springy steps in a social whirl around London.

As well as the nightly round of clubs and theatres, he also satisfied his sporting tastes. He went to Newmarket races – even travelling in the same carriage as a group of Scotland Yard detectives – and put what he said was 'a cool £250' on the Prince of Wales' horse Nunsuch. The jockey was the American Tod Sloan, inventor of the monkey crouch style of riding – leaning forward in the stirrups – and whose talent for winning races comfortably ahead of the field led to the cockney rhyming slang expression, being 'on your Tod' (all alone). With a combination of Nunsuch and Sloan, the Valet expected a bumper pay day. Nunsuch, however, started appallingly and was left at the post, according to the Valet. But he claimed not to have 'flickered an eyelid' when he saw his handsome bet go directly to the bookmakers. The Valet didn't leave Newmarket poorer. With the rest of his stake money he was able to win £2,000 on other horses. He also saw the Newcastle-born lightweight boxer Dick Burge flatten an opponent at the South London Palace in an exhibition bout. In the audience were more policemen he recognised – but who did not recognise him. 'My detective friends were in the house,' he said, before adding, 'but human nature is human nature and who could keep their eyes away from the ring to look for a needle in a haystack when Burge was about to knock out his man?'

The police were so inefficient that the Valet could probably have set up a jewellery stall outside Scotland Yard without being caught. Dew would claim, eventually, that 'we unearthed a piece of information which gave us something to go upon'. The word 'unearthed' suggests that the snippet came as a result of tireless digging. Given the audible chatter about his exploits around London, as well as his habit of constantly being seen in its best places, it is woeful in the extreme that Dinnie, Dew and Froest were among the last to learn about the Valet's carousing. Like

Nunsuch, the police were left at the post until the stories about the Valet's activities, offering anecdotal evidence of his involvement, were impossible to ignore. As Dew explained, as if expecting a round of applause for triumphantly finding a straight-edged piece of a jigsaw: 'His sudden excess of wealth seemed to coincide with the Paris robbery.'

The ponderous Scotland Yard detectives were still unable to bring him in for questioning. Although the geography of the Valet's jaunting was narrow – the Strand, Regent Street, Oxford Street, the hotels of Northumberland Avenue – the officers of the law could not locate him. 'He had vanished as completely as the jewels,' said Dew. 'It looked to us as though he had got wind of the fact that we were on his tail and had made a bolt.' It wasn't true. The police just kept turning up in all the wrong places – or

Walter Dew, who saw himself as Sherlock Holmes, but lacked the stained-glass mind of the fictional detective.

in the right places, but at the wrong times. Had he decided to be sensible, the Valet could have spirited himself away and hidden in the countryside or on the coast without ever being found. But the fortuitous break for Dinnie, Dew and Froest – a one-in-a-million stroke of luck which their pathetic groping scarcely deserved – was to have a star witness turn up on their doorstep. Dew called it 'a development of a nature quite unexpected' and added: 'We had a visitor at Scotland Yard. This was an actress.'

Returning from Paris towards the end of October, Maude had been debating ever since whether to tell the police the full story about the Dowager Duchess's jewels. Her motives were spiked by fear rather than inspired by altruism or a sense of public duty. She didn't want to find herself thrust into the dock as an accessory, forced to take prosecuting counsel through a humiliating step-by-step account of the carnality between her and her former lover. She saw the danger of being portrayed as aiding and abetting and willingly acquiescent to her boyfriend's compulsion to steal. If the French officer, who had politely dismissed her accusations against the Valet in Paris, realised his error and rechecked the records, Maude would find herself in the thick of the case. Scotland Yard would suppose that she'd been part of the heist from the beginning. How could she protest her innocence and extricate herself from accusations of complicity? If she was blameless, why hadn't she gone back to the French police and put her case more strenuously? And would Scotland Yard reach the conclusion that her original, panicky approach to the French force was the direct consequence of a squabble over the division of the jewels? Whichever way Maude imagined it, she saw nothing but trouble ahead – unless her version of events was believed from the beginning. To give it credence, she would have to offer it openly and voluntarily and leave nothing out. To do it, she needed the fuel of what Dew would describe as 'Dutch courage' – and so she reached for the bottle.

Perfectly attired but not demure in demeanour, Maude went to Scotland Yard and asked to speak to whoever was in charge of the Dowager Duchess of Sutherland's jewel mystery. 'I have some information for him,' she explained. Ushered into Dinnie's office, she told her story. Dew called the snap and sizzle of it 'amazing'. The facts of each adventure with the Valet – who, she said, called himself Harry Williams – tumbled slowly out of Maude, as though each sentence was forced. It culminated in the Valet's arrival at her hotel with the jewels, which she said were the 'most marvellous I had ever seen'. She added: 'I didn't know where he got them . . . but I suspected they had been stolen.' Maude went on to concede: 'I was so fascinated by them that I pleaded with him to be allowed to keep them just for that night. I had fully intended to give the jewels back the following morning. But, when the time came, I felt I could not part with them, and begged to be allowed to keep them a little longer. At this he became angry. There was a terrible scene, which ended with him taking the jewels from me by force . . . I was angry too – so angry that I went straight out and told the Paris police.' Maude's primary aim was completed before she finished speaking: she convinced Dinnie and Dew that she was guilty of nothing more than vanity. A knave rather than a villain, she'd been temporarily blinded by the beauty of the jewels. As Dinnie made clear in his report, Maude was in a 'somewhat intoxicated condition' and made a 'rambling statement'. Rambling or not, it was sufficiently coherent in minuscule detail – dates, times, recall of the appearance of the jewels – to convict the Valet.

Still in love, and still empty without her, the Valet set off in expeditionary spirit a day or so later to Maude's Langham Street home. He had no idea whether she was back from Paris; and certainly had no inkling about her meeting with Dinnie and Dew. On discovering she'd gone to Brighton, he took the train there and found her once more in the Cyprus Hotel. The meeting was awkward and tense and the conversation studded with hesitations. This brief, uncomfortable reunion essentially ended after Maude refused £40 from the Valet, who was trying to repay a fraction of his earlier financial debt to her as a sign of goodwill. There was nonetheless one thing he had to discover before leaving. He'd forgiven her for summoning the gendarme in Paris. But he had to know if she'd told Scotland Yard the same story about the theft. She proved that the cruellest lies are told in silence.

Maude regretted her betrayal of the Valet to Dinnie and Dew as soon as the words left her lips. Now guilty about it too, she spun him a highly implausible tale. Protecting herself against the possibility that she'd been seen in or around Scotland Yard, Maude reluctantly said she'd been inside the building without elaborating on who she'd seen there. A man called 'Halliday' had been bothering her, she explained weakly. She'd asked for police help in dissuading him from making further advances. The Valet was walking out of the door when Maude's maid Georgiana – who treated him with kindness and affection – whispered the truth in his ear. The news came like a knife to the stomach. The devastated Valet fled from Brighton on the early evening train.

Dinnie and Dew were still concerned that Maude's original account of what happened after the theft lacked a linear narrative. Scotland Yard had to make absolutely sure that she hadn't mistaken the Valet for someone else. With Dinnie clutching a buff-coloured folder – a list of the Valet's wrongdoings in file AG0909 – the two policemen visited Maude in Brighton almost a week after interviewing her in London. She immediately told them about the arrival and departure of her surprise caller. Dinnie listened and then handed her a series of different photographs. Did she recognise anyone? Were Harry Williams, Thomas Johnson, William Wilson and William Johnson the same man? he asked. She studied each face and features and nodded her head, aware now of the Valet's long chain of thefts well before she met him.

'The hunt for Harry,' said Dew, 'now started in earnest.'

In their conceit, the police assumed that capturing the Valet was a foregone conclusion. Patience, manpower and the constant staking out of places where he'd recently been seen were all that was necessary to haul him in front of a judge and make Dinnie, Froest and Dew headline heroes; perhaps the Dowager Duchess would show her gratitude by handing them the reward, too. After all, she would never countenance signing the cheque to Maude, who had spent a sleepless night both entangled with the thief and resplendent in her stolen jewels, like a nineteenth-century Queen of Sheba. But not for the first time – for it was a lesson difficult for them to absorb – did the police grossly overestimate their own skill and underestimate the Valet's. The combination caused further anguish for Dinnie, who had to try to explain to his superiors why the Valet perpetually outwitted his team when he was supposedly so close to capture. Dinnie was emerging as a Tantalus-like figure – for what was within his grasp moved away from him at the very moment he reached out for it. The Dowager Duchess and Sir Albert Rollit were unimpressed. With friends in high places, who took their power and influence for granted and who weren't used to being kept waiting, the length of Scotland Yard's inquiry was already unacceptable to them. More pressure was heaped on Dinnie because more strain was applied to those above him.

The Valet always knew things might ultimately fail to turn out in his favour. But, whatever the daunting odds against him, his mind was fixed on going down in a thundering fight. The last drop in the last bottle of champagne would be drunk before he'd give in supinely to Scotland Yard, even though 'all the biggest 'tecs in London . . . were on my track'. As if thumbing his nose at the police, he refused to alter or modify his routine. The allure of a good time far outweighed the consequences of capture. He still dashed around London's clubs, as if he was a respectable and affluent wheeler-dealer who had nothing to worry him except the next lucrative deal. He still took his attractive landlady to the theatre, as though courting her for marriage. And he still bought drinks for the house, enthusiastically waving a wad of notes in front of the barman to demonstrate that he could pay for them. Only one thing changed. In a further insult to – and as a further act of defiance against – the police, he now readily admitted to taking the Dowager Duchess's jewels. There was no longer any reason for him to hide the fact. 'By this time,' he said, 'everyone knew my secret and crowded around to drink my wine and tell me what a fine fellow I was.'

For Scotland Yard, getting hold of the Valet was like trying to catch a moth in a jar. As soon as the police approached, the Valet flew off and settled somewhere else. In the Palm Club, he was 'calling for magnums of champagne for my admirers' as further down the street the police were raiding a different establishment in the expectation of finding him at one of its tables. 'How I chuckled when I heard about that raid the following day,' he said. The drama was by no means an isolated incident. 'It was the same night after night,' said the Valet. The police raided a Piccadilly supper club, which the Valet had only just left. 'They got a £25 note which I had changed and, tracing it to me, they kept on raiding the clubs and narrowing down the chase.'

The following evening the Valet was in a cab headed for Rathbone Street. On the opposite pavement, he saw two police-men; one of them was Edward Gough. The Valet, knowing 'the friends I was going to meet had given me away', switched tack. 'My alert mind stood me in good stead, and pushing up the top-light with my cane, I told the jarvey to drive on up Regent Street, and await further orders,' he said. The detectives were equally quick-witted. Picking out the Valet through the carriage window, they hailed another cab and ordered the driver to follow it at a gallop. The wheels of the two cabs spun and rattled at speed, with the occupants tossed about inside like travellers over stormy seas rather than cobbled London streets. Aware that the police were seconds away from catching him, the Valet began to think of an alternative getaway. He could wait until his own carriage was obstructed by a pedestrian, or came to a halt in a dead end or because of a bad turning, and then try to make a run for it. Or he could swing open the door and leap into the chilly night like a cat burglar diving off a roof. As buildings and passageways rushed by, the Valet pulled himself up to the window and glanced all around him. 'I looked around for a way of escape,' he said. In the end there was no choice. He had to jump. It was an impossibly risky act. If he slipped on landing, he could break a leg or shatter an ankle. Worse, he could be trampled and crushed beneath the wheels of the policemen's cab, which was gaining on him. He ignored the danger of injury or death. 'Just as we were passing Conduit Street, I jumped from the moving vehicle,' he said.

In his short top hat and white spats, his cape afloat behind him like the black, flapping wings of a giant bird, he used his knowledge of London to dart in and out of its streets. 'I sped through the passage on the left, doubled back into Regent Street, and took another hansom to a club,' he said. The police gave chase, but, the Valet said, he 'was soon lost in the darkness'. At the end of the chase, he dusted himself off, walked nonchalantly into the bar and called for a magnum in celebration. 'The old fox had gone to ground,' he said, summing up the experience as 'grand fun'.

Only decades later did he regret his lack of intelligence and cunning. 'Looking back on these days and nights, I can only regard myself as a fool,' he said. 'But the utter recklessness of my nature, which enabled me to pull off jobs that would have frightened many another man, kept me from lying low like a wise fellow. The strange thing was that luck was with me and I had a grand run for my money.' The attention he received in the clubs puffed up the Valet's self-esteem. But, as he also accepted afterwards, it 'increased my confidence and led to my undoing'.

That 'undoing' arrived just 24 hours after the cab chase and his wonderful acrobatics. He never complained about it. He said instead: 'In the parlance of my profession it was a clean cop – clean, if you eliminate the element of treachery, which led some of my friends to tell the detectives about the house in which I was living quietly.' The Valet never found out whether Scotland Yard discovered him because of a stray, careless word overheard, through a promise broken or a confession teased, frightened or enticed out of someone he regarded as reliably safe. Dew offered no clues either. He would only ever deal in generalities, as if reading out a police statement. 'Information was brought to us that a man answering the suspect's description was living in an apartment house in Cathcart Road,' he said.

The Valet would never forget his final day and night of freedom or the way in which he was trapped.

He had taken Elman for a champagne lunch, telling her he would be collecting a further £4,000 in the afternoon. In the evening he went out for what he called a 'merry time with some of the boys'. By then the police were aware of his address and already planning to arrest him. The geography of his location favoured them. The house was at the bottom of Cathcart Road, which bent away to the right. The Valet was too far from the main thoroughfare to reach it by foot. He was too close to the bend to be able to dodge through any cordon that was properly organised. And the back of the house was blocked off by other properties. The police were confident that the Valet could only escape if he tunnelled out of the house.

The raid was timed for 8 a.m. At such an early hour, Dinnie rightly figured that the Valet would be at his most vulnerable. A good deal of alcohol would still be sloshing around his system, slowing his reactions. He would be tired and bleary-eyed too, less able to see them clearly let alone respond to the threat. The police feared the Valet might have a gun and be willing to use it. Froest, who liked firearms, was told to take along a weapon for protection.

The Valet was trailed to a nightclub and then trailed back home again. Once he went inside the house, Dinnie spread plain-clothes officers and a number of uniformed men in front of it to guard the exits. 'We were determined to make no mistake,' said Dew, who brought a selection of skeleton keys with him. 'We fully expected the door to be locked,' he added. What Dew found was the Valet's own key, which he had carelessly left poking out of the lock – a result of drinking too much wine. The door, however, was on its slim chain. That chain was never going to resist the heaving, burly bodies of two policemen, whose weight tore it off the frame of the door. The hush of daybreak was violently interrupted by the splintering of wood and the thump of boots on boards.

Elman and the Valet were in his room. Elman, 'startled by the sound of the tramping of feet', went to the door and found 'nine detectives, all carrying truncheons, rushing on to the landing'. Beside his bed, just as he began to undo his collar and tie, the Valet heard 'such a deafening row on the stairs that I knew it could only mean one thing – the police'. At the head of them were Dinnie, Dew and Froest.

Dew claimed to have reached the door first and 'gently' turned the handle, finding it neither locked nor bolted. 'We flashed our lanterns on the bed, expecting to see a surprised man lying there,' he said. 'The bed was empty.'

The Valet was standing halfway between the window and the iron fireplace. For a moment or two he contemplated jumping from the window as he'd jumped from the speeding cab the night before. But, staring out of it, he realised there was no point. He saw the policemen on the pavement in an orderly ring, like a noose. To leap in front of them would be as foolhardy as diving head-first into an empty swimming pool. The 15-foot drop could only cause him harm. If, by some miracle it didn't, there were enough officers to overpower him anyway. 'The house was surrounded,' said the Valet. 'Not a single avenue of escape. Not a million to one chance.' He resigned himself to the inevitable. Everything happened at speed. Dinnie, Dew and Froest were beside him. The handcuffs were slipped on his wrists before he could offer the least resistance. 'They never gave me an inch of room to turn in my chamber,' he said.

In retrospect the Valet recalled it vividly. He said the police 'rushed upstairs like a crowd of hurdlers at Lingfield making for the first fence' and that Froest – not Dew – slammed the door open just before he made a vain effort to lock it after hiding a ring, some loose stones and trinkets belonging to the Dowager Duchess. Dew remembered it vividly too: 'the sardonic smile on the Valet's lips'; the fact that he 'did not move as we seized him'; and a remark he made to Dinnie – 'It's all right inspector, I shall give no trouble.'

The distinguishing mark of the raid was the Valet's laid-back approach to it, as though it was his birthday and the police had arrived to take him to a surprise party. The Valet didn't shout or yell, kick or lash out, crouch in apprehension or even take a step back. He simply stood, hands by his sides, and looked the policemen directly in the eye – a symbol of pacification. There was no sign of strain or agitation in him. The Valet was almost tranquil. Such composure suggested that ice water, rather than blood, ran through his veins. But it suggested another quality too – the unflappability which enabled him to steal the Dowager Duchess's jewels in the first place. To Dew, the Valet's calmness was 'amazing'. He added: 'He must have known that if we succeeded in pinning the Paris robbery on him he would get a long stretch at either Dartmoor or Parkhurst, yet he didn't turn a hair.

I admired his bearing as, years later, I did that of Crippen when I arrested him on the charge of murdering his wife.'

The police hunted for the evidence of his guilt. Dew turned on the gas lamp, which threw tallow light around the room. In the pockets of the Valet's waistcoat, he found three diamonds. Further searching produced a leather purse containing four stones worth £1,500 and eight pearls valued at £2,000. Elman's jewel case – the battered tin box – was still on top of the wardrobe. The key was discovered hidden among the bedclothes. The box contained more of the Duchess's property, including an enamelled ring worth £300.

Amid the confusion and bustle, the Valet heard someone say: 'You have given us a run, Harry, and we are going to see you don't get away this time.' And he listened as Dinnie trotted through the necessary procedures before uttering the words he'd waited more than six weeks to speak: 'We are going to arrest *you* for stealing and receiving the Dowager Duchess's jewels.'

Dinnie took the Valet by the arm and led him downstairs and into the waiting Black Maria. He was taken to King's Road police station. 'Our march there was like a pageant,' said the Valet. Reaching for the perfect comparison, he added: 'They surrounded me the way they used to surround King Edward at the Derby when he led in a winner.' On arrival, he said there was already a crowd to see him because the news was 'all over town' and also because 'Scotland Yard had won, as it always will'. Early reports falsely said that Froest had been floored in a violent struggle while handcuffing him.

The Valet retained the stiffest of upper lips. He was undemonstrative about his plight, as though detached from the scene around him. He glanced from Dinnie to Dew and from Froest to the other policemen who milled around and gawped at him. 'You never saw a prouder lot of men in your life,' he said, recalling the self-satisfied smiles on their faces and the relief of the principal officers, who could now report the good tidings to the Dowager Duchess and to the newspapers. Providing the perfect punchline, the Valet summed up what his apprehension meant to Scotland Yard.

'I was the catch of the season,' he said.

Chapter 10

If I could have just one more kiss

Walter Dew would always remember a peculiarity about the arrest and jailing of Harry the Valet. It was the conspicuous lack of thought the jewel thief displayed for his own future and his total preoccupation with someone else's.

Dew came to understand the powerful attraction Maude Richardson held for the Valet. He recorded it as though not able to believe what he was witnessing. The handcuffed man in front of Dew and Walter Dinnie ought to have shown the normal, anguished reactions of the arrested criminal – a sweating fear for himself, the heart-racing, nervy apprehension about what would happen when his case came to court, a boiling resentment against Scotland Yard and, most obviously of all, spitting outrage and contempt for the informants who had led the police to his hideaway. In the circumstances, he should have been pouring vitriol over Maude – cursing her mendacity, promising to get even with her and then providing a convincing but contrary account of the theft, which implicated her sufficiently for the police to begin to doubt her version of events and question her innocence. The Valet had none of those reactions. He was not vociferously bellicose, and there was no sewage spill of hate. Dinnie and Dew waited for an outburst of counter-accusations against Maude. It never came. As Dew explained it: 'Even the production of the stones left our prisoner unconcerned – at least about himself.'

Dew said that the Valet's 'only thought' was of Maude. He asked about no one except her. Dew added: 'He began to ply us with questions. Had we seen her recently? Was she all right?' The Valet begged for any information the two policemen could provide for him – however scrappy or inconsequential. He was obsessed with Maude, and indifferent to what faced him now. Indeed, he seemed to take extreme comfort from the knowledge that she would be called to give evidence in court, which would enable him to be close to her again. 'I can't make out why she has given me away,' he said, constantly repeating the line, 'I love her still – in spite of what she has done to me.' He sent a message to her via Dew: 'Tell Maudie I want to see her. She must come to me. I do not care if I do five or seven years for this job. I will come to see her the moment I get out, and I will divide my last penny with her.' Dinnie and Dew were surprised by something else too. The Valet was already running up the white flag of surrender. He made it clear that he would 'take what is coming to me' with neither complaint nor resistance. 'What do you suppose I'll get for this?' he asked them. He answered his own question before either policeman could offer a response – and without bleating about it. 'I suppose it will mean a "fiver",' he added, as though the length of the stretch was immaterial to him.

Dinnie and Dew's first task was to try to wheedle the whereabouts of the rest of the jewels out of the Valet and to discover which fences had handled and disposed of them on his behalf. So few of the Dowager Duchess of Sutherland's jewels had been found that it was assumed the Valet must have hidden the rest or passed them to an associate for safe keeping in case of his detection. He had so little cash on him – one note of £200, another for £100 and two for £10 each – that Scotland Yard figured the jewels must have been stored secretly. Dinnie and Dew probed away in the belief that the Valet – in return for the clemency of a lighter sentence – would point them in the direction of this buried treasure, as if marking a map with the letter X. But from the start the Valet laid down his own ground rules for interrogation; and there would be no negotiation. He would not blab or squeal to the police. He refused to draw anyone else into the crime. There was a code among thieves, and he would not break it. Had he done so – naming Kammy Grizzard, for instance – then the Valet would have put himself in danger. If he even whispered Grizzard's name he might not have got out of prison alive. So he told Dinnie and Dew instead: 'You won't get a word out of me. I don't care if I get a lifer for it – I'm not going to split.' When Dinnie asked him, 'How did you get the jewels?' The Valet replied, 'some of them I bought' – an excuse no one was ever going to believe.

The inconclusive sparring went on. Dinnie and Dew put each predictable question to the Valet, who was stubbornly resolute. He responded with silence, lies or incomplete replies. The police, who had taken so long to find and arrest him, now couldn't persuade him to speak to them.

The Valet was charged with the theft of £25,000 to £30,000 worth of jewels from the Dowager Duchess, of which just a tiny fraction – £5,000 – had been recovered.

For the newspapers, the story had everything which guaranteed that the reading public would be ravenous for it: a rich dowager duchess protecting her dark past, the array of jewellery she'd lost and the frantic manhunt across London to reclaim it, which had dominated Scotland Yard's operations day and night for more than a month and a half. No truer conclusion was ever reached than the opening sentence of the *Daily Telegraph*'s coverage of the Valet's trial: 'Romance to a greater or lesser extent is invariably associated with jewel robberies.' A further godsend for editors was that the perpetrator had a catchy sobriquet. It was gleefully reported in the

The court artist does his work. Harry the Valet is impassive as the Duchess of Sutherland condemns him from the witness box.

Daily Mail that Harry the Valet was more than a run-of-the-mill opportunist chancer who had suddenly got lucky. The newspaper called him 'one of the cleverest jewel thieves in Europe'. He was both prolific and proficient and his firecracker personality jumped off the page. He was – as Anthony L. Ellis later documented in his book, *Prisoner at the Bar* – the type of thief regarded as: 'Incautious, open-handed, careless of money, a free-liver and too fond of wine and women'. In short, he was the sort of criminal about whom the ordinary reader wanted to know more. The man already known to the police now became known to the public too. He was half venerated as a criminal star, a cult anti-hero. A three-deck headline in the *Mail* was proof of the endless fascination and grudging respect he aroused.

AMAZING CAREER
HARRY THE VALET'S MANY GREAT COUPS
DUCHESSES I HAVE ROBBED

The accompanying report did more than verge on the worshipful. It read like a love letter. He was called 'one of the most notorious criminals of his generation', as though the newspaper deplored the principle of it but applauded the skill involved in making him so. The *Mail* added: 'His capture is one of the most important the police have made for years.' The bold statement was qualified in several ways. The paper said the Valet was already established as a 'genius' and 'quite a master in his profession', the sort of 'skilled thief who would not waste his time on small game'. These were the days before photographs were regularly published, so the *Mail* broadly sketched out his appearance as well as his character, establishing him in the imagination as 'a genteel thief' with a 'grand air about him'. He was an 'assured' and 'substantial' figure, 'like a man in a good way of business'. It didn't stop there. 'He has a frank, engaging look. He dresses neatly and without flash. And there is shrewdness in his smile which suggests a man with a good story or two up his sleeve,' it concluded.

Joyfully the *Mail* unrolled his life as a criminal, as if chronicling the career of a highly decorated soldier – a brave champion of the guard, too. 'This man has been concerned with a vast number of jewel robberies,' it said, and had 'reduced the profession to a science'. The article unveiled facts that had previously been available only to the police and to the Valet's victims: the contacts book he kept of the aristocracy's wealth and movements; his specialisation in London's railway stations; the one-man raids he carried out on the Northumberland Avenue hotels; his mistake over the Duchess of Devonshire's jewels; the long list of successes which made him a fortune; the source of his nickname ('the pupil outstripped the master,' it said admiringly); and the way in which Scotland Yard had strived to hold him in check throughout most of the 1890s 'without catching him in anything but his smaller coups'. The Valet could not have hoped for a better press. He was hoisted on to a plinth.

Far from being cast as a crook, he was painted as both number one on Scotland's Yard's list of the most wanted jewel thieves and as the feisty underdog who had bravely pitted his brain and two hands against the organised might of the police machine. Incredible though it may seem, the Valet even aroused sympathy – not that he wanted any – for the way he'd been brought down, as though Dinnie and Dew had contravened the rules of engagement by acting on the information given to them by his former lover. The Valet further endeared himself to newspapers such as the *Mail* by coming across as engaging and interesting – a gentleman scamp rather than a gutter scoundrel, a Jack-the-lad with a sly wink rather than a beastly or deviously cruel figure with a malicious streak. The Valet's own counsel, Gerald Geoghegan, confessed that his client had 'never done an honest day's work in his life' and specialised in 'the lifting up of unconsidered trifles at railway termini'. This frankness won the Valet esteem rather than condemnation. It proved again that the average man and woman viewed jewel-taking from the mega-rich as a victimless crime.

According to the adulatory *Mail*, the Valet made 'a good deal of money', which he instantly spent. 'He lost several thousand at a gambling club in Oxford Street,' it went on. 'His tastes were lordly. He was satisfied with nothing short of the best dishes and the choicest wines and at a West End hotel his bills were frequently £50 a week.' The average yearly income for artisans was £150 to £300.

It was immaterial to the *Mail* that he took highbrow satisfaction from his crimes and enjoyed life's low pleasures from its profits. The fact that he was colossally vain, liked to dress well and frequented London's night spots meant he cut a glamorous, dashing figure. The point was sharpened when it became known that he was even paying – obviously with money raised from the sale of the pilfered Dowager Duchess's jewels – for a special cell in Holloway as he awaited trial. For six shillings a week, he was moved into a superior class of cell, which gave him more room in which to wander, a comfortable bed and chair, a desk and a side table and lamp. He also paid to have his food sent in rather than eat whatever mush the jail's cook concocted and then served on battered tin plates. It was all very cosy, and so very reminiscent of the Duchess's own stay in Holloway, another titbit in what was hailed by the *Mail* as a 'smashing story'. As the *Mail* stressed, the Valet came to dominate the trial as though he was a celebrity topping the bill in his own show: 'The prisoner looked so important a person that there was nobody to be pitied unless it was the Duchess for the loss of her jewels,' it said. It continued: 'He showed a beaming pride as his achievements in larceny were related. He smiled with an air of conscious skill when counsel said he had beaten the police. He smiled again when . . . [it was] hinted that he was no novice in crime. And he smiled more pleasantly when the rival barristers offered their own accounts of the crime, each as the only true and authoritative version. But he was content to have it understood that he knew better than either, and he offered no correction'. It was as if the Valet had become 'the sole arbiter of the proceedings', added the *Mail*.

The case of the Valet and the Dowager Duchess of Sutherland could so easily have been set to music by George Edwardes and performed at his Gaiety Theatre. It would have been a more appropriate backdrop for this freakish production than Bow Street – a spacious but dull, oak-panelled room – or Clerkenwell Sessions, much grander with its multi-tiered seating and high, moulded ceiling and the brightly coloured coat of arms fixed to the wall. The Valet's trial deserved to be framed by ornate gold plasterwork and heavy curtains, lit from every angle and with a full orchestra to play the cast in and out of the witness box. Again, the headlines endorsed that fact, wringing every drop of melodrama out of it, as though it really was starting a long run on the Strand:

SENSATIONAL STORY
EXTRAORDINARY REVELATIONS
THE GREAT ROBBERY AND HOW IT WAS DONE
SUTHERLAND GEMS ROMANCE

The Valet made his first appearance in a hearing at the Bow Street court on 29 November. His curtain call came at his sentencing, which was held at Clerkenwell Sessions on 18 January. From start to conclusion, the preliminary hearings and the trial created immense interest. As the *Mail* reported, there were 'several curious features' about the proceedings too, as if hinting at some baroque conspiracy around it. But the case was more like a detective novel in which there are numerous red herrings; key lines and sometimes entire pages of the text missing; or in which the principal information doesn't fit with earlier established facts.

First of all, the police made no attempt to establish the Valet's true identity or to trace his background. Asked to give his name, the Valet replied: 'William Johnson.' At various stages he was also referred to in court as Thomas, James, Jackson, Wilson and Jones – but, significantly, never Henry Thomas. The *Mail* said: 'He greeted them with an equal smile. If he had a preference it seemed to be for Harry the Valet.' The police were simply content to let him use whichever alias he saw fit, as though his name had no bearing on the shape of the case or his previous misdemeanours.

Asked to give his address, he said: '5 Mornington Crescent' – a tall, imposing property in Camden that had been chopped up into apartments. Six years later the painter Walter Sickert would move two doors down and begin painting his Camden canvases and nudes there. According to Dinnie, who researched it, the Valet had stayed 'for only a few weeks' before moving on to Cathcart Road.

Asked to give his profession, the Valet said: 'A dealer.' Dew remarked, as though the description amused him: 'He was – in stolen goods.'

The evidence was marked by contradictions and evasions as well as outlandish, unproven claims by Maude who, bizarrely, was allowed to disguise her identity too. As she stepped into the witness box, her name and address were handed to the court on a slip of paper and were not revealed for 'special reasons', which were never specified. She was given the name Mrs Ronald and described as 'the wife of a man of blameless character' and as a 'woman of means'. The newspapers began calling her 'the mysterious lady of fortune' or 'the veiled lady of mystery' before the *Mail* revealed she was a former Gaiety Girl actress. The most striking thing about her performance was this: her public statements never matched her private feelings – a state of affairs of which only Dinnie and Dew were aware because each policeman had to deal with her simpering on an almost daily basis before, during and after the trial.

Edith Elman also used a pseudonym. She was referred to as Sarah Morris, a fact she disclosed exclusively to the *Echo*, which published a disclaimer at the foot of her interview. Elman, avoidant and oblique, insisted that her connection with the Valet was 'quite an innocent affair' and 'from the moment he became her guest to the day he was arrested he never alluded to the robbery of the Duchess's jewels or mentioned where he got his money from'. She had no idea why her battered tin box had been used as a repository for the stolen jewels and hidden on top of the wardrobe in the Valet's room.

As for the Dowager Duchess, who sat through six of the seven days of court questioning, the Valet observed that she 'seemed to take a keen interest in my personal appearance'. It was as if she had eyes for him alone.

The Valet found it impossible to be quiet or to stop smiling, whatever was said about him. If he thought his own counsel was speaking out of turn, he repeatedly corrected him and then grinned in the direction of the public gallery. He seemed to believe the courtroom was a stage on which he could show off like a vaudeville comedian, nodding at and nudging the audience into applause. He never had to be coaxed into speaking. As well as blabbing out the odd inconvenient truth, he interjected when questions were asked of witnesses. When, briefly, the Dowager Duchess identified items of her jewellery – claiming that some of the settings had been altered – he responded to her name and appearance by repeating the line 'I've seen her before' as if it was a catchphrase.

The newspapers loved it all. But the police had reached the point where they just needed to have the affair tightly closed, sealed and put away in a place where the Valet could be forgotten. It was as if firmly shutting the lid on this particular case was more important than establishing the rounded, crystal picture of it. For to do so might prove highly embarrassing to them and to the Duchess. Scotland Yard worried that a prolonged trial would highlight the stops, hesitations and inefficiencies of their investigation. The newspapers and the public would ask why the Valet hadn't been found and locked up far earlier. The Dowager Duchess worried that she'd be tarred all over again, as one story after another was dragged out about the shots which ended her first marriage and the feud with the Sutherland family which defined the second. Memory Lane was not a route she wished to take. She wanted everything done briskly, an opinion both she and especially Sir Albert Rollit strenuously conveyed. The fact that such haste created loose ends did not concern her; nor did it seem to trouble Scotland Yard.

There was not even a flicker of anxiety or trepidation on the Valet's face. Wearing a light brown suit, he came into the court at Bow Street smiling and looked at the front row of the spectators in an amused way. The spectator's gallery overflowed as the public

*The accused at the bar: Harry the Valet, left, and Moss Lipman hear the charges
read out to them after the theft of the Dowager Duchess of Sutherland's jewels.*

strained for a look at his face. The Valet took off his bowler hat
and laid it on the shelf of the dock.

Beside him was Moss Lipman, who had had the misfortune to
call at Cathcart Road as the police were still rearranging the furniture, pulling up floorboards and looking for hidden passageways or
hollows in the wall where the jewels might have been kept.
Scotland Yard assumed Lipman was guilty by association. An
unflattering drawing of the two men, published in *Lloyd's Weekly
Newspaper*, gives Lipman a quiff, a pinpoint nose and a solid,
square jaw. He is resting his arms on the dock rail. The artist has
made the Valet look old enough – though he was only 45 – to have
personally known Methuselah. Lipman protested his innocence,
and the Valet said nothing to contradict him. Ever since the
robbery Lipman had been 'on and off' in the Valet's company, said

Dew. Lipman countered that he had an alibi for the day of the theft. He was in London and could prove it beyond doubt. The police eventually had to concede that there was nothing to link him to the Gare du Nord; and nothing to tie him to the disposal of the jewels either. He'd done nothing more than take advantage of the Valet's drinks-for-all generosity – on which basis a quarter of London would have to be arrested. Reports of the trial rightly called Lipman a 'minor personage'. The Valet scathingly said of him that he cried 'like a baby' after his arrest. It was one of the few flickers of distaste he betrayed for any of the participants in the trial.

The case properly began when the Dowager Duchess took her oath. Her hair was tied back and she wore a ribboned hat decorated with a bunch of violets, a coat with prominent shoulder pads and a thickly knotted scarf. She buried her white-gloved hands in a fur muff. She made it seem that the monetary aspect of the case interested her far less than the theft itself, which she regarded as a personal insult. She pulled a long, disapproving face marked by a sullen glower, as if it pained her to be called to court – though she was scarcely unfamiliar with its rules and rituals. With a stern gaze, she dutifully went through her account: the way she'd asked the maid to take care of the jewels (she referred to the servant only by her surname – 'Perkins'); the movements of the footman (whom she didn't name at all, as though he was an irrelevance); her journey alone to the Gare du Nord; and of stepping from compartment to platform to greet Henri de Blowitz. Asked whether she shut the carriage door behind her, the Dowager Duchess said she couldn't remember. She retold the story of the 'staring man' and admitted: 'I did not recognise him but he was certainly not the prisoner.' Throughout her testimony, the Valet smiled broadly.

A jewel merchant, Louis Gaboril Duperri, of Garrard in the Haymarket, informed the court that pearls he had once set into a collarette for the Dowager Duchess were those found on the Valet. A special wax he had used was still traceable, he said. Another dealer in precious stones, Walter Ellis Mallett, picked out an emerald he had sold to the Duchess shortly before she left for Paris. It was also discovered in the Valet's possession. And a general dealer, Howard Levy of Hackney, who identified the Valet as Mr Jackson, said he had been hired to organise the making of a ring, pin and a stud from eight diamonds, two brilliants and an emerald. Levy asked no questions, assuming Mr Jackson was a respectable businessman who had been pleased with previous work he had carried out for him. A second casual acquaintance of the Valet's, Thomas Hinton of the Brown Bear Inn, repeated what he'd told the police before the arrest at Cathcart Road. He'd given the Valet a cheque for £500 in exchange for gold. He believed the Valet was Mr Jones, a 'very nice man whom when he was not drinking whisky drank champagne by the bottle'. The Valet smiled again, as though recalling in that moment the pleasure of every mouthful.

As each piece of evidence was presented and recorded – all of it guaranteeing the police a conviction and the prisoner a long jail term – the Valet reacted as though it no longer mattered to him. Partly, this calmness was integral to his approach, as if he had been born with it in his genes. But it was also because he knew he had only himself to blame for his circumstances. After his arrest, the Valet had remarked wistfully to Dinnie: 'If I hadn't been a fool and got drunk, you wouldn't have found me.' The idea must have played on his mind, because he added another sentence to support it: 'You would never have got me if it hadn't been for women and drink.' It was true. The uncorked bottle and a pair of fluttering eyelashes were the essence of his downfall. He could never resist either, and a combination of the two always led to trouble. The prime example of it came next.

Maude Richardson proved the Valet's assessment of his own

failings to be absolutely correct. She went into the witness box as if expecting the thunderclap of applause. She came to topple him showily dressed in a costly fur coat, a white satin blouse and heliotrope. From her wide-brimmed hat with its half-veil sprang a plume of black feathers. A tight belt accentuated the slimness of her waist and the size of her chest, which she thrust out as if to advertise two reasons why the Valet was drawn to her in the first place. The *Daily Chronicle* made a point of dwelling on her 'buxom appearance'. Maude had a face like a porcelain doll. 'She has a wealth of golden hair, tender mouth and rose pink complexion,' said the London *Star,* as if reviewing a solo turn rather than reporting a court case. She was also suffering from a bad cold, which lowered her voice and made it appear harsh and slightly rasping. The Valet brightened even more when she stood across the courtroom from him. He appeared galvanised, and gave the ends of his moustache an extra twirl with first finger and thumb to impress her. He knew what was on its way, and yet he listened without ever grimacing or shirking away from the bad news.

Maude ticked off each stage of her exhilarating journey with the Valet – the first meeting in London, his arrival in Brighton with the bottle of champagne and a more plausible manner than ever, his pursuit of her to Ostend and his spasm of jealousy there, which led to the attempted shooting, his imprisonment and the bail she paid on his behalf, the couple's jaunt across the border from Belgium into France and their eventual arrival in Paris. With the back of her hand laid daintily against her forehead, as though playing a role, she talked about frequent quarrels – mostly over cash. 'I paid the bills,' she said, telling a half-truth. 'He had no money . . . he was like a leech . . . he never left me alone,' added the woman who voluntarily went to his cell in Bruges to release him. She maintained she funded him 'out of her usual generosity' until the relationship disintegrated. Her account meandered to its climax – the evening when he found her at a table at the

Casino de Paris and later presented her with the Dowager Duchess's jewels.

Maude described the jewellery, including a pearl necklace 'about four or five yards long', an emerald ring, a bangle with a gold ball attached, another ring, a diamond collarette 'as long as your arm', and a cross 'like an Egyptian Star'. She added that the diamonds from the star had been 'abstracted and were in a piece of tissue paper'. When she talked about the pearl necklace, she stretched out her arms to convey the length of it. She said that, after showing her 'the stuff', the Valet had confessed straight away that the jewels belonged to the Dowager Duchess. She plunged in the bodkin by adding something more. The Valet implied he'd become entangled in a sexual liaison to obtain them. Maude told the court: 'He said to me, "If you want to get anybody's jewels, you only have to get around the maid first, and that is not too difficult."' She paused before remarking in a reflective way, 'I've found out it is not too difficult for a man to get around a maid.' Maude then claimed – as if entirely blameless for sleeping in the jewels – to have contacted the police in Paris early the following morning to 'protect my life'. She insisted he'd attempted to shoot her again in her room for refusing to hand the jewels back. In closing, Maude conceded that she did not tell the Valet she had 'given him away' after his arrival in Brighton in early November. When he found out 'behind my back', she said, he called her a 'dirty rat and a few other odds and ends of that sort' before striking her in the face, 'nearly knocking out one eye and left me nearly dead on the sofa'. She recalled him leaving her with a terse goodbye: 'I am going abroad to foreign parts. I shall never see you again.'

She wittered on, pumping her account with hot air. Each chapter of her story was relayed with 'reluctance and impatience', said a report. If there was a pause between questions, she was brusque and rude, urging counsel to 'go on, go on'. She constantly snapped her fingers, as if the clicking sound was meant to add emphasis to each statement. At one point, Maude was so testy that she turned around and sat down in the witness box, staring away from the bench. She was ordered to stand up and face the court. After further questioning, Maude struck her hand forcibly on top of the box and then went into a hacking coughing fit. Water was hastily brought and she took the glass in both hands. When she admitted sleeping in the Dowager Duchess's jewels, the Valet shouted with perfect timing: 'I had a job to get them away from her.' The court fell about laughing. Most remarkable of all were Maude's glances towards her former lover. Her words cut through the notion that she still felt something for him. Her facial gestures did not. Whenever she made a point she nodded to the Valet in what the newspapers regarded as 'a friendly manner'. In return the Valet 'glowed with happy reminiscences – and smiled'.

In a supplementary interview with the *Daily Mail*, Maude put forward her version of events more strongly than ever and damned the Valet completely. Asked why she had 'put him away', Maude said she was 'in dread that any moment he might drag her into complications over the robbery'. Her knowledge of it, she added, 'was a secret too dangerous to keep'. She repeated her account of the Ostend shooting and his 'handiness with a revolver,' producing what the *Mail* described as a 'pretty little watch' with dents on the cover, which she insisted had saved her from death. 'You think I exaggerate when I talk of shooting, but what do you think of this?' Running her fingers across the watch, she said that the Valet 'tried his best to kill me when he fired this shot and I was only saved by this . . . and my other jewellery'. She added that the Valet made another attempt to 'dispose' of her in the same way. 'I complained to the police of the threats to murder me,' she said, 'but all the satisfaction I got was the assurance that if he did so he would be locked up.' Maude wound up her verbal attack by separating herself entirely from the Valet. 'He has been wanting me to go and see him in prison. I don't intend to go,' she said.

To Dinnie and Dew, Maude's hostile and bitterly exhaled emotional responses in court, and on page three of the *Mail*, simply did not square with her emollient attitude towards the Valet in their company. What appeared in the newspaper was a cock and bull story, and a malicious piece of whimsy too. The discrepancy was noted by Dew, who explained: 'While Harry was awaiting trial [she] became something of a nuisance to Dinnie and myself. She was continually sending telegrams to the Yard offering more information. On each of these occasions I went to see her, only to find she had nothing of value to communicate.' He added: 'It was only with the greatest reluctance that she went into the witness box. At each hearing Harry would plead with me and with other officers to be allowed to see the woman whose evidence was sending him to penal servitude. She was just as anxious to see him.' The Valet, chivalrous and discreet towards Maude, made it clear to his counsel that he didn't want her cross-examined.

The newspapers never warmed to her. She gave off 'all the airs of the gilded cocotte', said one. In general it was implied she'd carefully shaped the evidence to reflect well on herself. She presented it in such a way as to make her look like a hostage to the Valet's controlling and scheming in Paris. But he didn't seem to mind.

The damage was now done. At the trial itself, which began on 4 January, Geoghegan took hold of the defence as best he could. He was described as 'one of the greatest natural orators at the Bar'. But there was a rider to this tribute. Like most such men, he was 'exceeding hard to stop' once his tongue slipped into top gear. Geoghegan was Irish and he relied on his brogue and the lilt of his voice to charm and flatter a jury, as if trying to massage and soothe them into submission. He drank hard liquor (he died prematurely because of it) and refused to take the cases of criminals accused of murder because the thought of losing, which meant his client would swing from the hangman's rope, left him queasy and depressed. In 1885, when he was briefed to defend a man accused of murder and rape, he backed out of the trial fearing the consequences of defeat. The Valet nonetheless called Geoghegan 'a fine pleader and a very estimable gentleman'. But he accepted that his situation was already hopeless because the prosecution witnesses – with Maude the most prominent of them – had already made it so. 'What could he say in mitigation of such an offence as mine?' asked the Valet of Geoghegan, aware that the routines and rigmarole of the court – necessary hoops to be jumped through – were only delaying the inevitable. However long the process, and however long-winded the pleas in mitigation, he was going to jail. The Valet therefore decided to enjoy his moment in the spotlight.

Geoghegan tried two lines of counter-attack against the prosecution, led by Richard Muir, who was then still awaiting his knighthood. The Valet wantonly sabotaged the opening attempt to reduce his prison term. Geoghegan played the romance card, claiming that the poor, lonely and love-struck accused 'only stole the case of jewels so that he might make up the quarrel between himself and the woman'. He added that taking the Dowager Duchess's gems was no more than 'a temptation acted upon' – a spur of the moment theft inspired by devotion and lust. He urged the court to treat it as an 'ordinary railway theft', ignoring the value of the case, and then strived to portray the Valet as more of a bumbling amateur than a hardened professional criminal. This was rather like arguing that Nelson wasn't much of a sailor and had only messed around in boats. To the Valet, it was a slur on his talents, as though he'd exaggerated or inflated them. He couldn't let Geoghegan's charge be placed in the written record of the proceedings without challenging it – whatever the repercussions. 'I've pulled off 20 greater coups than this one,' he boasted unbidden from the dock and said it as if he couldn't understand why so much fuss was being made over a mere £25,000 to £30,000. Geoghegan pressed on regardless. He tried to reaffirm that the theft hadn't been premeditated. The Valet, however, made it clear he'd gained precious details of the Dowager Duchess and her jewel case from within the Hotel Bristol during her stay. It was as fatuous as sawing off the branch you're sitting on. As Dinnie wrote in the report he submitted for the files at Scotland Yard – and for colleagues in Paris – the Valet had admitted that 'he alone committed the theft of the jewels, but has stated that someone attached to the Hotel Bristol . . . supplied him with information in relation to them'.

It left Muir with an easy job. He only had to remain upright and coherent to complete it, but he still prepared exhaustively, scribbling notes on stiff oblong cards. Each line was in a different colour to differentiate between the threads of his forensic examinations. When, a decade later, Dr Crippen heard that Muir was prosecuting his case, he admitted: 'I fear the worst.' Muir was called 'ponderous and relentless'. His biographer, S. T. Felstead, summed up his approach – the gradual accumulation of facts and an economy in speech when it came to disclosing them. 'He made it a virtue to use the fewest possible words in the clearest possible manner,' said Felstead. 'He never descended into theatrical effects.' Against Geoghegan, Muir hardly needed to break sweat. Here was another success he could add very simply to his ever-lengthening curriculum vitae.

The Valet, who began by deferring his plea, had no option but to plead guilty. But he smiled as he did so.

The judge, James McConnell, postponed sentence in the hope that the Valet could be persuaded to change his mind and tell the police where to find the rest of the jewels. McConnell did so despite the advice of the exasperated Geoghegan. Not only aware of his client's mulish tendencies, but now also with first-hand experience of them, he told the judge it would not be of the

'slightest use to take that course'. The police had already tried and failed, added Geoghegan. Neither the prospect of a tougher sentence nor the incentive of a more lenient one had made any difference to the Valet. As politely as possible, Geoghegan tried to tell the judge that he might as well complete the final formality of the case without dragging everyone back into court later in the month. No sooner were the words spoken than the Valet was unable to resist adding his own final paragraph to his counsel's comment. It wouldn't make any difference if the judge sent him down for 'fifty-five years', he said. He would say 'nothing'.

Judge McConnell was an optimist – albeit a misguided one. Whatever Geoghegan's view, and however much the Valet

Sir Richard Muir, who prepared for every case with a military-like precision and was admired by contemporaries and feared among the criminal profession.

protested otherwise, he thought another two weeks in his paid-for Holloway cell might bring him to his senses.

He didn't understand Harry the Valet at all.

The man of 'many names and resources' waited for sentence. Dew was sent to interview him for the umpteenth time, knowing full well that the Valet would remain mute. 'The view in police circles is that he is looking forward to recovering the rest of the spoils when he has done his time,' insisted one report.

Questions still remained, but no one was bothered about foraging for answers. Foremost among them, as the London *Echo* said, was his real identity: 'As to the prisoner's real name there is some doubt,' it pointed out, as if urging someone in Scotland Yard to resolve the matter without delay. There was also doubt about the credibility of Edith Elman, whose protests of innocence were a masterwork of evasiveness and never properly tested because the Valet declined to offer evidence against her. Elman's account of her strictly innocent relationship with her boarder fell into the category of fairy tale. She was, after all, in the Valet's room during the police raid on Cathcart Road and waiting for him to undress. Her claim to be unaware that he'd stolen the Dowager Duchess's jewels – and was slowly selling them – is too fantastical to be believed. She'd been his perpetual companion for several weeks, a period in which the hunt for the jewels – and the figure responsible for stealing them – was constantly in the newspapers. The Valet drank enough to have let something fatally incriminating slip from his lips. Also, by his own admission, he was freely confessing to the theft shortly before his arrest. Either Elman was particularly dense or she stuffed a wad of cotton wool in each ear.

Maude's story was garnished by violence, designed to arouse the court's sympathy. It was as if she'd been brutishly bullied into spending two months bed-hopping with the Valet – coerced into paying his bail and his bills, forced against her will to accompany

valuable heirlooms,' she said. The swoop for them was a split second away from taking place when the Valet sped into the carriage and out again, and beat them to the gem case. 'Audacity won where skill and finesse had failed,' she added. Chicago May's account carries the mark of authenticity because of the statements Sir Albert Rollit gave to the police in both Paris and London, and the evidence his wife supplied at the Valet's trial. He talked about a figure looming alongside them on shopping expeditions. She became fixated on the 'staring man' she saw standing on the platform at the Gare du Nord. That is why the Dowager Duchess could never visually connect the Valet to the crime. The man she saw – and the man Rollit sensed had been following and constantly scrutinising them – belonged to Gleason's gang, which was pulled together for the specific job that the Valet interrupted.

How different everything might have been for him. Gleason nearly saved the Valet from the pain he subsequently endured – all of it caused by Maude.

She developed a taste for litigation. Adding one coda after another to the Sutherland gem theft, she kept the Valet's name as well as her own in the newspapers.

Maude's first prominent reappearance in print came less than a month after the Valet was sentenced. Near the end of the court case she suggested that some items of jewellery, which had been returned to the Dowager Duchess of Sutherland, actually belonged to her. In February she pressed her claim more strenuously. She asked for the jewels to be examined independently to settle the argument. Maude said two stones in particular – a Cape diamond and a pearl – were taken by the Valet to be valued and never given back to her. The diamond was formerly the centre stone of a ring, she added, and sat beside two sapphires. The pearl was originally at the heart of another ring and flanked by diamonds. She had bought it in Australia. The Dowager Duchess went through the motions of being diplomatically pleasant. Rather than abruptly saying no to her demand, she explained that Maude had been 'unfortunate' in her choice of the stones. As Maude persisted, the niceties turned to bare-knuckle defiance. Preparing for a holiday in Monte Carlo, the Duchess emphasised that the stones had been put under the microscope before the trial. Provenance had been emphatically settled in her favour, she said, before adding, as if to swat the irritant away: 'Not only did Maude Richardson have every opportunity of proving what was her property, but the expert who went over the trinkets afterwards was able to assign them all to their proper places. No stones were given to me that had not been carefully examined and fully identified.' Asked whether she would allow Maude to look at the stones again, the Duchess replied tartly: 'Most certainly not. The jewellery is mine.'

No sooner had the Dowager Duchess fought successfully on one front than she had to fight on another. Maude also insisted that she – rather than Walter Dinnie, Walter Dew or Frank Froest – deserved a slice of the reward for finding the jewels, which her greedy eyes had first seen when the Valet presented them to her. Sir Albert Rollit was served with a writ in which Maude demanded £5,000. The Dowager Duchess repudiated the claim that she had anything to do with their recovery or the discovery of the Valet. Indeed, her reluctance to part with the jewels forced the police to race down a series of blind alleys in pursuit of them. In response to this stonewalling, Maude farcically wrote to the Home Secretary, Sir Matthew White Ridley, urging him to intervene on her behalf. Ridley, a Conservative as well as a friend of Rollit's, ignored her. The writ flared up in the newspapers and then faded away. It was impossible to take seriously.

Maude was undeterred. Next, she irrationally turned her ire on Leopold II, the King of the Belgiums. The case was so novel that it produced laughter, then bafflement and finally almost struck dumb those who heard about it. She was determined to recover the £120 bail she'd handed to the Belgian courts to free the Valet. Her argument rested on a technicality. When he was supposed to be appearing in a court in Ostend, he was already in custody in England, which made it impossible for him to travel. Maude thought she had 'good ground' on which to reclaim her money because the Valet had not deliberately fled Belgium. This ignored the irrefutable evidence that she'd willingly left the country with him. Another writ ended in another failure.

Her preoccupation with the legal profession continued, as if she thought solicitors were underpaid and she needed to constantly contribute to their financial well-being.

By August 1899, she was accusing a crabby, 57-year-old widow called Edith Shadgett of clearing her flat of furniture and stealing jewellery and other items worth £150. These included two diamond solitaires, a silver tray and a mirror. Maude said she found them missing after returning from a fortnight's seaside break in Margate. There was a further complication because Maude disclosed that she'd allowed Shadgett to pawn other jewellery for her. She had not, however, given her blessing for the removal of other possessions. These were taken on 'false pretence', she maintained.

Maude was living beyond her means in a furnished London flat in Berners Street, which she rented for £16 a month. The *Daily Mail* reported that she gave a 'ludicrous exhibition' of herself in Marlborough Street court. Maude claimed Shadgett was her maid; Shadgett counter-claimed correctly that she was her landlady and occasional travelling companion. She shouted from the dock: 'Since when was I your housekeeper?' Again, Maude gave evidence 'in a very incoherent manner'. With her composure dissolved by drink, her display in the witness box was almost identical to her performance in the Sutherland jewel case. The *Mail* noted she was caught 'frequently stopping to snap her fingers and sway'. At one point she was told that the charges against Shadgett would be dismissed 'unless you give your evidence in a sensible manner'. Maude bristled at the order. 'What do you want now?' she said to the magistrate, turning from side to side as she said it and listing, like a capsized ship. Another bout of finger-snapping – and more 'antics' – followed. She swallowed her words, making them almost inaudible, or sometimes her replies came in irritable, staccato bursts. She also answered questions with questions. Asked how much rent she owed Shadgett, Maude asked counsel: 'How much do you make?' When the accused was bound over for a week, the magistrate said that he hoped the caterwauling Maude would be fit to give her evidence properly. 'You do as you like,' she told him. 'You can kick her out but she will be charged again.' The *Mail* concluded: 'With this remark, she sailed pompously out of court.' Shadgett was sent for trial and found not guilty.

The Valet followed all this from afar, every day hoping for a perfumed letter from Maude which never came.

What he received instead was a visitor at Lewes Prison in early 1900. He prayed it was Maude. It was actually a clerk from the firm of solicitors representing her estranged husband, Harry Andrew. The Valet was being cited as co-respondent in their divorce. Confusingly, he was named on the court documents under the aliases of Johnson and Williams. In almost a year, no one had taken the trouble to find his birth certificate. He accepted news of Maude meekly, as if grateful to know what was happening to his beloved. And, as though imploring the clerk to understand his pain, the Valet said that he was *still* unable to work out why she had given him away. The problem of Maude was insoluble to him, and it made no sense at all. 'He loved her even then, in spite of what she had done to him,' remarked the clerk.

The Valet's trial had been covered by every newspaper in the country. It was impossible to avoid. One reader who took particular personal interest in it and claimed to be 'surprised one morning' by the tantalising story as it unravelled was Andrew. He began to register the extent of his wife's infidelity with the jewel thief. Thinking of her savings as much as her reputation – and sensibly realising, too, that Andrew would file for divorce after the trial was over – Maude got her retaliation in first. She spoke publicly about the money she had loaned to Andrew during both their courtship and the marriage. Only two days after the Valet was sentenced at Clerkenwell, she published a small notice in several morning newspapers in which she declared:

Take notice that I, Louisa Andrew (Maude Richardson) am not responsible for the debts of my husband, Lieutenant Harry Andrew, late of the 42nd Gordon Highlanders (Black Watch) and of Hawkley Uplands, Liss Hants – Louisa Andrew.

The idea was to send a warning message to Andrew. In a mud-slinging contest, she could match him clod for clod. The notice was sufficient to delay, but not to dissuade, Andrew from taking her to court. Divorce was rare and costly. Rare because couples tended to muddle along in miserable marriages rather than face shame and ignominy as the dirty laundry of their lives was strung out in the newspapers. Costly because the financial and emotional consequences could be dire; especially so for women, who voluntarily surrendered everything to their husbands – property, chattels and money as well as body and soul – by saying 'I do.' The 1857 Matrimonial Causes Act, an appallingly biased and unfair document which stripped women of basic legal rights, allowed husbands to sue for divorce on grounds of adultery alone. If a woman wanted to sue her husband, however, she had to prove adultery as well as at least one of the following: cruelty, bigamy, incest, bestiality or desertion. The social consequences of divorce for a wife were rejection and shame. The stigma of divorce meant the prospect of finding another husband – or even another role in life – was remote. She was a pariah, which explains why 1900 saw pitifully few divorces – just 560. Those which reached the courts were often juicily reported.

From the beginning Maude was embroiled in a rearguard action because the evidence against her was conclusive. Her former maid, the Valet's friend Georgiana Summers, spoke about the liaison with 'Harry'. She added that Maude 'used to drink', alluding to an alcohol dependency which would soon become obvious and was caused by one misfortune after another and a succession of bad choices: the strain of her rushed, inappropriate marriage, her husband's departure after one night of the honeymoon to join Henry Cavendish's African expedition, then his fourteen-month absence in Africa, his refusal to live with her again on his return, the publicity of her association with the Valet and the subsequent court appearance. Maude was trapped in a cycle of depression and hysteria. She could take no more. To the newspapers, she'd become a 'woman with a past' – a none too subtle code for someone with loose morals or no morals at all; an actress, moreover, who'd taken advantage of the libertine attitudes of the Gaiety Theatre to wallow in drink and lasciviousness and had allowed the stage-door Johnnies to provide her with gifts in return for favours.

Andrew appeared in court with his moustache thickly waxed. The ends were twisted and upturned into the shape of quarter-moons. He had short sideburns and his black hair was swept back. His shirt collar almost reached his chin, as if he was using his dress to suggest he was High Church. He was certainly trying to pass himself off as high-minded and upstanding, a soldier-gentleman and a fearless explorer who was the hapless victim in an unsavoury affair. Andrew said that letters he'd received from his wife during their separation made him question her mental stability. In one she wrote about being starved and robbed in a medical home, adding that 'Your mother would have had me dead now and you would have come back with Cavendish and enjoyed yourself at the Jubilee Club.' Andrew insisted that he assumed she'd been drinking – a claim, since there was no previous evidence to support it, that he could only make with knowledge gained well after the event. The more he tried to cast himself as the 'man of blameless character', which is how the court had described him during the Sutherland trial, the more he came across as an old-fashioned cad and bounder. The court was appalled at the money he'd borrowed from Maude, including the £100 she gave him to arrange the wedding. He claimed she had savings and investments in the bank from her stage career, which brought her an income of £300 to £400 per year.

His wife's solicitor asked Andrew: 'You did not provide her with a single penny for her maintenance except what she might have or what she might make?'

'No,' he replied without adding a word to his answer.

As for his wife's career, it was put to him bluntly: 'As a man of the world, did you not know the life she had led?'

'Yes,' he replied, again without further elaboration.

Foundation cracks began to appear in the holier than thou structure that Andrew had built around himself. These widened considerably as the court heard about his disappearing act to Africa. Andrew pretended he had not known of the invitation from Cavendish when he asked Maude to marry him. He wasn't believed, and found the divorce suit backfiring on him. He was labelled as someone who 'knew the life [his wife] was leading and knew how she had obtained the money which she had lent him, and yet he went away, leaving her absolutely unprotected'. The judgment of the court was that Andrew's conduct in wilfully separating from Maude had 'conduced' to her adultery with the Valet. Andrew's petition was dismissed; he was ordered to pay costs of £100.9s.

Even victors are by victories undone, and Maude did not escape without a further wide, dark stain on her character. In the public eye, she was now a drunk, a serial philanderer and prone to outbursts of instability.

Of the two of them, the Valet had the better reputation.

For Harry the Valet, jail was a condition to be endured rather than a problem to be solved, because time is nothing, but experiencing it is everything. He spent the next six years in three prisons before his release: Lewes, Dartmoor and Portland. Dartmoor was the toughest regime in the bleakest surroundings – sombre, greenish-grey stone and a wild-looking landscape surrounding it. 'It really is a prison,' wrote Arthur Griffiths, the author and former Inspector of Prisons. It was a 'place of durance and confinement', he added. Writing an article on jails for the *Pall Mall Gazette,* Griffiths sat with the Valet in his cell and spoke to him about 'the psychology of criminals and their methods'. The visit broke the long, dull days of routine at Dartmoor. Those who were taken through the mists and high tors of Devon moorland, and then passed beneath the great stone-built archway of the jail, were immediately fastened into a regime of repetitive toil.

The orderly day, driven by the clock, began at 5 a.m. when more than 1,000 men rose to the strike of a bell and the release of the cell doors for breakfast – a pint of gruel or porridge, tea and a loaf of bread – and then a chapel service at 6.55 lasting exactly a quarter of an hour. The Valet and the rest of the inmates were always searched and counted before work began. Supper was served at 5.15 p.m. and the lights turned out at 8 p.m. With the finery of his wardrobe packed away – 'ready for wear when I came out if the fashion had not changed', he said – the Valet wore a 'broad arrowed canvas, which chafed my skin'. He sewed in the tailor's shop and tried to be philosophic: 'I was a model prisoner, recognising that the man who cuts up rough and is not amenable to discipline, is picking a rod for his own back.' He added

*Bleak and desolate, Dartmoor Prison's strictly regimented routine forced
prisoners such as Harry the Valet to toe the line or face tough consequences.*

gloomily, as though it needed to be spelt out, that 'The life at a
convict establishment such as Dartmoor is in sad contrast to my
life in the West or in the bright capitals of Europe.'

He was nonetheless treated as a celebrity by his fellow inmates.
After the vivid descriptions in the newspapers, and his devil-may-
care approach to his imprisonment, the Valet found himself feted.
Dartmoor's equivalent of the red carpet was rolled out for him.
The prison grapevine hummed with expectation. Everyone wanted
to talk to him and listen to his stories. One question followed
another. Just how beautiful was Maude? What did she look like
after covering herself in the Dowager Duchess's jewels? How had
he managed to dodge Dinnie and Dew for so long? The prisoners
also wanted to know about his other escapes and narrow scrapes.
Very cleverly the Valet let it be known that he was still a well-to-
do gent with enough money to return to luxury as soon as the
inconvenience of his uncomfortable sentence was over. Without

explicitly saying so – in case a nark passed the information on to the prison warders – he gave the impression that the remainder of the Duchess's jewellery was hidden in a safe place and just waiting for him to reclaim it. The other prisoners thought he might share a portion of it with them if he was treated as minor royalty. They acted as servants for him, fussing over his needs. He said he 'refused to allow my head to be turned by the adulation of my fellow convicts', and added: 'the poor fellows looked on me as a sort of hero, and even smuggled me their own bread, which I always tried to refuse and there were sometimes fights to get near me at exercise. Even the prison officials themselves had a very tender heart towards me.'

At the end of his sentence, the Valet said, he was both 'older and wiser'.

This was true only up to a point. He was indisputably older. The 45-year-old who went into prison re-emerged – his 50th birthday well behind him – considerably wearier than before. But he was no wiser – a fact which became apparent all too soon.

Chapter 11

The eyes of a man with murder in his heart

Of all the things contemporaneously written about Harry the Valet and his theft of the Dowager Duchess of Sutherland's jewels, the most prescient appeared in the *London Letter*, a column of gossip and opinion syndicated to Britain's provincial newspapers. The dilemma the Valet would confront after his release from prison was encapsulated in a solitary paragraph. 'One of the single features of his career has been the good fortune he has had,' wrote the anonymous author, who also pointed out a truism. 'Now that his record contains an entry of penal servitude, he will not escape so easily for the future.' The prediction proved to be devastatingly accurate.

The Valet's previous jail sentences had been comparatively short and unpublicised. He was always able to slip back, unnoticed and unannounced, into the criminal ways of his past without interference. It was different now. Every policeman in London knew the Valet as Walter Dew described him: a man 'particularly fond of diamond merchants'; knew, too, how to recognise him from Scotland Yard's description; and also knew where to look for him. No matter which alias he used, the Valet would find it impossible to avoid capture for all but the most ordinarily minor or trivial thefts, which would never restore his former fortune. He couldn't ghost into and out of Hatton Garden and the restaurants around it, or frequent the de luxe hotels or the railway stations, without being spotted instantly. Fame and notoriety, which the Valet initially embraced as due recognition of his skills, had become the chief obstacle to earning a good, dishonest living. He struggled to accept it, or to come to terms with the implications. The solution was to move out of London and operate elsewhere. But he was so tightly allied to the city that he could not contemplate leaving it. It was his home and he couldn't imagine abandoning it.

With freedom from jail, at the end of 1905, came other realities. He walked back into a different London from the one he'd left. In six years the world around him had changed, and was still changing substantially as he stared at it: the old Queen was dead, the new King had taken her place, the age of the motor car and powered flight had begun, and Britain was being remodelled in fashion, culture and social beliefs to fit a fresh century and the different attitudes which came with it. Progress was everywhere, and he found it disorienting. The sights and sounds of London managed to be simultaneously familiar and alien to him.

The Valet was no longer the most celebrated and emblematic of the gentleman jewel thieves. That distinction now belonged to the fictional Raffles, already imprinted on the minds of the reading and theatregoing public in titles such as *The Black Mask* and *A Thief in the Night*. E. W. Hornung's first book to feature Raffles, *The Amateur Cracksman*, was turned almost immediately into a play that matched its wide appeal. Raffles was rich and living in Albany. The Valet was almost penniless and living where he could. There were no rock-solid certainties on which he could rely any more. And there was no vast stash of the Dowager Duchess's gems for him to claim either. Only a few odd items remained to be cashed in. On his return from Paris, desperate for money and security, he'd sold most of the jewels to rapacious fences such as Kammy Grizzard, who recognised that the Valet was negotiating from a position of weakness and so exploited him. The publicity of the theft winnowed out his options. The jewels were described in such detail in the newspapers that no legitimate or semi-legitimate businessman could ever handle them. The Valet admitted as much as he remembered the various deals he had cut with the untrustworthy Grizzard. 'I had put a little fortune of jewels into his hands – and not always at my own price,' he said. By the time of his arrest at Cathcart Road, the most precious of the jewels were already gone and almost all the money raised from them had been spent. The Valet couldn't tell the police the location of the jewels; he simply didn't know where to find them.

And there was no Maude Richardson for comfort. Absence had not enhanced Maude's feelings for him. The Valet had brought her nothing but prolonged and very public anguish, and she wanted no more to do with him. From his cell the Valet despondently accepted the scale of his foolishness over Maude. He could not even write to her. From choice as much as financial necessity, she regularly changed addresses, which made finding her impossible.

He dwelt on lost chances. With the Dowager Duchess's jewels, he could have turned himself into a wealthy man. He could also have chosen a wife from a hundred or more women – all of them exactly like Maude. If he'd left Paris within hours of taking the jewels, and disposed of them sensibly, how different life would have been. The Valet had been fundamentally stupid over Maude, unable to let go because he couldn't rationalise the relationship or see how disabling and damaging it had become for each of them. In a strange way he and Maude had been too alike to ever get along – both too restless, independently headstrong, self-absorbed and over-fond of their own ways. The love between them was too light to carry the weight of their expectations.

But the image of her would not lie still in his mind.

The Valet had to reconcile himself to another truth too. Prison had fatigued him, wasting his body and blunting his mind. His prime was past. Like the clothes he'd worn when cavorting around London – the cape and spats – he was out of fashion. The energy and headlong momentum that once propelled him across the city was all but spent. He'd survived his jail term, but emerged with the spark inside him extinguished. His movements had become cumbersome and clumsily improvisational, though he stole the odd wallet when he could. These were often taken with sluggish, ungainly lunges. Others escaped him because he moved too early or too late – frustrating and stressful for someone whose timing was once so impeccable. No longer was the Valet able to look down at everything from the comfortable vantage point of success. He had to muddle and grub along as best he could. It was a chaotic and incoherent existence, which in April 1908 eventually led him back into court and fulfilled the prophecy of the *London Letter*.

The Valet was on the hunt in the Viaduct Station Hotel in Holborn. 'I saw a pocket book sticking out of a man's coat,' he said. He assumed it contained diamonds or banknotes. A decade earlier he would have stolen it as easily as plucking a petal from a flower. Now, with his reactions slower, his co-ordination rustier and less reliable, the result was disastrous. The touch of his hand on the wallet was too heavy. Its owner felt the tug and jarring of his pocket and made a counter-move as the Valet tried to dodge clear of him. 'I was tripped up by the mark,' he said. He was arrested after stumbling, as if drunk, across the room. The failure confirmed that there could be no more hair's-breadth escapes or magical last-minute reprieves for the Valet. Those were the good old days, and long gone. He was diminished, the hands not able to take cleanly what the eyes saw or what a lifetime's instincts compelled him to snatch.

The Recorder of London, Sir Forrest Fulton, took a none too

The eyes of a man with murder in his heart

Sir Forrest Fulton, who always tried to teach a lesson to repeat offenders
unless mitigating circumstances were attached to their crimes.

lenient view when the Valet appeared before him at the Old
Bailey. Regarded as a 'competent and careful Judge' who was
'hardly to be ranked against the greatest of his predecessors',
Fulton was urbane and usually fair, but also toughly orthodox in
doling out his punishments. He did not care for repeat offenders.
Fulton tried the unfortunate Adolf Beck in that dreadful case
of mistaken identity, demolishing the defence's protests that
the accused had been confused with someone else. Fulton said
he thought it 'irrelevant anyway', and found himself looking
ridiculous as a consequence. The error made Fulton compassionate
on occasions; he could sometimes be persuaded to look kindly on
a criminal if there were extenuating circumstances surrounding his
crime. But he saw none when weighing up the Valet's slapdash
theft. In front of him was a habitual offender, who would go on
stealing repeatedly unless the stiffest correction was made to the
course of his life. The defendant – known to him as William
Johnson – had used yet another alias in his feeble striving to hide

his previous crimes. He'd told police his name was Thomas Williams.

The Valet supposed he would get a light sentence because the wallet contained neither diamonds nor notes. The only things inside it were five penny stamps. He hadn't taken into account his reacquaintance with Walter Dew, who was put in charge of the case.

Dew was never likely to forget the Dowager Duchess or the Valet. He recognised his old foe immediately. 'How different were the circumstances,' he said, hardly able to believe that 'the man noted for his spectacular crimes . . . was standing in the Old Bailey charged with stealing an empty pocket book from an overcoat'. After the guilty verdict, Dew went into the witness box and read out the Valet's long criminal history, repeating to Fulton the line that the Valet had heard so often: 'He is one of the cleverest jewel thieves in Europe.' The man about whom it was said no longer took it as a compliment but a curse. The phrase reminded Fulton that a mild rap across the knuckles would be unacceptable in dealing with him; he deserved Justice's big, clunking fist. Dew thought the Valet had been 'unlucky' to find the pocketbook empty and 'still more unlucky to get caught'. He sounded as if he half regretted his demise. It was as though the Valet was a once-great athlete who had played on for one season too long. Fulton delivered his verdict – five years: one year for each penny stamp. As the Valet readily accepted, the sentence had nothing to do with those stamps. In the dock was no ordinary thief, but Harry the Valet. The Sutherland jewels 'thrust me into the limelight again', said the Valet. He knew Fulton was making him pay for the theft for a second time.

Sir Forrest Fulton and Walter Dew intended to drive him out of crime for ever. But it did not work. The destructive impulse remained. No length of sentence could ever dissuade him from giving up his profession. He knew nothing else. The Valet was shamed at the Old Bailey. He'd looked a ruined, pathetic figure – washed up and washed out, paraded as someone to be mocked rather than feared for his criminal prowess.

But, as his sixtieth birthday loomed, pride became paramount to him. He needed to restore his reputation and prove a point. To Scotland Yard, who assumed his best was behind him. To his fellow criminals, who no longer respected him. And, of course, to himself. Anyone else would have accepted defeat. Not the Valet. He sought a final major coup – a last spectacular and headline-grabbing hurrah to ease him into an idyllic, secluded and sedentary retirement. In May 1912, just a few months after being let out of prison again, he was checking the movements of society hostesses in the same methodical way he would check the form, odds and the recent performances of a racehorse. 'A paragraph I chanced upon made me sit up suddenly and put on my thinking cap,' he said. It was no more than a snippet. The paragraph, buried at the bottom of a column, said that Jai Singh Prabhakar, the Maharaja of Alwar, would be visiting Britain for the London season. He was due to arrive at Marseilles in two days' time. The jewels he was bringing with him were described as 'gems worth a King's ransom'. The Valet said: 'The minute I finished reading the news I made up my mind to gain possession of the Rajah's State Jewels, and the only thing that concerned my mind for the next hour or two was how and where I was to capture them.' He rated the task as a 'colossal one'. The Maharaja of Alwar was well insulated against crime and criminals. 'But there was no reason,' the Valet insisted, 'why I should not repeat my triumph in connection with the Sutherland jewels.' He cited his 'experience of Europe and the ways of wealthy Indian Princes' as the reason for such confidence. From distant memory the Valet dredged up close studies he'd previously made into the behaviour of maharajas who had savoured the sights of Europe. He said: 'When he arrived at Marseilles he would sigh for the delights of Paris after his long sea voyage, would make straight for the Meurice Hotel in the Rue de Rivoli, the favourite caravanserai of every Eastern potentate scouring Europe, and then, when satiated with visits to the Folies Bergère, Maxim's and other Parisian resorts he would come to London by the Calais–Dover route, which is the quickest . . . the question was where I was going to pinch those jewels.'

The Valet ran the route through his mind and decided to head directly for Marseilles. 'I reckoned the Maharaja and all his retainers would be less settled than when they got to Paris. There would be a greater element of danger if I left the job till Dover.'

The Maharaja of Alwar, whom Lord Halifax considered was a victim of schizophrenia, a sadist, a pervert and contained evil within him.

Within three hours of reading about the Maharaja, he'd packed two suitcases and hailed a hansom cab, which drove him to Victoria station. From there he caught the train to Folkestone, crossed on the overnight boat and arrived in Paris at 4.30 the following afternoon. He booked into the Hôtel du Nord for a 'wash and brush up' before boarding the night express to Marseilles, which he called the 'most wonderful port in Europe' He arrived there at 6 a.m. He was sure the Maharaja would book into the Louvre Hotel. He was right. The Valet found him already in residence with his entourage. A number of balconies ran along the front of the bedrooms. The Valet glanced up and saw eight or nine turbaned figures smoking cheroots on one of them. 'The balconies delighted my heart,' he said, 'because I saw the possibility of getting into the bedroom of his Serene Highness without too much trouble.'

There was trouble, however. The hotel, full of 'the aroma of Dahl, Kejeree and other beloved Indian dishes', was crowded; the Valet could only get a room on the top floor. He also discovered the Maharaja took his meals in his apartment, which meant he seldom left it. After leaving to buy a newspaper, the Valet returned from a kiosk opposite the hotel to see the head porter, accompanied by three of the Maharaja's servants, heaving luggage out of the lift. 'At once I jumped to the conclusion that he had made up his mind not to delay his journey to Paris any longer.' The Valet made an excuse to explain his own abrupt departure and got his luggage suitably arranged too – marked for Cannes and taken to the railway station. For an hour and a half he waited for the party to appear on the platform.

Well aware that the Maharaja, who claimed to be descended from the Sun God, was spiteful, ruthless and viciously unpredictable, the Valet carried out his surveillance with extreme caution. Edward Wood, Lord Halifax, would later tear apart the Maharaja's character in a coruscating portrait which conveyed what he reckoned was the 'evil' within him. As Viceroy of India, Halifax regarded the Maharaja as: 'A strong and baleful personality, a tall man of reptilian beauty and remarkable achievements, a philosopher, a scholar and fine orator'. But he viewed him with disgust and also believed him to be 'a victim of schizophrenia . . . a sadist . . . a pervert . . . whose continued presence on his throne was thought by many to be an affront to public decency'. Halifax explained: 'He was commonly supposed to have murdered more than one person who had crossed his path, and was said to have tethered a recalcitrant polo pony to the side of a hill in the hot weather, and made daily visits to watch it dying of thirst. He was a man who could literally produce a shiver in those who encountered him.'

The Valet saw the Maharaja – wearing a grey European suit and a white silk turban – and called him 'strikingly handsome'. Accompanied by his secretary and a gaggle of servants, who carried umbrellas, parasols and walking sticks decorated with beaten gold, his luggage was sitting on handcarts and drawn by the uniformed footmen of the hotel. The Valet's gaze fell on one thing alone. 'A big cash box took my eye at once. It contained, I conjectured, the loose money of the Maharaja, his jewels and other treasures. I began to think quickly about how I might get it.' The Valet said the job was 'not easy – for I was single-handed'. He also sensed that the servants' devotion to their master would be so great, and the penalty of losing any treasure so severe, that the slightest mistake would be fatal for him. The word 'fatal' was a particularly poignant and crucial one. For if the Maharaja, rather than the police, caught him, the Valet would breathe his last. The machinations began. 'Imagine me dancing about on the platform trying to give the railway servants or anyone else who might be about the impression that I was one of the party,' he said. As the luggage was loaded on to the Paris-bound van, he saw one servant collect the cash box and put it in a compartment of the train. 'I decided it was now or never. I waited till he turned into another carriage.'

The Valet entered the carriage through one door, picked up the box and walked out of the other side. He hurried down the long corridor of the train and emerged almost directly opposite the barrier near the booking office. The porter, checking tickets, was engrossed like everyone else in the departure of the Maharaja. The Valet asked him for directions to buy another ticket. The porter thrust his thumb over his shoulder and allowed the Valet to pass. Without a moment's delay he headed for the station courtyard and hailed a fiacre. 'I jumped in and told the *cocher* to drive as quickly as he could to the centre of the town, explaining that I wanted to retrieve something I had left behind at my hotel and be back in ten minutes before the train for Paris got under way.' The Valet asked to be taken to the Hôtel du Monde in the Rue de la Paix. He told the driver to wait for him. He got into the hotel and rushed to the back exit, which he knew led into a 'sort of backwater'. He was now in the lower part of Marseilles. 'I made for a seaman's lodging house where I had done business on a previous occasion. The barman was quite delighted to hear I had some jewellery to sell.'

The Maharaja was so rich that in the 1920s he could walk into a Mayfair showroom and pick out a Rolls-Royce Phantom II Tourer. The salesman had regarded his customer snootily, refusing to take the attempted purchase seriously. In retribution the Maharaja bought all seven cars on the forecourt and stipulated that the salesman should escort them back to India. When the cars gleamed in front of his palace, the Maharaja ordered that each one should be used only to collect waste and store other rubbish. The cars became the most expensive dustbins in the world. The man who now owned them had made his point. So, as the Valet opened the jewel box in a bedroom at the lodging house, he glimpsed the merest fraction of the Maharaja's fortune.

In the case he found a pearl necklace made up of four rows of stones. 'They were all graded. They sparkled with a light I have seldom seen in pearls,' he said. In each partition of the box, he found something different – gold studs, loose diamonds and rubies 'which shone with a lustre which made me long to run them through my fingers like a miser. I was delighted beyond measure at the extent of my haul.' He estimated the jewels were worth £100,000 – a sum which made the Dowager Duchess's gems, taken fourteen years earlier, almost insignificant in price and quality. Still carrying his trusty canvas bag embroidered with the letter S, he slipped it over the box and told the barman where the jewels had come from. The nervy barman accepted three gold studs as a bribe before recommending a fence to him – a man called 'Jean Coquellin', who was the Marseilles equivalent of Kammy Grizzard.

The Valet called on Coquellin and found him out on other business. He buried and marked the box beneath bushes in a nearby wood, and returned to wait for the fence in his own drawing room. At 11 p.m., after the Valet had retrieved the jewels, Coquellin appeared. 'From the first I must say I did not like the look of Jean Coquellin,' the Valet admitted. He described him as 'young, short, not over-intelligent', and said Coquellin had 'an eager-eyed, crafty, evil look about him which betokened treachery'. Wearing what the Valet thought was a 'comical' blue beret askew on his head, Coquellin was equally suspicious of the Valet. He told him: 'It's not safe to talk here. My servant is very suspicious and might overhear us talking. Let's go into my shed at the bottom of the garden.' Inside the shed, at the point at which the Valet was about to open the box, his body stiffened, like a line of stretched rope, after 'the weirdest scream I have ever heard in my life' broke through the air. 'It froze the blood in my veins, and jumping back from the bench with a startled look in my eyes, I was about to make for the door, thinking the place was haunted,' he said. Coquellin pulled him back by the arm and laughed in his face. The scream had come from a donkey. The Valet, regaining his composure, opened the box and withdrew the pearls. After letting the fence inspect them, and about to re-wrap the chain in tissue paper, he 'saw something which startled me more than the donkey had done'. He said: 'The eyes of Coquellin burned like two pieces of hot coal.' The Valet was intimidated. 'As much as I know about psychology, it took me some time to discover he was mad,' he said before asking: 'Have you ever looked into the eyes of a man who plans murder in his heart?' The rest was a blur. In the half-darkness Coquellin grabbed the pearls. Afraid, the Valet reached for a stick from a nearby bench with the intention of killing before being killed. Coquellin ran, vanishing into the unlit house, and returned with a revolver.

'If you don't hand over the jewels,' he said to the Valet, 'I am going to kill you.'

The Valet replied: 'You can kill me if you like and get the jewellery. But sooner or later the thing will be found out and you will be guillotined for it. Why not be sensible and work with me?'

Coquellin listened and ratcheted up his threat. Now he demanded money as well as the pearls.

'Not on your life,' said the Valet. 'The necklace is mine. I want it for myself. You can have some money and part of the other jewellery.'

Tucked beside the Maharaja's jewels was 1,000 francs in notes. 'You can have five hundred of it,' the Valet told Coquellin, who also had a handful of gold studs tipped into his hand in a bid to extinguish his temper. The promise and the ploy had no effect. The Valet said: 'He appeared to want all the money, and being by this time a bit unnerved, I did not know what to do. My great desire was to get rid of the incriminating box, and I suggested we should go in the direction of the sea so that I could weigh it with stones and throw it in.'

Coquellin had another idea. He demanded that the two of them walk to Marseilles, where the jewels would be sold and the profits split. Coquellin was still clutching the revolver, so the Valet agreed to lead the way. The box was eventually thrown in a sewage drain during the long trudge into the city, which took almost six hours. Arriving at 6 a.m., and finding an open café, the two men quarrelled again across one of its tables. As Coquellin, yelling wildly, began to complain about duplicity, the Valet swept up the jewels and fled with them. Coquellin chased him to a fountain opposite the zoological gardens. But, as a tram passed by, the Valet leapt on it – leaving his stranded 'partner' gesticulating angrily at him as he receded into the distance. Out of breath, heart pumping and without sleep, the Valet sought any respite he could find. 'I resolved to delay my departure for a day or two in case the police, en route for Paris, should be on the alert. It was a great mistake,' he said.

After sleeping in a small hotel, he returned to the centre of Marseilles. Coquellin was waiting for him. The Valet persuaded the mentally unstable fence to accompany him to another café. But Coquellin – for reasons the Valet was unable to explain because it appeared so senseless – had brought company with him: the police. 'On looking round, I saw a number of men closing in on me,' said the Valet, 'and I recognised the game was up. My pockets were full of jewels.' He made a token effort to elude his pursuers. 'Turning swiftly round, I sped through the door of the café on my right, tried to get to the garden and, finding no exit, ran upstairs, where I was met by a woman carrying a pail of water, who barred my way to the roof. There was nothing for it, but to dash downstairs again.' The detectives met him there with a pair of handcuffs.

The Valet told them his name was Henry Williams. Reporting on the theft, *The Times* was not alone in failing to connect the theft to the man who had once robbed the Dowager Duchess of Sutherland. It did no more than describe the thief as bearing 'a typically English name' – without enlightening its readers about the name itself. The Valet was variously described as 60 years old (untrue); from London (true); born in 1854 (untrue); part of an 'organised criminal gang' (also untrue) and with previous convictions for taking jewels (very true). The Paris-based *Petit Journal* was more explicit. On its front page, it called him a 'professional expert' and a 'correct gentleman' who had volunteered his criminal record with 'imperturbable composure'. It added that 'the misfortune' of the Maharaja was 'the main topic of conversation' in Marseilles.

Just like the Dowager Duchess, the Maharaja wanted no publicity – though for entirely different reasons. The Valet was charged only with stealing jewels from a secretary. The newspapers reported that the Maharaja 'showed no emotion over the loss', valued the jewels at only £24,000 and continued on to England after reporting the theft in Avignon. The decision to downgrade the theft masked more than wounded feelings. Conscious that news of it was sure to find its way back to India – he could hardly censor the French press – the Maharaja felt that any report which said his jewels had been stolen would make him appear far less intimidating to those he ruled with such vicious authority. He didn't dare allow the theft to make him look susceptible to common crooks. 'The sensational affair was hushed up,' said the Valet, aware of the benefit that brought its consolations: 'It probably saved me from being sent to Devil's Island for life.' The Valet, who had expected to crown the arc of his career with no more than a 24-hour stay in France, was sent down for five years in Nîmes. 'For some time my place of residence would be a castellated building with high walls,' he said.

In a coincidence, which sounds so contrived as to make it unbelievable, the Dowager Duchess of Sutherland fell ill as the Valet began his sentence. She died two weeks later, aged 63. The long obituaries and accompanying news reports did not gloss over the controversial landmarks of her life – the 'famous will case sequel', the prison term 'in luxury' and the theft of her jewels at the Gare du Nord, which placed her 'prominently before the public' again. The thief responsible for it settled into an unchanging pattern of meals, work and sleep. He was back in a tailor's shop, sewing and trimming and mending.

But far worse was to come.

The Great War was still being fought in the churned mud of France and Belgium when the Valet completed his sentence. On his release, at the beginning of 1917, he tried to raise some funds for his journey home. His lack of practice proved decisive. 'I snatched a bag containing £500 in change from a [Thomas] Cook's man at the railway station,' he revealed. By his own admission, he 'bungled the job' and was easily caught.

Only twenty days after leaving his cell, he was returned to it. 'I was sent back for another stretch of five', he said.

By the time he limped back to England – nine years after tearing off to Marseilles for his rendezvous with the Maharaja of Alwar and those enticing jewels – prison had begun to sow the rank seeds of failure in him. The Valet was virtually destitute; he had just enough money for his passage home – though, of course, no roof of his own when he got there. 'The French authorities turned me out of their country without a bean,' he said. 'I arrived in London in the early hours of a Sunday morning with only a franc in my pocket – cold, hungry and miserable, and out of tune with English life.' A cloud of gathered doubts returned with him. He seemed to be in a condition of irreparable decay.

By now the motor car had taken over almost completely from the horse-drawn cabs and hansoms. Red double-decker buses rattled across Westminster Bridge. Trams slid through the streets on cables. The soldiers who returned home from the war were burdened by guilt and tried to cope with memories of the carnage

and the loss of family and friends. The generation which immediately followed them were the Bright Young Things, the
pleasure-seekers and socialites, the gilded butterflies and the
extravagant smart set. These were the people not old enough to
have fought in France but certainly old enough to have been
influenced and partly blighted by the repercussions of it, and
convinced that the only antidote to its miseries and a dull fate was
a good time. The twenties were about to roar with the bohemian
flair of jazz and its new dances, the flamboyance of the flappers
and daring fashions. Again, the Valet was adrift; and this time he
was elderly and out of kilter. London was another city now; and
not his own. But he needed money, a place to sleep and the faint
glimmer of blue skies to come to sustain him.

Out of what he called 'sheer desperation', and full of quivering
uncertainty, he walked to Stoke Newington in the anticipation
that one person would give him a bed or enough cash to find a
room. Kammy Grizzard had a reputation for supporting criminals
who found themselves in dire straits. He marked it down as a
favour to be cashed in at a later date, which was advantageous to
a man who always needed someone to do his bidding. The Valet
arrived at Grizzard's door tired and dishevelled, far removed from
the spic and span man who had once defiantly occupied the dock
at Clerkenwell and asked Judge James McConnell for his extensive
wardrobe of clothes to be waiting for him on his release. Grizzard
was not at home. The Valet tramped all the way across London
again to Brick Lane, where he thought the fence would be
entertaining friends. He was told Grizzard had gone to Aldgate.
The Valet looked more bedraggled than ever, and his feet ached.
Grizzard neither expected nor wanted to see him. He treated the
Valet dismissively – certain that he could be of no further use to
him. As he told Grizzard about his plight, the Valet received no
reassuring signals. He said Grizzard was 'standoffish and unsym-
pathetic'. Just to get rid of him, Grizzard took two shillings out of

his jacket pocket and flipped them at the Valet, the coins spinning into his hand. 'It was an insult I never forgot,' he said. The Valet accepted the charity because he had no choice. But he waited for an opportunity, which he knew would come soon enough, to repay the slight with interest. 'I was determined to get my own back,' he said.

His chance came a few weeks later in Hatton Garden. From a distance he saw Grizzard in a taxi, leaving with two men he recognised as jewel thieves. He followed them to a hotel in Whitechapel, where he lingered as Grizzard met two more of his agents. 'For about twenty minutes I waited outside till the two came; then giving them time to settle down, I simply walked in and, with a quiet, "Kammy, I want a bit of my own back", I lifted the handbag he had beside him on the adjoining chair, and was out of the bar before he could realise what had happened.' Inside were jewels worth £500. He sold them to one of Grizzard's rivals in Brick Lane. 'It was a risky thing to do,' admitted the Valet. 'I might have had the whole underworld roused up against me, but for some reason Kammy was frightened of me; probably my audacity had scared him stiff, and beyond a threat or two I never heard from him again.' Another reason was the 54-year-old Grizzard's own failing state of health. He had bad eczema and diabetes, a condition which was slowly worsening. Early signs of tuberculosis were evident too. While the Valet occupied his cell in Nîmes, Grizzard had been locked up for his part in the Great Pearl Robbery of 1913, which involved snatching sixty-one pearls – insurance value £130,000 – in transit from Paris to London. The sickly Grizzard became another victim of Richard Muir's exhaustive prosecution technique. He was given a seven-year sentence and spent most of the latter half of it in hospital. He retained a grip on his cohorts, but was less able now to deploy it. The Valet had struck Grizzard when he was enfeebled; too physically brittle to strike, too fragile to concern himself with retribution.

Triumph over Grizzard, whatever the circumstances, restored a modicum of confidence to the Valet. At Victoria station he saw a 'beautiful woman' accompanied by two servants. 'As she was carrying the bag herself – that is how the game is given away – I knew it must contain something valuable.' When she laid it down, the Valet swept in and found it contained £800 worth of valuables. Soon, he said, as 'befitting a man of my position I was living in great style'.

According to the Valet, life became sweet again. He insisted his rise was as sudden as his fall had been. Back came the smartest suits and the handmade shoes. Back came the frequent visits to new clubs and silver service restaurants. Back came the whisky and the bottles of champagne. He re-established himself among the criminal fraternity. Scotland Yard had to watch him with the vigilance of twenty years before. The whiskered veterans had gone: Walter Dew retired, basking in the fame and financial comfort that capturing Dr Crippen had brought him; Walter Dinnie emigrated to New Zealand where he became Commissioner of Police; Frank Froest wrote critically acclaimed and popular who-dunnits, which were among the first books to include authentic accounts of police procedure.

The detective assigned to his cases was Edward Gough, whom the Valet regarded as 'the only live-wire I ever really feared'. He was 'alert and zealous' and dogged, as if he'd made the appre-hension of the Valet his sole reason for becoming a detective in the first place. The Valet found it hard to hide from him. 'Wherever I went Gough was always in the background,' he said. 'If a jewel robbery took place, no matter whether I had a hand in it or not, he would find out where I was living and force me out.' Whether it was the theft of a diamond traveller's leather bag (value £700), nimbly lifted from the luncheon room of a Camberwell hotel, or the disappearance of a wooden box with metal bindings containing jewels and a plate (value £3,500) from the cloakroom of King's Cross station, the Valet headed Gough's list of suspects.

In a club in Haymarket, he was trapped in a 2 a.m. raid involving fifty policemen who were intent on prosecuting anyone caught for illegal gambling. Along with a group of other gamblers he was marched to Vine Street station, and then taken to Marlborough Street court next morning. If Gough came to hear about it, the Valet thought, he'd be arrested for previous thefts which the policeman suspected he'd carried out but could not prove. He had to get away. 'I watched for my opportunity and, edging towards the door of the court, I suddenly darted into the passage, ran swiftly into Oxford Street, where, hailing a taxi, I drove as far from the court as possible.'

A few weeks later Gough picked up the Valet and arranged what his victim said was 'quite a little reception in my cell' at Vine Street. 'About three hundred detectives of the "new school" came to familiarise themselves with the features of Harry the Valet,' he remembered. Gough filed them through the cells to make sure everyone knew exactly what the Valet looked like. 'In the course of this chat,' said the Valet, 'it made it all the more difficult for me to continue the work I had been doing on this side of the Channel.' Gough could not find enough evidence to press further charges. The Valet was let off with a five-shilling fine for fleeing from Marlborough Street court. But the added attention from Gough forced him to lie low. Within a few months the detective had worn him down. The Valet said: 'The man with the immaculate clothes and his uncanny trick of turning up when I least expected him became a menace to me. I saw him at the breakfast table, he loomed up in front of me at dinner, I dreamed at nights that he was chasing me over the roof or round and round the first class saloon of the boat to Boulogne. It was insufferable and I knew that unless he retired from the service or I retired from the business, it meant another spell of penal servitude, which was not for a man of my age and expensive habits. I wanted to end my days in comfort.'

The Valet began to feel a melancholic nostalgia for the past; for the way things had been in his halcyon days, as though he'd led a rustic life. Sentimentality is almost always a lie, but crime definitely was different now, and the criminal had to be a different – and far younger – breed to adapt to it. 'Business, owing to the changing fashion of life, was not what it used to be,' he said, as if it was so unfair. Time had rushed by. First he was 20. Then 30, 50 – and now 70. The years coalesced, making it impossible to separate them or to know how the passage of each had occurred. He spoke like a solid Victorian, trapped in an age which he neither cared for nor understood and who preferred gas lamps to electric light, horses to engines, the music hall to the picture house. Morals and manners had changed and adjustments were torturesome for someone so dug into old ways which had an appealing simplicity. The new ways just seemed exotic and outlandish.

'The advent of the motor car made a great difference to me,' said the Valet, reflecting on fundamental change. 'Formerly, when any member of the aristocracy planned a visit to the country, they went by rail. Now the limousine was drawn up at the front door of Berkeley Square or North Audley Street. The jewel box was carried by the butler and before you had a chance to get near it the car was spinning along on its way to the open country.'

As if raising his hands above his head to signal his defeat by Gough, the Valet added: 'Because my adversary did not seem like retiring, I decided that I must. Wherever I went Gough seemed to get on my track generally an hour or two late, but with such unfailing regularity that I felt it was only a matter of time before he ran me to earth.' A career which began with the lifting of a gold pocket watch ended because of the diligence of a detective, who was only a squealing infant when the Valet served his sentence in Pentonville in the mid-1870s. He resolved to give up crime entirely and 'go quietly' into the night – just as he had done when

Dew and Dinnie arrested him at Cathcart Road. After doing so the Valet claimed: 'On the whole I am happier [because] I am finished with crime.' He sounded like Prospero abjuring his magic, asking to be pardoned and set free.

He was emphatic that in retirement 'I do not touch a penny which I do not make honestly'. He also explained: 'The police, recognising virtue, whether it is forced on a man by circumstance or conscience, left me alone.' Gough faded from his nightmarish dreams, and the Valet insisted, as if to reassure everyone of his new-found probity: 'I have lost the feeling which every criminal, even the most successful, has – that there is always a hand dangling over his shoulder as he walks along the street.'

Putting a full stop to his story – and suggesting that crime can pay – he said he possessed 'sufficient capital to keep me in luxury all the days of my life' and was living in a 'little cottage in the country'. The rest was silence. With those words the man called Harry the Valet and known as Williams and Johnson, Thomas and Jones, Jackson and Matthews – and who said his real name was Henry Thomas – just disappeared from public view, as if vanishing into one of London's famous peasouper fogs. No one heard from him again and he left no footprints to follow.

Which was exactly the way he wanted it.

Afterword

Look your last
on all things lovely

The truth – rarely pure and never simple – always sat in one of those hard to reach places where Harry the Valet was concerned. He preferred it that way, a fact sharpened by his memoir in the *Weekly News,* which contained deliberate obstructions, evasions and downright falsehoods. The Valet was convinced no one would ever be able to unearth some of the salient details of his life, which – even near its end – he remained unwilling to share. The most significant was his real name. He had good reason to believe that anyone who tried to uncover it – Scotland Yard and nosy criminologists alike – would be unsuccessful.

In the late nineteenth century, and during the opening decades of the twentieth, it was difficult to find out the identity of someone who wanted to remain anonymous. Family records were incomplete or inaccurate. The fundamentals of the census return – name, birth-date and birthplace – were frequently contradictory, inconsistent or wrong. The reliability of the census hinged on the ability of those who gathered the information for it: discrepancies in the intelligence, diligence and enterprise of the field force of enumerators were matched by discrepancies on the page. The government only required that enumerators should be 'temperate, orderly and respectable'. They were told to conduct themselves 'with strict propriety'. Some found themselves intimidated by what one compiler called 'some very nice language at my expense', which meant the forms were rushed affairs. The information given on them could be unreliable for a number of other reasons: ignorance, carelessness, lack of thought or deliberate dissembling. A brave soul in Cornwall voluntarily disclosed that he was a 'retired smuggler' – he lived just doors away from a 'retired customs officer' too – but for the most part anyone who had something to conceal told lies and got clean away with it. No exhaustive checks or cross-checks were made to disprove the evidence. Bigamous marriages, illegitimate children and incest were consequently camouflaged. A father's name was often left off or invented (he'd be given an untraceably ordinary name and occupation) if he was either unknown to the mother, which was common, or if the child was born out of wedlock. These sealed records were hard to source even for Scotland Yard, and occasionally harder still to decipher because the legibility of handwriting varied. This wasn't the only difficulty when it came to tracing the Valet. Although he counted as hot copy, the newspapers were frequently erratic too. Names in court were misheard and so misspelt in print. Aliases were given, protecting those who stood in the dock or the witness box. There were also so many newspapers – in myriad editions – that it became a test of patience and an act of perseverance to jigsaw individual reports together to produce a coherent narrative.

Time has simplified and clarified. Now it is possible to make the dry bones of history dance, digging up and dragging to the surface what the Valet strived to keep buried for so long. Not even someone of such shadowy complexity can hide completely in a digital age when ancestral records and historic newspapers share cyberspace, and an archival dive into Victorian ink is possible through microfilm and bound volumes. What emerges emphasises how much the Valet sought to cloak his real name – even when it seemed unnecessary to do so. None of the crime anthologies or articles which highlighted the Valet's theft of the Dowager Duchess of Sutherland's jewels as a famous crime ever managed to get to the core of him. George Dilnot's *Great Detectives*, which appeared over eighteen months after the Valet's pieces in the *Weekly News*, claimed he was Harry Villiers, and said he 'wore the name with an air as he wore his clothes', adding that he had been 'held up to the world as a sort of super-Raffles'. In his 1934 book, *Prisoner at the Bar*, Anthony L. Ellis settled on the name William Williams for the Valet. Even Walter Dew's 1938 autobiography *I Caught Crippen*, which became an instant best-seller and added to the policeman's stellar celebrity, lazily called him either Harry or William Johnson. The Valet was just too much of a puzzle ever to be solved back then.

His account in the *Weekly News* was designed to make money. But it served another purpose too. Aware of his own mortality, he was anxious to confound and correct the authors who had written about him. The newspaper offered more than the chance to leave a record of his life: it enabled him to put his own slant on it, laying false trails which were then impossible to contradict, and to compete against the unauthorised versions. Some of these were wildly off the mark and either ignored or reported statements at his trial inexactly.

'The confessions of Harry the Valet' is rather like William Morgan's celebrated 1682 map of London. Just as Morgan depicted a slightly sanitised London after the Great Fire, capturing the city the way he imagined it – with the streets wider, the parks more spacious, the prisons and workhouses unmarked and St Paul's Cathedral already built – so, in places, the Valet shaped the landscape of his life to fit an ideal. He omitted some things from his story, slid others into it and in parts gave distinctive shading to his past. The odd lie was packaged as truth to suit his agenda and to protect him from further police intrusion. On the whole, however, the Valet's confession withstands scrutiny. It is – again like Morgan's map – substantially accurate, packed with verifiable detail and finely records most of the contours and cardinal points. It is also painted with watercolour brightness.

Precautions were nevertheless taken. If the Valet believed anyone from whom he'd stolen was still alive, he would not name them, such as the Maharaja of Alwar. Or he would disguise them, such as Countess Howe, who lost her jewels on the way to Cowes. Or he would refer to them by pseudonyms, such as the love of his life. Maude Richardson appeared on the page under neither her stage name nor her real one, Louisa Lancey. The Valet referred to her instead as Hetty F——. He declined to date some thefts. A few more were rolled forward or backwards along the time-rail of his career. He wanted to ensure that Scotland Yard could never resurrect and reopen cold cases and hold him accountable for them.

He indulged in only four glaring pieces of fabrication – each of them a whopping fib.

The first came in the retelling of his theft of the Dowager Duchess of Sutherland's gems. He disingenuously claimed that, as he arrived at the Gare du Nord, 'the last thing in the world I was thinking about was jewels'. He insisted he was 'only scanning the face of every Englishwoman I saw coming towards me' in the search for Maude. It wholly contradicted the evidence he unwillingly gave to Dew and Walter Dinnie about skilfully gleaning inside information about the Dowager Duchess's move- ments at the Hotel Bristol. It also went against his boast, which he made time and again to improve his standing, that he thoroughly researched each theft before carrying it out and reduced his crime to a mathematical science.

Far worse – the second untruth – was his invention of Mary,

who supposedly became his wife in 1874 at St Luke's Church and whose death he said turned him from a casual participant in crime into someone determined to become a prime exponent of it. This was a piece of fiction. The Valet could not have returned home to the picture-framing shop in Great Arthur Street and heard his mother tearfully recount the circumstances of his wife's death. The shop in Great Arthur Street was sold before the end of the 1860s. And his mother died in 1869 – five years before he claimed the conversation with her took place. The Valet did marry – but not until February 1882, at St Mary's Church in Lambeth. His bride was Katherine Clee, the daughter of a Cambridge stonemason. She died alone in 1891 of cirrhosis of the liver. She was 33. Her death certificate includes another fantasy. Her occupation is described as 'Wife of a valet to a foreign gentleman on travel'. The line covers the Valet's obvious desertion of her. He never had been a gentleman's valet, but the pretence explained away the long absences to her friends and the rest of polite society. The masquerade was far preferable to Katherine than admitting that her husband was a jewel thief – for 1891 was also the year in which the Valet went to jail for stealing a wallet from the Holborn Restaurant.

In seeking to understand why the Valet was so coy about the Dowager Duchess's gems, and so anxious to invent one wife and hide another, it's relevant to remember what Rousseau said: 'It is not the criminal things which are the hardest to confess, but the ridiculous and the shameful.' To argue that he merely stumbled across the Dowager Duchess and her jewel case is easier than admitting that a ruinous and uncontrollable love drove him to a desperate deed; a deed, moreover, that he orchestrated purely because of that passion and which led to his downfall. Far better – and far less embarrassing – to maintain that the major calamity of his life was motivated by what he called the 'old instincts' of thievery rather than the even older instincts of sexual attraction.

The Valet and Maude are proof that the hottest love often leads to the coldest end. For the striking thing about his 'confessions' is the way she drops out of the story shortly after his arrest. He does not discuss Maude's appearance in court. He does not refer to his repeated pleas to see her, which Dew and Walter Dinnie remembered and wrote about. Nor does he talk about his most magnanimous gesture of all – allowing Maude's evidence to go unchallenged, as though he was too gallant, too weak or too scared of upsetting her to refute its most blatant exaggerations. And he makes no reference whatsoever to his continued reaching out for her, the awful waiting for a letter or a visit. Maude is never mentioned again once his trial ends, as if he'd been able to cauterise his feelings for her instantly and without discomfort. The real reason is more banal. She simply fell into the Rousseau category of 'the shameful'. In particular, letting her damn his character in the witness box without so much as a token protest suggested he was like a lapdog, still entranced by his mistress's presence, however much she despicably neglected or mistreated him. There is no doubt that the love-drunk Valet sobered up in prison, where he passed through the long transformative stages known to anyone who has loved and lost and allowed both of these states of heightened emotion to consume them. The longing and painful ache for Maude became a hurt bewilderment at her indifference and lack of affection. It then turned, slowly at first, into resentment and anger. This led to the realisation that he'd been a simpleton all along; and also that what he'd experienced was a superficial crush – not love but merely the desire for it. What came next was humiliation – a deep blush whenever he thought about his insane over-reactions to her, and blank incomprehension about how he'd allowed himself to degenerate into such an awful, enfeebled state. In love there is always one that kisses and one that offers the cheek. The Valet always took the subservient role, and came to realise and regret it.

The abominable treatment of his wife and his refusal to acknowledge her was different. It grew out of guilt and expediency.

Judged at its brightest the Valet was taking poetic licence in uprooting Katherine from his life. Judged at its worst – which is the way in which we are compelled to see it – the act was duplicitous and coldly calculating. But it doesn't take much of an imaginative leap to conclude that the terse exchanges he pretended to have with the fictional Mary were actually those he had with Katherine. Instead of 'living happily together' for a while with Mary, he did so with Katherine. The rest of the relationship followed the pattern that the Valet outlined in his articles. When, as he conceded, 'married life began to pall a little', he drifted shiftlessly back to pubs and his beery friends, the racetrack and his beloved horses. The quarrels he quoted with the disconsolate Mary, who challenged him about his drinking and gambling, were those he surely had with Katherine too: especially her fear that 'something dreadful' would happen to him and the barbed reminder of his promises not to return home at all hours. The chauvinist, uncaring way in which he warned her off must have been delivered to Katherine as well – his claim that 'a man must have friends' and that it was 'a mistake when a wife tries to interfere'. Simply replace Mary's name with Katherine's and you get an idea of the atmosphere in the marital home.

The Valet admitted that he killed his wife 'by inches'. But the fact that he called her Mary rather than Katherine was only partly to do with his extreme shame. It was also because he could not risk highlighting her existence. For anyone who knew he'd married her would also be able to discover his real name. And the Valet could not bring himself to give up the secret he most cherished – which became his third lie.

In the *Weekly News*, he revealed only a half-truth, as if subscribing to Byron's opinion that 'there should always be some foundation of fact in the most airy fabric'. He *was* Henry Thomas

– but even in conceding this he gave away only his Christian and middle names. Indeed, the only document on which his middle name appears is his marriage certificate.

The Valet's full name was Henry Thomas Sands.

On the 1861 census, he appears as an eight-year-old at 24 Great Arthur Street in St Luke's. By 1871 – with the family fractured after the death of both parents – he is living with his sister Maria and her husband George Cosburn at 5 Park Cottage in East Ham. And in 1881 he appears as a visitor at 26 Panton Street, Cambridge, with Katherine Clee and her family. The couple are falsely listed as having already married, and he is similarly falsely listed as being 25. Within a month of the census being taken, Katherine's father, Charles, was sentenced to four months' hard labour for receiving stolen goods. There is no record of the goods which the police found in his possession or of their supplier. The chief suspect, however, is obvious in retrospect.

The 1871 census describes the Valet as an apprentice stone-mason, which was also the trade of his sister Maria's spouse. The census taken in 1881 calls him a clerk. But on his marriage certificate, which also corrects the inaccuracy over his age, he becomes a commissioning agent. His signature at the bottom of the marriage banns is beautifully crafted – a lovely array of loops and loosely flamboyant strokes, as though calligraphy was impor-tant to him. There is another piece of clinching evidence. Moss Lipman, who stood beside him in the dock, is revealed not as a friend or associate but as his nephew. Lipman's mother was the Valet's sister, Mary Ann, and she married her husband Benjamin, a general dealer, in the early 1870s after the two of them, like the prospective Mr and Mrs Sands, passed themselves off as man and wife on the previous census because the lovers already had a 12-month-old child.

The Valet not only concealed his real name in the *Weekly News*. He hid his real circumstances, too, which became lie number four.

The surface appearance of serenity and breezy contentment which he tried to convey – and buff to a shine in the final paragraphs of his last article – was a sham. What lay beneath it was gloom and disillusion. He was playing a part again – just as he'd once done to infiltrate the aristocracy or look inconspicuous as he lingered around first-class rail compartments.

At the end of his life he didn't own a 'little place in the country' where he could watch the drowse of sunset from his window and marvel at the cathedral of trees around him. And certainly he didn't have 'sufficient capital to keep me in luxury' for the rest of his days either. The clues are found not between the lines of his words, but in the photographs of him in the *Weekly News*. In the first he is sitting at a desk and peering over a pair of round-framed spectacles, which have slid down to the bridge of his nose. The face is slightly gaunt, revealing hollowed cheeks and a crinkled forehead. His pallor seems to be the colour of china clay. The hair, once so abundant, has receded on the crown. The moustache is straggly and misshapen; slightly unkempt too, as though a shaky hand has lost control of a cut-throat razor. The eyes are heavily lidded, the pupils as dark as shards of coal. His mouth is wide and thin, but on the brink of breaking into a lopsided smile. With a half-puzzled expression, he stares directly at the camera, as if he wasn't quite prepared for the shot and the photographer has caught him unawares. All that he had been – a wealthy man about town – is missing from his pose, bearing and clothes; he looks as if he has shrivelled inside his suit. But all that he'd become ought to have been clear to anyone who looked hard enough at each image. He was like a candle that had burnt down, leaving only the flickering existence of a tiny flame. If you stare hard enough, it's still possible to conjure up the image of a much younger Valet, handsome enough to captivate Maude and impress the newspapers during his trial with both his cheeky countenance and good looks: the bright eyes and once-firm line of the jaw can be superimposed on to the faded reality.

By the time the *Weekly News* signed him up, the Valet's great days were over. The passing years had stolen all things from him one by one. First to go was his talent, which died long before his body. Now he was living on scraps; all he had left was whatever he could remember. There was no longer a rail of fine suits and a separate shelf for his selection of bowler and coachman hats. There was barely a case or a bag in which to store his belongings. He lived week to week, each of them formless and featureless, and wandered nomadically from one lodging place to another. The man who used to think nothing of spending £50 on food and champagne and dined in London's leading restaurants was surviving on a few shillings and taking his meals in greasy spoons. He'd gone from wine to moonshine and from high life to low life. His most frequent home was an eight-by-seven-foot cubicle in a run-down corner of Camden Town.

The Rowton Houses – which became cockney rhyming slang for trousers – were described as 'the working man's hotels', but were in reality hostels, a very decent dosshouse for the impoverished, the damned, the down at heel or the transient workforce of labourers and builders that passed through the capital because of a shortage of work in the provinces. Their creator was the politician and philanthropist Montagu William Lowry-Corray, the first and last Lord Rowton. He was a man of 'considerable wealth and some distinction' and a lifelong bachelor, who sometimes 'blushed at my self-indulgent life' of town mansions and country weekends. He was exactly the sort of figure that the Valet would once have targeted – a well-to-do, always finely dressed gentleman with a wallet full of notes. Rowton was 'profoundly shocked' by the state of the homeless hostels in London, which he studied on behalf of a charitable trust. He decided to build his own. His aim was outlined in what became known as the Rowton

House rhymes, written by the author W. A. Mackenzie. One includes the verse:

> Enter here and hide your fear, your sin, your sorrow
> Buy a bed: perhaps you may be buying slumber

George Orwell stayed in a Rowton House during his research for *Down and Out in Paris and London* in 1932 and called them 'always full to overflowing'. Orwell regarded them as the most superior of the hostels; though, of course, he'd become accustomed to living rough for the sake of his literature and on behalf of his social and political beliefs. Luxury for him was a bar of carbolic soap.

Those who slept in a Rowton House passed through a clanking turnstile after buying a shilling ticket for the night. The ticket entitled the holder to a bed, a chair, a chamber pot, and storage and hooks for clothing. There was no adornment or flourish, but each house was arranged like a hotel. A resident could get his hair cut in the barber's shop, light a cigarette or pipe in the smoking room with its wooden bench-type seats or read books and newspapers in the library at polished teak tables. Meals were taken in a wide, long dining room with sixty-four tables which could seat 512 men. There was a communal wash house. The near-destitute weren't patronised or lectured. But there were strict rules to obey and woe betide anyone who broke them. These included no cooking, no spitting, no singing in the cubicle, no gambling and (virtually) no alcohol. But it was possible to obtain three adequate hot meals a day for 2s. 3d. there.

The Valet stayed at Camden's Arlington House – a vast, red-brick edifice of turrets studded with serried rows of tiny windows and spread over six floors and a basement. Built in 1905 it became the last and the largest of the six Rowton Houses. The Valet occupied one of 1,003 beds. By the time of his arrival in the mid-

1920s Arlington House was full of ex-servicemen, sent by charitable institutions, as well as the unemployed and the unemployable, who bundled themselves into its warm rooms.

He was coping with absolute loss – of position, prestige and glamour – and the fact that he'd now become what he had always dreaded being: an anonymous, drab, doddering figure. He was no longer the Valet. Instead, he was the ailing, brittle and very plain Henry Sands – the one person he'd always strived not to be. Given his lifestyle, and the fact that he'd spent almost two decades in various jails, it was remarkable that he'd lived so long; especially in an era when the average lifespan for men was 64 to 66, preventive medicine wasn't advanced and there was no National Health Service.

But death was waiting to claim him.

On the morning of 5 November 1929, he complained of chest pains. The porter of Arlington House took him to St Pancras Hospital and registered him there at 10.47 a.m. A few hours later the man who was Harry the Valet – society crook, jewel thief extraordinaire, lover of a Gaiety Girl – died, aged 76.

There is a scribbled note of his admission. It looks a hasty piece of work, the doctor's handwriting an untidy scrawl of poorly shaped letters, words that run into one another and crooked sentences that threaten to spill out of the box allocated to them. Amid this storm of ink, it is difficult to understand the messages contained within the note. You squint at it. You turn the page as though tilting it at an angle might make reading easier. You have to stare hard and trust in guesswork. The construction is also terse, as if whoever wrote it was sending a telegram. One short phrase stands out because it captures a final sorrow. It constitutes the Valet's last recorded words. The doctor writes:

States no friends

This is clearly the Valet's answer to a doctor's question. In response to it he had to admit that there was no one to care for him or to say goodbye. At his funeral a week later, there was no one to mourn either. As he had nothing to leave, there was no will. And as he knew no one – and no one then knew him – there was no death notice. The only survivor of the Sands family was Mary Ann, who did not die until 1935. The likelihood is that she distanced herself from her wayward brother as soon as her son Moss, who died in 1910, became embroiled in the theft of the Sutherland jewels.

On the Valet's own death certificate he was classified as a stonemason – another answer he gave either to further questioning from the doctor or to Arlington House on his admission there. The refuge was primarily 'home' to current or retired tradesmen; and in such a confined space – where meagre possessions might go missing easily – he dared not own up to having been a thief. But this last description of him is the essential Valet – true but not entirely the full truth and also the statement of a singular and irrelevant fact that obscures much more pertinent ones.

He occupies a pauper's grave in the Islington and St Pancras cemetery: 190 acres which border Coldfall Wood and the North Circular Road. The graveyard's focal point is a Gothic-style Episcopal Chapel, cruciform and made of Bath stone and Kentish Rag. The tip of its spire rises above the leafy boughs of oak and ash trees, pines and yews, hawthorns and limes. In between the meandering pathways and avenues wildflowers poke up from beside graves. The Valet lies in section 7U in grave number two, which overlooks Viaduct Road. The visible graves in this part of the cemetery – only a two-minute walk from the main gate – are weather-beaten stubs of grey stone: worn, chipped and rough. Some have sunk almost completely beneath the lush, tufted grass. Others list and lean as if a mighty hand has pushed them. The inscriptions have been rubbed away so that once-tender epitaphs are incomplete or indecipherable, and names have to be pieced together from an alphabet that Nature has eroded. Tiptoeing through it, you realise that in most of these graves are men and women no longer spoken of, who lived lives which are no longer remembered and can never be brought to mind again because the ravaging sweep of rain and the bite of hard frosts has made them unidentifiable.

The Valet's grave is beneath an impenetrable thicket of scrub, leaves and brambles. Overhanging the ground are heavy branches of trees to shade it, as if offering it an added layer of camouflage. It is a supreme irony that the man who hid so expertly in life is now undiscoverable in death too.

There is a further irony. For Maude's death was almost identical. She left London and moved to Brighton, where she felt so at home. At the end of a life of too much alcohol, she was taken from her rented, three-storey terraced home in College Street to Elm Grove House, an austere and formidable-looking former workhouse with the architectural embellishment of a clock tower. In 1930 it became a specialised refuge for the aged and infirm, which is what Maude had become. She died there in March 1932, under her married name of Louisa Andrew. She was 69 and impoverished to the degree that no memorial marks her resting place in the City Cemetery, which sits behind a wall of Sussex stone and flint. It is logged only in letters and numbers: ZGF 101. The roof of Elm Grove can be seen from the approximate site of her grave, somewhere in an immaculately neat, well-clipped expanse of lawn. Beyond the trees, the town dips and curves towards the sea, where boats with sails as white as freshly laundered linen track the shoreline.

On Maude's death certificate there is no mention that the frail, delicate and prematurely elderly woman it describes was once an actress, a beautiful magnet for the stage-door Johnnies and the paramour of Europe's foremost jewel thief. In the space reserved

*Maude Richardson, who could never recapture her reputation – or
her beauty – in her final, declining years.*

for her occupation, she is referred to as 'the widow of Lieutenant
Andrew'. Like the Valet's, the death of a performer who once
adored publicity and acclamation went unreported.

The jewel thief and the actress each looked their last on all
things lovely without the wider world being aware of it.

Arthur Conan Doyle once had a dejected and bored Sherlock
Holmes complain to Dr Watson that 'life is commonplace, the
papers are sterile; audacity and romance seem to have passed for
ever from the criminal world'. He forgot Henry Sands – aka Harry
the Valet – who was both audacious and romantic. He seems an
astonishingly fictional creation, as though he was born on the inky
page rather than in mid-Victorian England. He was Raffles made
flesh and could have been a character in *'The Red-Headed League'*

or '*The Noble Bachelor*'. It's said that E. W. Hornung based Raffles on the poet, penal reformer and criminologist George Ives. But, like anyone else who picked up a newspaper in late 1898 and early 1899, Hornung will have read of the Valet's theft of the Dowager Duchess of Sutherland's jewels, and did so while he was actually writing or rewriting *The Amateur Cracksman*. He surely felt he was experiencing wondrous pre-cognition; or reached the conclusion that real life was partly imitating his imagination.

The Valet's end was wretched. The path towards it, however, was lit with bright flares, which illuminated one of crime's braver spirits and a man who could out-posture Narcissus. We are able to say of the Valet what Keats once said of Burns: 'We can see horribly clear in the works of such a man his whole life, as if we were God's spies'. After studying the Valet's works and life, the verdict has to be that here was someone who co-operated in his own downfall through a fatal weakness for excess and extremes. In this process of dogged self-destruction he turned his career into a wreck and himself into a piece of wreckage. But it's equally clear that he wanted it no other way and was prepared to live on no other terms. He was creative, persuasive and intelligent enough to have been successful in a legitimate role almost of his choice. But he deliberately chose crime because he was first rate at it and did not want to be second rate at anything else. Most of all, he did not want to be ordinary. It explains why he treated jewel thievery like a competitive sport, and regarded himself as a sportsman.

Like every life it was full of might-have-beens. There were decisive moments when he could have pulled away from crime. At several stages he had enough money to cut an alternative route for himself in which pilfering gems would have been unnecessary. He could have shed his criminal ways as easily as a suit of old clothes. But the key to understanding him is that his imperative – like a central fire within – was pure enjoyment and visceral thrills. To most it seemed a shallow existence. To him it represented fulfilment. The dark talent of stealing jewels and cashing in on the profits came naturally. This never left him because it was embedded in the marrow of the man.

In old age, as he dwelt on the remembrance of things past, he tried to pretend it wasn't so. 'If I saw the Koh-i-noor diamond lying in the front garden,' he said, 'I would fetch the nearest policeman to carry it back to its place among the Crown jewels.'

No one who knew Harry the Valet ever believed a word of it.

Acknowledgements

Finally, I would especially like to thank (as ever) my agent Gráinne Fox for her advice, patience and good humour; my editor at Century Ben Dunn (who dispatched me on the hunt for Harry the Valet); Century's Jack Fogg and Briony Nelder, and finally Emma Grey for the wonderful cover depiction of The Valet.

Author's Notes

For anyone studying the 1920s, it's fortunate that the pages of most newspapers of the era were smothered in words – small, dense type, which often difficult to read for those (like me) without perfect vision, but crowded with detail and colour. 'Harry the Valet' wrote six articles for *The Weekly News*. They constitute a 'mini' book. I imagine the first part alone, covering a broadsheet page and three quarters, would fill nearly a dozen pages of one of today quality papers.

The opening piece, published on March 27 1926, was called Confessions of Harry The Valet: Told by Himself. The second (April 3) was sub-titled: How He Carried Out a Great Coup. The third (April 10) was Inside Story of a Famous Jewel Robbery. The fourth (April 17) was How I Robbed Famous Actress. The fifth (April 24) was Midnight Interview with Armed Madman. The final part was headlined How I Robbed Kammy Grizzard and sub-titled: Unceasing Vigilance of Famous Sleuth Forces Me to Retire. The articles are descriptive and vivid, and also contain the dialogue which I quote between him and Maude and his other associates. He also figures in several books, mostly prominently Walter Dew's I Caught Crippen, Blackie 1938; C L McCuler Stevens' Famous Crimes and Criminals (Stanley Paul undated), Anthony L Ellis'

Prisoner at the Bar: Story-Studies of the Criminal Mind (Heath Cranton, 1934) and N Connell's Walter Dew: The Man Who Caught Crippen (Sutton 2005).

Some of the police who chased him figure in George Dilnot's: Great Detectives (Geoffrey Bles 1927). The Valet – and Grizzard – each feature in James Morton's Gangland: The Early Years (Time Warner 2003). Grizzard is also in the biography of Richard Muir (listed in the books section)

The newspapers latched on enthusiastically to The Valet's story.

It is worth pointing out that the coverage of some of those in the Commonwealth was comprehensive. In certain cases these papers seemed to use every line sent to them from London by Fleet Street reporters or agencies. Below is a breakdown of the sources – apart from The Valet's own story and the books already mentioned – which I found most useful (other than those which appear in the main text).

BOOKS

The sights, scents, customs, working and business life of London from the mid-Victorian to the 1930s:

Arthur M: Lost Voices of the Edwardians, Harper Collins, 2006

Ackroyd, P: London, The Biography, Chatto 2000

Baedeker, K: Baedeker's Guide: London and its Environs 1900, Old House Books

Best, G: Mid-Victorian Britain, 1985

Booth, C: The Life and Labour of the People of London, 1903

Diamond, M: Victorian Sensation, Anthem Press, 2003

Dickens, C (junior), Dickens's Dictionary of London, 1888; Ensor, R: England 1870–1914, OUP 1936 and subsequent editions

Fay, C R, Life and Labour in the Nineteenth Century, Nonsuch 2000 (first pub 1920)

Fletcher, G: London Overlooked, Hutchinson, 1964

The London Nobody Knows, Hutchinson, 1962

Hart-Davis, A: What the Victorians Did for Us, Headline 2001

Harvie C and H C G Matthew, Nineteenth-Century Britain, Oxford, 2000

Hattersley, R: The Edwardians, Little Brown, 2004

Hodgson, G: People's Century, BBC, 1995

Jackson, L: A Victorian Dictionary of London, Anthem Press, 2007

Low, D M: London is London, Chatto and Windus, 1949

Paterson, M: Life in Victorian Britain, A Social History of Queen Victoria's Reign, Running Press 2008

Picard, L: Victorian London, The Life of a City 1840–1870, Weidenfeld 2005

Sweet, M: Inventing the Victorians, Faber, 2001

Taylor, D J: Bright Young People: The Rise and Fall of a Generation 1918–1940, Chatto, 2007

White, J: London in the 19th Century, Vintage, 2008

Wilson, A N: The Victorians, Hutchinson 2002

—— After the Victorians, Hutchinson, 2005

—— London, A Short History, Weidenfeld, 2004.

The Victorian poor, middle and upper classes:

Debrett's (Various Years)

Greenwood, J: The Wilds of London, 1874

Mayhew, H: London Labour and the London Poor, 1851

Rose, J: The Intellectual Life of the British Working Classes, Yale 2001

Thomson, E P: The Making of the English Working Classes, Victor Gollancz, 1963

Thomson, J: Victorian London Street Life, Dover 1994

Crime, punishment, pick-pockets and the role of the police in Victorian Britain

Browne, D G: The Rise of Scotland Yard, Harrap, 1956

Camp, J: Holloway Prison, The Place and the People, David and Charles, 1974

Chesney, K: The Victorian Underworld, Penguin (third edition) 1974

Dell, S: The Victorian Policeman, Shire, 2008

Dickens, C: Oliver Twist, Folio Society Edition, 2004

Dilnot, G: The Story of Scotland Yard, Houghton Mifflin, 1927

Felsted, S T: The Underworld of London, John Murray, 1923

Forsythe, W J: The Reform of Prisoners, 1830–1900, Croom Helm, 1987

'Gentleman George', Raffles in Real Life, Hutchinson (undated)

Goodwin, J C: Sidelines in Criminal Matters, Hutchinson, 1923

Griffiths, A: Mysteries of the Policing of Crime: Cassell, 1899

Hargrave, L A: The Story of Crime: From Cradle to the Grave, TW Lawrie, 1908

Illustrated Police News, The: London's Court Cases and Sensational Stories, Wicked 2002

Kingston, C: Dramatic Days at The Old Bailey, Stanley Paul, 1929

Leach, C: On Top of the Underworld, Sampson Low (undated)

Lock, J: Tales from Bow Street, Hale, 1982

McLevy, J: The Casebook of a Victorian Detective, Canongate, 1975

Macintyre, B: The Napoleon of Crime, The Life and Times of Adam Worth, Harper Collins, 1997

Mayhew, H, Kimber W, London's Underworld, 1950 (first pub 1862)

Mayhew, H: Binny J: The Criminal Prisons of London, 1862

Palmegiano, E M: Crime in Victorian Britain, Greenwood, 1993

Reith, C: A Short History of the British Police, OUP, 1948

Smith, P T: Policing Victorian London, Greenwood, 1985

Taylor, D: The New Police in Nineteenth Century England, Manchester University Press, 1998

—— Crime, Policing and Punishment in England 1750–1914, Macmillan

Thomas, D: The Victorian Underworld, John Murray, 1998

Wensley, F P: Detective Days, Cassell, 1931

Williams, A, Head V, Prooth, S C: Criminal Masterminds, Futura 2007

Whitmore, R: Crime and Punishment in Victorian Times, Batsford, 1978

Vigar-Harris, H: London at Midnight 1885

Victorian 'CSI' and the history of forensic medicine

Browne, D G and Tullett, E V: Bernard Spilsbury: His Life and Cases, CBA 1952

Camps FE with Barber R: The Investigation of Murder, Michael Joseph 1966

Veavon, C: Fingerprints, Fourth Estate, 2001

Evans, G: The Father of Forensics, Icon, 2009

Galton, F: Finger Prints, Macmillan, 1892

Guy, W A: Principles of Forensic Medicine, History Press reprint 2001

Henry, E R: Classification and Uses of Finger Prints, 1899

Rose, R: Lethal Witness, Sutton 2007

Victorian railways and stations

Betjeman, J: London's Historic Railway Stations, Capital Transport, 2002

Clapham, J H: Economic History of Modern Britain: The Railway Age, 1926

Dimbleby, D: How We Built Britain, BBC 2007

Freeman, M: Railways and the Victorian Imagination, Yale, 1999

London's Railways Map, 1897, Old House Books (undated)

May, T: The Victorian Railway Worker, Shire, 2008

Simmons, J: The Victorian Railway, Thames and Hudson, 1991

The home life of the Victorians:

Calder, J: The Victorian Home,1977

Cassell's Household Guide (various);

Dutton, R: The Victorian Home, Bracken Books, 1964

Enquire Within Upon Everything, 1890, Old House Books, 2003

Flanders, J: Consuming Passions, Leisure and Pleasure in Victorian Britain, Harper, 2006

Hill, T E: The Essential Handbook of Victorian Etiquette, Bluewood (undated)

Mitchell, S: Daily Life in Victorian England (second edition), Greenwood Press, 2009

Newton, C: Victorian Designs for the Home, V&A 1999

The Saturday Book, various editions

No Author, Enquire Within Upon Everything, 1890, Old House Books

200 Years of the Census, Office of National Statistics pamphlet;

The Victorian stage

Bantock, G, Atlato, F G: A Gaiety Girl, McQueen 1896

Dawes, E A: The Great Illusionists, David and Charles, 1979

Haddon, A: The Story of Music Hall, 1935

Hollingshead, J: Good Old Gaiety, Gaiety Theatre Company, 1903

Hyman, A: The Gaiety Years, Cassell, 1975

Jupp, J: The Gaiety Stage Door, Cape, 1923

Steinmeyer, J: Hiding the Elephant, Heinemann, 2003

Van Kemph, B: Gaiety Girls, unknown

The Victorian race-meetings and gambling

Ashton, J: A History of Gambling, 1898

Black, J: The English Press 1621–1861, Sutton 2001

Binstead, A and Wells, E: A Pink 'Un and a Pelican, Bliss Sands, 1898

Hudson, D: British Journalists and Newspapers, Collins, 1945

Paxman J, The Victorians: Britain Through the Paintings of the Age, BBC Books, 2008

Victorian and early 20th century Brighton:

Adland, D: Brighton's Music Halls, Baron, 1994

Gilbert, E M: Brighton: Old Ocean's Bauble, Flare Books, 1954

Musgrave, C: Life in Brighton, Faber, 1970

The Duchess of Sutherland and her circle

Bell, Gilbert T: A Prospect of Sutherland, Berlinn, 1995;

Drummond, D: Taylor and Humbert, 1782–1982, Taylor and Humbert, 1982;

Hough, R: Edward and Alexandra: Their Private and Public Lives, Hodder, 1992

MacGregor, A A: Land of the Mountain and the Flood, Michael Joseph, 1965

Paget, Lady: Embassies of Other Days, Hutchinson, 1923;

Strathnaver, Lord, ed: Dunrobin Castle: Jewel in the Crown of the Highlands, Heritage House, 2003

The legal figures

Felstead, S T and Lady Muir: Sir Richard Muir: A Memoir of a Public Prosecutor, Bodley Head, 1927

Marjoribanks, E: The Life of Edward Marshall Hall, Victor Gallancz, 1929

Miscellaneous books/articles:

Birkenhead, Earl of: Halifax: The Life of Lord Halifax:

Charmley, J: Splendid Isolation? Britain and the Balance of Power, 1874–1914, Hodder, 1999;

Hibbert, C: Edward VII A Portrait, Allen Lane, 1976

O'Faolain, N: The story of Chicago May, Riverhead Books 2005

Robb, G: Parisians: An Adventure History of Paris, Picador, 2010

Sharf, F A: Expedition from Uganda to Abyssinia, 1898: The Diary of Lieutenant R G T Bright, Tsehai, 2005

Sharpe, M C: Her Story, Macauly, 1928

Sheridan, M: Rowton Houses, 1892–1952, Rowton Houses Ltd, 1956

Vane, H: Affair of State: A Biography of the 8th Duke and Duchess of Devonshire, Peter Owen, 2004

Wade, J W: The Royal Mail: Its Curiosities and Romance, Harper 1885 and 1889

Chicago Daily Tribune:

January 16, 1898: Monte Carlo and its throngs of fashionable folk

The Harmsworth Magazine:

Jewel Wearers and how they wear their jewels, F Nevill Jackson, Vol II, Feb–July 1899;

The Times:

June 25, 1925: Sir Forrest Fulton obiturary; August 3, 1891 and January 27, February 6, 16 and March 15: Various stories on 'Monte Carlo' Wells.

New York Times:

November 25, 1895: Behind the scenes at Monte Carlo; March 6, 1898: A Glimpse of Monte Carlo; September 6, 1908: Gaiety Love Match; July 16, 1911: Death of Duchess of Devonshire

The Pall Mall Gazette:

A Day at Dartmoor, A Griffiths, Vol XXII, September–December, 1900

The Scotsman:

July 6, 1903: Last of the Gaiety Theatre

The Star (New Zealand); June 2, 1903:

Walter Dinnie: Smart Performance of New Zealand's Police Commissioner Elect

OS Map: Pitlochry and Loch Tummel

Lord Rowton by Richard Farrant

NEWSPAPERS, MAGAZINES and DOCUMENTS
The theft and trial:

Belfast News-Letter:
October 19, 1898: The Robbery of the Duchess of Sutherland's Jewels; Bristol; October 20, The Jewel Robberty:

Daily Chronicle:
November 30, 1898: How the Clue was Obtained; December 22, 1898: Story by An Anonymous Veiled Lady; January 5, 1899: Duchess's Jewels;

Dundee Courier and Argus:
October 19, 1898: Daring Jewel Robbery;

Freeman's Journal and Daily Commercial Advertiser:
October 19, 1898: The Great Jewel Robbery: No Trace of the Missing Property;

The Echo:
December 7, 1898: Prisoners in the Dock Today; December 8, 1898: Johnson's Life in London; December 9, 1898: Curious Legal Points; December 21, 1898: An Important Lady Witness; December 22, 1898: Witnesses Name Suppressed; January 4, 1899: Johnson's Plea; January 5, 1899: Ardlamont Monson; January 18, 1899: The Duchess' Jewels

The Graphic:
October 29, 1898: Untitled

The Guardian:
October 19, 1898: The Dowager Duchess of Sutherland's Jewels: A Reward of £4,000 offered; November 30, 1898: Police Court Proceedings; December 22: Evidence of a Mysterious Stranger;

Illustrated Police News:
December 10, 1898: Smart Recovery by Detectives; December 31: The Great Robbery and How it was done; January 7, 1899: Harry the Valet; January 14: Prisoner Refuses to Give Their Whereabouts;

The Leeds Mercury:
January 6, 1899: Politics and Society
Lloyd's Weekly News:
December 8, 1898: Johnson's Trial
Daily Mail:
October 18, 1898: The Dowager Duchess of Sutherland's Jewels;
   December 15, 1898: Her Grace's Story of the Sinister Stranger;
   December 22, 1898: Johnson's Mistresses Tells How She
   Betrayed Him; December 24, 1898: A Gaiety Girl Decked Out
   in the Duchess of Sutherland's Jewels; January 5, 1899: Where
   is the Rest of the Plunder?; January 6, 1899: Amazing Career:
   Harry the Valet's Great Coups; January 12, 1899: Maud
   Richardson's claim; January 13, 1899: Interview with the
   Dowager Duchess of Sutherland; January 19, 1899: Harry the
   Valet Obdurate;
Daily News:
October 19, 1898: The Stolen Jewel Mystery: How the Thieves
   Made their Haul; November 29, 1898: Some of the Booty
   Recovered.
News of the World:
December 4, 1898: Smart Capture of Two Men; December 18:
   Duchess' Version of the Robbery; December 25: How to Steal
   Jewels – You only have to get around the Maid
Nottinghamshire Guardian:
December 17, 1898: Strange Stories of Johnson
The Manchester Times:
October 21, 1898: Dowager Duchess of Sutherland's Jewels
   Missing;
Mercury and Daily Post:
October 19, 1898: Great Jewel Robbery, Daring Thieves at Paris
National Archive:
Report of the theft of the Duchess of Sutherland's jewels from
   Paris: HO 144/522/X73341

Daily Northwesterner:
November 26, 1898: The Duchess of Sutherland: A Woman of Fortune
The Pall Mall Gazette:
October 18, 1898: Duchess of Sutherland Robbed: Thieves at French Railway Station
Police Gazette:
November 9, 1898: Duchess's Stolen Jewels – a Clue
Reynold's Newspaper:
October 23, 1898: The Dowager Duchess of Sutherland's Jewels Stolen; December 4, 1898: Alleged Thieves Captured; December 11: Remarkable Story
Western Mail:
October 19, 1898: Dowager Duchess Robbed; October 20: London Letter, The Duchess' Jewels; January 8, 1899: Sutherland Gems Romance;
The Standard:
October 19, 1898: The Jewel Robbery in Paris: Details of the Affair; November 29: The Duchess of Sutherland's Jewellery: Two Arrests in London; December 15, 1898: Duchess' Evidence; December 22, 1898: Remarkable Disclosures;
The Scotsman:
October 19, 1898: Jewel Robbery at Paris
The Sun:
December 14, 1898: Duchess' Stolen Jewels; December 24, 1898: Mysterious Witness A Gaiety Girl; January 4, 1899: Prisoner Pleads Guilty; January 18, 1899: Harry the Valet Sentenced;
The Star:
December 14: The Duchess' Jewels; December 21, 1898: Duchess Stolen Jewels; January 18, 1899: Seven Years;
The Star (New Zealand)
February 23, 1898: Harry the Valet; February 28, 1899: Too Clever for Scotland Yard

The Standard:
January 5, 1899: Trial of Accused; January 19, 1899: Harry the
Valet – seven years;
The Times:
October 19, 1898: Jewel Robbery in Paris; thereafter, November
30, December 15, 22, January 5, 19, 1899
The Daily Telegraph:
November 29, 1898: Important Arrest; November 30: Prisoners in
Court; December 15, 1898: Lipman Discharged; December 22,
1898: A Mysterious Lady; January 5, 1899: Romantic Story of
the Great Robbery; January 19, 1899: The Sutherland Jewels:
Western Mail:
December 23, 1898: Sensational Story
Western Australian:
January 9, 1899: Johnson's Life in London
Other thefts and events:
Aberdeen Weekly Journal:
July 31, 1893: Countess Howe's Jewels
Atlanta Constitution:
April 27, 1908: Criminal Who Stole: Very Cunning International
Criminal Again Sentenced
Belfast News-Letter
August 17, 1889: Florence St John
Brisbane Courier:
April 21, 1893: Duchess of Devonshire's Jewels
Bristol Mercury and Daily Post:
July 31, 1893: Countess Howe
Daily News:
August 18, 1889: Florence St John
The Era:
October 26, 1889: Theft of St John's jewels
Hampshire Telegraph and Sussex Chronicle:
August 5, 1893: Jewel Robberty at Portsea

Illustrated Police News:

October 24, 1889: Theft of St John's Jewels; March 11, 1893: Robbery of the Duchess of Devonshire; August 5, 1893: Countess Howe.

Jackson's Oxford Journal:

August 5, 1893: Countess Howe's Jewels

The Morning Post:

August 2, 1893: The Last Jewel Robbery

Nelson Mail:

October 2, 1893: Countess Howe's Jewels Stolen

New York Times:

January 9, 1899: Duchess of Devonshire

North Eastern Daily Gazette:

March 6, 1893: Daring Attempt

Nottinghamshire Guardian:

March 11, 1893: Duchess of Devonshire

Daily Express:

May 7, 1912: Maharaja's Jewels: British Suspect Detained at Marseilles

Daily Mail:

March 7, 1908: Criminal Courts: 'Harry the Valet – back in court'; April 3, 1908: Notorious Jewel Thief Sentenced; May 7, 1912: Maharajah's casket: Jewels Stolen from a Train.

The Daily Telegraph:

October 16, 2004: Bejewelled carriageways (Maharajah)

The Times:

May 7th, 1912: Theft of Maharajah's jewels

Poor Law Records:

St Pancras Hospital

Maude's legal battles and career

Birmingham Daily Post:

January 24, 1900: Sequel to Jewel Robbery

Daily Mail:

March 10, 1899: Claim against a Monarch; May 16, 1899: Maud (sic) Richardson's Writ; August 8, 1899: Echo of a Great Robbery; August 15, 1899 Untitled;

Daily News:

August 15, 1899: The Alleged Jewel Robbery

Leeds Mercury:

January 14, 1899: Untitled: January 19, 1899: Untitled

Lloyds Weekly News:

January 28, 1900: Andrew v Andrew

Marlborough Express:

March 9, 1899: An Aden Marriage and its Sequel

Morning Post:

August 15, 1889: Untitled

National Archive:

Andrew v Andrew Divorce Papers: J77/672/422 and J77/665/238

The Penny Illustrated Paper and Illustrated Times

February 10, 1900: Andrew v Andrew

Western Mail:

February 4, 1899: Maud Richardson claims part of the reward; January 24, 1900: Maud Richardson and her Husband;

Reynold's Newspaper:

August 13, 1899: Singular Conduct in Court; August 20, 1899: Maud Richardson's Jewels; January 28, 1900: The Actress and the Officer.

The Standard:

March 2 1899: Untitled; January 24, 1900: The Sutherland Jewel Robbery; January 27, 1900: Andrew Questioned;

The Star:

March 3, 1900: Antecedents of Harry the Valet's Betrayer; March 22, 1900: Maud Richardson's Divorce

The Times:

January 24, March 15 and May 8 1900: Andrew v Andrew Divorce

Duchess of Sutherland and her circle

The Evening Times:

April 19, 1893: The Imprisoned Duchess;

Glasgow Herald:

March 1, 1889: engaged in Florida: September 23, 1892: Death of Duke of Sutherland; September 27 1892: Funeral of Duke of Sutherland; April 19, 1893: Sutherland Will Suit: The Dowager Duchess Sent to Prison for Contempt; June 22, 1893: Sutherland v Sutherland hearing; June 8, 1894: Sutherland v Sutherland settlement; November 13, 1896: Marriage of the Duchess Dowager of Sutherland;

Guardian:

October 18, 1898: Daring Theft From a French Mail Train; December 10, 1892: The Sutherland Heirlooms;

Daily Mail:

May 29, 1912: Late Duchess of Sutherland

Hull Daily Mail:

November 13, 1894: Duchess weds Albert Rollit

Illustrated London News:

October 1, 1892: The Late Duke of Sutherland;

Inverness Courier:

September 23, 1892: Death of the Duke of Sutherland;

April 21, 1892: The Dowager Duchess of Sutherland Sent to Prison; April 28: The Dowager Duchess of Sutherland: A Luxurious Prison Life

The Times:

October 10, 1883: Death of Arthur Kindersley Blair; September 24, 1892: Death of the Duke of Sutherland. Announcement of funeral, letter from doctor and funeral coverage on: September 26, 27, 29, 30: Trial and imprisonment of the Duchess of Sutherland on April 19, 1893, April 20, 21, 22. May 20, 1893: Release of Duchess of Sutherland. High Court of Justice re Sutherland v Sutherland June 13 and 14, 1893; High Court of

Justice re settlement: June 8, 1894 and December 21, 1894;
August 14, 1922: Death of Albert Rollit.

Moray and Nairnshire Express:
December 1, 1888: Death of Anne, Duchess of Sutherland
The New York Times:
October 18: 1898: A Duchess Loses Diamonds;
Northern Times:
July 4, 1935: The Blair Death Mystery
Perthshire Advertiser:
October 6, 1883: Death of Arthur Kindersley Blair
The Scotsman:
August 2, 1912: The Late Duchess of Sutherland's Estate
The Westminster Budget:
December 2, 1898: The Duchess's Stolen Jewels

I am very grateful to the following: Matthew Richardson, Sheridan
Atkinson, Kristy Davis of the Raymond Mander and Joe
Mitchenson Theatre Collection, Marie-Claire Pontier of the Archive
Department in Nimes, the Jerwood Library of the Performing Arts,
Rebecca Jackson of the Staffordshire Record Office, Mark Aston of
Islington Local History Centre, Stephen Horlock of The Woodville
Lodge, Dr Quintin Colville of the National Maritime Museum,
Yvonne Bell of the AK Bell Library, Paul Dew of the Metropolitan
Police Museum, Chris Waters, Mike Vince of the Police History
Society, Laura Ibbett of the Cambridgeshire Archive, Nicole Lauriol
of the Nimes Tourist Board, Shona Milton of the Brighton History
Centre, Bridget Howlett of the London Metropolitan Library, Sam
Johnston of the Dorset History Centre, Barry Turvin of the Railways
Archive and the staffs of the British Library, the British Library
Newspaper Archive and the National Archive.

Index

Blair's death notice 149–50
on Duchess of Sutherland's
imprisonment 160, 161
on Duke and Duchess of
Devonshire 81–2
on Duke of Sutherland's funeral 157
on Florence St John 62
on the theft of Maharaja's jewels
260–61
see also Blowitz, Henri de
Torquay, Devon: Sutherland Tower
152
Toulouse-Lautrec, Henri de 77
Trentham, Staffordshire 148, 154,
156, 157
Tummel Bridge, Scotland 149, 150
Twain, Mark: *The Tragedy of
Pudd'nhead Wilson* 110

Valet, the *see* Sands, Henry Thomas
Vanderbilt, Cornelius, II 155
Vanity Fair: portrait of Edlin 107
Viaduct Station Hotel, Holborn 250

Victoria, Princess 77
Victoria, Queen 16, 76, 22, 82, 110,
113, 148, 248
Victoria Hotel, London 94
Victoria station 52, 265

Wales, Prince of *see* Edward VII
Wallace, Edgar 9
The Man at the Carlton 9
Wasp (magazine) 64
Waterloo station 52
Weed, Edwin Gardner, Bishop of
Florida 154
Weekly News 16
'Life Story of a Super-Crook' 3,
16–18, 65, 269, 271–8
Wells, Charles ('The Man who Broke
the Bank at Monte Carlo')
100–101
Windsor: The Willows 160
Worth, Adam *56*, 56–7

Zanzibar, Sultan of 122